THE ENGLISH NOVEL OF HISTORY AND SOCIETY, 1940–80

THE ENGLISH NOVEL OF HISTORY AND SOCIETY, 1940–80

Richard Hughes, Henry Green, Anthony Powell,
Angus Wilson, Kingsley Amis, V. S. Naipaul

PATRICK SWINDEN

St. Martin's Press   New York

All rights reserved. For information, write:
St. Martin's Press, Inc., 175 Fifth Avenue, New York, NY 10010
Printed in Hong Kong
Published in the United Kingdom by The Macmillan Press Ltd.
First published in the United States of America in 1984

ISBN 0–312–25439–3

Library of Congress Cataloging in Publication Data

Swinden, Patrick.
  The English novel of history and society, 1940–1980.

  Includes index.
  1. English fiction – 20th century – History and criticism.
2. Historical fiction, English.   3. Social history
in literature.
I. Title.
PR888.H5S94   1984   823′.081′09   83–40520
ISBN 0–312–25439–3

For Martin and Anne Bygate

Contents

Preface and Acknowledgements

This book is neither a general history of the novel in England since the Second World War, nor a compendium of essays on six novelists of the period, arbitrarily selected at the whim of the critic. Each of the novelists I have written about at length has been selected on the basis of his ability to satisfy three requirements.

The first of these was that his reputation was made, or substantially added to, in the years following 1940. Obviously this applies to the writers included in the last three chapters, because their first novels were not written until after that date. I think it applies to the other three because, although they had produced interesting work before the war, the novels on which their reputations now rest were written later. (Or, in the case of Hughes, his reputation would have been a very different one – based on the single novel *A High Wind in Jamaica*. Perhaps the same applies to Henry Green and *Living*.)

The second requirement was that there should be no argument about the fact of the reputation itself: i.e. it might be possible to argue that the reputations of any or all of these writers have been inflated, but it is not possible to argue that they do not have a reputation. Therefore what they have written is important in a literary historical sense, even if not in a more strictly literary critical one.

The third requirement was that they should not be, generally speaking, bad writers. As a matter of fact I think three out of the six have written what I would consider downright bad novels. Most novelists, even the best, do – from time to time. But what seems to me good in their writing is good enough to warrant their being taken seriously as novelists of society. It is for this reason that I have not included essays on such writers as Evelyn Waugh and Ivy Compton-Burnett, whose best novels it seems to me were written before or during the War. Paul Scott and Iris Murdoch I have written on elsewhere. Other contemporary novelists with high reputations I have ignored not only because of pressure of space, but because those reputations seem to me to have been built on insecure foundations. I should add that this doesn't necessarily apply to novelists younger than V. S. Naipaul, since I have seldom felt able to provide a sound judgement on them – not having had enough material to work on, or not having lived with it for a sufficient length of time to feel that I really know it.

As a result, this book does not seek to advance any particular argument about directions in which English fiction has travelled since the war. Nothing, that is to say, beyond what I have written below and in my Introduction about the persistence of a certain kind of fiction – innovatory in some of its detail, but deeply traditional in its basic aims and approaches to character in society – from the nineteenth, into the (late) twentieth century.

In all other respects there is only the shadowiest of polemical purposes here, and that is more evident in the introductory survey than in the chapters given over to the study of individual novelists. Instead, I have tried to make of each of these chapters as penetrating a study as I can of the work of the writer in question, paying close attention to what I take to be representative examples of his work from different phases of his career post-1940. Each chapter therefore should read like a short book on the novelist concerned, attempting a comprehensive evaluation of his work in the light of a survey of all that he has written during the period, and a detailed analysis of some of his novels.

This is a history of what seem to me to be the most interesting developments in the novel of history and society since 1940. No doubt part of the reason for this is that I think it is into novels of this kind that most of the imaginative life of our literature has gone during the pasty forty years. In my Introduction I seek to give reasons for this. But it does mean I have not been able to examine some of the more strikingly experimental fiction of recent years, even where, as in Muriel Spark for example, it has a basis of sorts in social comedy. I hope my comments on Beckett and Golding will go some way towards justifying this principle of exclusion, which has little to do with intrinsic value, much more with a sense of relevance and proportion.

Readers may be puzzled by my references to each of the three parts of Richard Hughes's *The Fox in the Attic* and *The Wooden*

Shepherdess as 'novels'. There is ample evidence, however, in Hughes's own comments on *The Human Predicament*, that he thought of them as 'units' within the whole (unfinished) sequence that might be better described as 'novels' than as anything else. I have found it convenient to describe these sub-units as novels both for relative ease of reference, and as an indication of the density of events and relationships which are described within them.

I should like to make the following acknowledgements: to my colleagues in the Department of English at the University of Manchester, where early versions of some of this work were read at staff and student seminars; to the *Critical Quarterly* for permission to reproduce essays on Anthony Powell and D. M. Thomas, which now appear as parts of chapters in this book; to the New Fiction Society for affording me the opportunity to discuss some of my views on modern fiction at their offices in Book House, Wandsworth; and to Macmillan Press for permission to reproduce the paragraphs on V. S. Naipaul's *A House for Mr Biswas* which, in an abbreviated form, first appeared in my book *Unofficial Selves: Character in the Novel from Dickens to the Present Day* (1972).

I should like to offer more personal thanks to John Bayley, Betty Blanchet, C. B. Cox, Felicity Currie, Kathleen Fisher, Damian Grant, Stephen Haxby, Raymond Snape and John Stachniewski – with all of whom at one time or another I have discussed some of the writers and some of the issues that are the subjects of this book. My wife, Serena, has offered her own views and, as always, I have often had to modify my own in the light of them. Penny Evans has been as patient and as efficient as ever at the typewriter.

The author and publishers wish to thank the following who have kindly given permission for the use of copyright material:

Gillon Aitken, on behalf of V. S. Naipaul, for the extracts from *A House for Mr Biswas*.

William Heinemann Ltd and Little, Brown and Company, for the extract from *The Soldier's Art* by Anthony Powell.

David Higham Associates Ltd, on behalf of Richard Hughes, for the extracts from *The Wooden Shepherdess* and *The Fox in the Attic*.

The Hogarth Press, on behalf of the author's Literary Estate, for the extracts from *Party Going* and *Caught* by Henry Green.

Martin Secker & Warburg Ltd and Academy Chicago Publishers, for the extracts from *Hemlock and After* by Angus Wilson.

Martin Secker & Warburg Ltd and Viking Penguin Ltd, for the extracts from *The Middle Age of Mrs Eliot* by Angus Wilson.

1 Introduction

To have written this Introduction fifteen, even ten, years ago would have required much more of a defensive strategy than is needed in present circumstances. In 1965, it was felt, the English novel was dwarfed by literary events outside these islands. Arguably the greatest 'English' novelist of the period was Samuel Beckett, an Irishman living in Paris and writing in French; possessed of a vision of what T. S. Eliot had earlier described as 'the horror, the boredom and the glory', such as no other contemporary English or even Anglo-Irish novelist would have or could have aspired to. Eliot died that year, but Pound, Auden and MacDiarmid lived on, carrying into the 1970s the vitality of the poetic *avant garde* of the twenties and thirties. By contrast the great experimentalists of the modern novel had all died years ago: James in 1916, Conrad in 1924, Ford in 1939 and Joyce and Virginia Woolf in 1941. Lawrence had returned from New Mexico only to die at Vence in the south of France in 1930. In the fifties and sixties there was no living testimony to the creative energies released in the novel in the first half of the century – only Beckett translating the Joyce inheritance into French; and Forster, the most approachable and least evidently revolutionary of the moderns, who had not published a new novel since *A Passage to India* in 1924. Meanwhile Saul Bellow in Chicago, Alain Robbe-Grillet in Paris, Patrick White in Australia and Günter Grass in West Germany were demonstrating how the novel form might be adapted to confront the realities of the mid twentieth century, in ways that seemed to be untranslatable into English literary practice.

A tradition, pulled loose from its early twentieth-century moorings and seeking to re-anchor itself in the Victorian and Edwardian experience, seemed doomed to extinction. Too many English novels betrayed a sort of imaginative anaemia and provincialism that was much commented on by foreign writers

1

and readers. The matter is crystallised in a few words from one of the characters in Barbara Pym's novel *Excellent Women* (1952):

> I wondered that she should waste so much energy fighting over a little matter like wearing hats in chapel, but then I told myself that, after all, life was like that for most of us – the small unpleasantnesses rather than the great tragedies; the little useless longings rather than the great renunciations and dramatic love affairs of history or fiction.

One wonders who 'most of us' are in this passage. People like Mildred (who is speaking) and Dora (who is spoken about), or people like their readers too, who are presumed to be wisely and realistically nodding agreement with the sentiments expressed? In her most widely acclaimed novel, *Quartet in Autumn* (1977), Pym makes the whole story revolve around the efforts of one elderly lady to return a used milk bottle to another elderly lady. Is this another of those 'little useless longings' that make up most of our lives, and to which we are therefore expected to pay the kind of attention not willingly spent on Grass's neo-Nazis or Solzhenitsyn's labour camps?

Elizabeth Bowen writes that 'when one remembers habit it seems to have been happiness', and one sees what she means in the context of a view of life that fails to relate private feelings that are conversable about the public catastrophes that seem not to be. It remains a fact, though, that Solzhenitsyn is perfectly well able to remember habits acquired in the labour camps and cancer wards of Gulag without thinking for one moment that 'it seems to have been happiness'. Not that even the most extreme experiences don't on occasion promote scenes of happiness and personal satisfaction, but the sort of wise aphorism enunciated by Miss Bowen's character, based on a deplorably limited view of life, points to much that was unsatisfactory about the English novel during the immediate pre- and post-War years.

Elizabeth Taylor, another genteel but rather tougher minded writer in the provincial tradition, saw what was wrong. One of the characters in *A Wreath of Roses* (1949), a painter called Frances Rutherford, broods on the inadequacy of her art, its inability to come directly to terms with what is most demanding, most serious, and most true about life:

She closed her eyes and bunches of roses were printed for an instant, startlingly white upon the darkness, then faded, as the darkness itself paled, the sun from the window coming brilliantly through her lids. Trying to check life itself, she thought, to make some of the hurrying everyday things immortal, to paint the everyday things with tenderness and intimacy – the dirty café with its pock-marked mirrors as if they had been shot at, its curly hat-stands, its stained marble under the yellow light; wet pavements; an old woman yawning. With tenderness and intimacy. With sentimentality too, she wondered. For was I not guilty of making ugliness charming? An English sadness like a veil over all I painted until it became ladylike and nostalgic, governessy, utterly lacking in ferocity, brutality, violence. Whereas in the centre of the earth, in the heart of life, in the core of everyday things is there not violence, with flames wheeling, turmoil, panic, chaos?

It is a Woolfian perception that neither Frances nor any other of Elizabeth Taylor's heroines can resolve in Woolfian aesthetic terms. The evidence not in the paintings erupts in the novel in the person of Richard Elton, a psychopath who almost kills the heroine and does kill himself at the end of the tale. Of course, we don't believe in him. He is not a vitally credible character. But his presence in the story shows us that Mrs Taylor is, like Frances, aware of disturbing and violent forces that fail to penetrate the immaculately even surface of her prose. In the end both Frances's speculations and Elton's physical presence are aberrations from the civilised if somewhat eccentric behaviour that is the norm of Elizabeth Taylor's fiction.

I do not think we should be in too much of a hurry to underrate the achievements of Bowen and Taylor, or of their male equivalents, such as L. P. Hartley and, latterly, Francis King. All of these novelists have performed a service by placing English fiction in a sort of quarantine – depriving it of the wider and deeper perceptions displayed in some of the competition from Europe and America; but protecting it from a great deal of inferior writing that looked as if it contained such perceptions but in fact possessed nothing of the kind. Perhaps the best way of putting this is to say that for every Saul Bellow one could count a hundred Kurt Vonneguts or John Barths; for every Alain Robbe-Grillet, a hundred inferior practitioners of the *nouveau roman*. At least one can say that what Bowen, Taylor and King professed to understand, by and large they understood – and, although a far cry from the whole truth of whatever matter they were dealing with, it was worth understanding. Bad linguistics and worse philosophy aren't worth understanding at all, even when they do call themselves *Giles Goat Boy* and *Slaughterhouse-5*.

However, the gravest threat to the survival of the English novel as a serious literary form came from closer to home than either France or America. Beckett was the lone survivor from the great days of the twenties and thirties. During the early fifties he had written, in France, his important sequence of novels, *Molloy*, *Malone Meurt* and *L'Innommable*. In the same year that he published *Malone Meurt*, *En Attendant Godot* was performed in Paris. Translated in 1954, and performed in London at a time when the English theatre was taking on a new and vigorous lease of life, the play became a *cause célèbre*. And this in turn awakened interest in Beckett's novels. Consequently *Molloy* and *Malone Dies* were published by Calder and Boyars in 1956, and *The Unnamable* followed in 1960. These novels were all translated by Beckett himself, and word got around that the translations were the final realisation of Beckett's intentions. A condition of their appearing in pure, unmetaphorical, un-Romantic English was that they should have been written in French first – just as Conrad had had to think in French and then translate the sentences into English when he committed them to paper (with very different stylistic results). So we had a great experimental English (well, Irish) novelist among us again. The link with Joyce had been reforged. The impulse to experiment with literary forms, under the guise of writing novels, was renewed.

In fact, though Beckett was a junior associate of Joyce in Paris back in the thirties, and though there is a sense in which his novels represent an extension of the stream-of-consciousness techniques deployed in certain sections of *A Portrait of the Artist as a Young Man* and *Ulysses*, in significant respects Beckett's work is profoundly opposed to Joyce's. In the final analysis it is on *Ulysses* that Joyce's claim to have written something of considerable and permanent literary value rests. And the greatness of *Ulysses* does not, in the end, have much to do with myths, matrices and street-maps of Dublin. It has to do with Joyce's supreme ability in many parts of this novel to produce the illusion of life. John Fowles has written that only one ambition is shared by all novelists, and that is the 'wish to create worlds as real as, but other than the world that is'. He might have gone on to say that the more a novelist can make the 'realness' of what is 'other' convince us, paradoxically, of the familiarity of the world we are invited to contemplate, the more satisfactory it will appear to be. That is what Joyce has done. Through the reality of his portrayal of Dublin on that June day in 1904 he has habituated us to what is 'other', making strange things familiar and familiar things strange. But they are things – or people, places, times of day. That is what is felt to be real, other, and familiar in Joyce. Can the same be said of Beckett?

Turning to the second of Beckett's novels, *Watt* – written in English in 1944 – we would be hard pressed to give an affirmative answer. Concluding the first part of this novel, Watt speculates in the following terms on something that has recently (?) happened to him:

> To conclude . . . that the incident was internal would, I think, be rash. For my – how shall I say? – my personal system was so distended at the period of which I speak that the distinction between what was inside it and what was outside it was not at all easy to draw. Everything that happened happened inside it, and at the same time everything that happened happened outside it. I trust I make myself plain.

What Beckett, or Watt, is confessing here is the extreme solipsism of his philosophical position. I am reminded not so much of a novelist of external details and surfaces – the kind of novelist Joyce was in the best parts of *Ulysses* – as of a discursive poet in the high Romantic tradition. More specifically I am reminded of Hazlitt's review of *The Excursion*, in which he says of Wordsworth that 'The power of his mind preys upon itself. It is as if there were nothing but himself and the universe. He lives in the busy solitude of his own heart; in the deep silence of thought.' Except that in Beckett the universe has also disappeared as an entity separate from his own mind. But it did the same thing, intermittently, for Wordsworth too; for Wordsworth told his friend Bonamy Price that 'There was a time in my life when I had to push against something that resisted, to be sure that there was anything outside me. I was sure of my own mind; everything else fell away and vanished into thought.' Certainly Beckett's heroes live in the busy solitude of their own hearts. Or 'minds' – since the frenzy of Beckett's characters is an intellectual frenzy, breaking against the bars of a rationalist's prison. Again, Wordsworth speaks (in *The Prelude*) of the 'self-sufficing power of solitude', just as Beckett's Unnamable speaks of solitude as one of the three things in his life he had to make the best of. The others were the inability to speak and the inability to be silent – each of them also a recognisable Wordsworthian trait.

All of Beckett's characters have the same problem. Molloy, for example: 'Not to want to say, not to know what he wants to say, not to be able to say what you think you want to say, and never to stop saying, or hardly ever, that is the thing to keep in mind, even in the heat of composition.' Malone and Murphy say much the same thing, and indeed there are moments in *Molloy*, *Malone Dies* and *The Unnamable* when the speaker confuses his co-identity with other speakers in the trilogy and previously published works by Beckett. The speakers, let alone the 'characters' they invent to speak about, have no reality separate from their creator. They are simply names on which Beckett confers the responsibility for passing his time – until Godot comes along or the author gets to the end of the number of pages available, or he simply runs out of breath. It is an Irishman's despair: nothing to do but tell stories to pass the time. If they do pass the time. The Unnamable thinks they don't even do that: 'no point in telling yourself stories to pass the time, stories don't pass the time, nothing passes the time, that doesn't matter, that's how it is, you tell yourself stories', etc. Notice, you tell *yourself* stories. There's nobody else to tell them to, so distended is the personal system of even so empty and shrunken a personality as this one. But his voice and his 'person' contain everything there is to talk about – stories, lists, ideas: 'If this noise would stop there'd be nothing more to say.'

Is this remotely what we feel about Joyce's Dublin? If the noise stopped, do we feel that there'd be nothing more to say – about Bloom, about Molly, about Stephen? Literally, of course, there wouldn't be. But literature is a constant battle against literalism. Joyce's language, in spite of its Flaubertian origins, beckons us to a world we are convinced lies beyond it, a world 'as real as, but other than the world that is'. There is nothing beyond the words Beckett's protagonists speak. Only the darkness Malone fears. For, as Winnie says in *Happy Days* (buried up to her neck in sand), 'I do of course hear cries, but they're in my head surely.' The cries

Bloom heard in *Ulysses* were not only in his head or, the book having been written, in his author's head either.

In the middle 1950s, however, it seemed to many *avant-gardistes* in this country that that was where they ought to have been. For Beckett was related, as a sort of taciturn visiting uncle, to a school of French writing, the *anti-romanciers* or *nouveaux romanciers*, who placed great emphasis on the element of private indulgence that went into making fictions. For them, Beckett had blown the gaffe. Ignoring the fitfully disturbing power that issued from Beckett's intellectual despair, they took over what might be called the transparency of his writing – i.e. his unwillingness to hide the fact that writing was what he was doing and that the fact that he was doing it was the most important fact about its being done – and made it into a formal principle of their own fictions. I have written elsewhere* that this is a sterile intention, to be taken seriously at all only in so far as it emphasises a certain purity of motive (being honest about the truth) or issues in the expression of feeling, often obsessional feeling (see Robbe-Grillet's *La Jalousie*), completely at variance with everything it professes to be. Nevertheless the vogue for the *nouveau roman* crossed the Channel during the sixties and created a market for films by Chris Marker, Jean Luc Godard and others which would have kept no one but the most ardent Francophile awake had it not been for the excellent camera work and editing, which made it difficult for anyone to believe that nothing of significance was going on beneath it. The fall-out of this misguided movement *against* the novel remains with us in novels by English writers such as B. S. Johnson, Christine Brooke-Rose and Gabriel Josipovici. So far as I know no one reads them, but their theoretical *raison d'être*, displayed in much-praised critical books such as Josipovici's *The World and the Book*, has a seductive fascination, and might, some day, lead someone to forge a way through such intriguingly-named anti-novels as *Christie Malry's Own Double Entry, Such*, or *The Inventory*. Clearly, however, this was not a direction in which any sensible reader of English fiction would want to go. And there were siren voices calling from elsewhere in the sixties.

Mainly from William Golding, the most widely acclaimed home-grown escapologist from the constricting provincialism of

* See my *Unofficial Selves: Character in the Novel from Dickens to the Present Day* (London, 1972) ch. 3.

the Hartley–Bowen–Taylor school. Like Beckett, Golding is a
writer of considerable stature. This is not the place to enquire at
all closely into where his strength as a novelist lies. But it clearly
has to do with speculations such as this one, made by the hero of
Golding's third novel, *Pincher Martin* (1956), as he clings to his
rock in the mid Atlantic:

> There was at the centre of all the pictures and pains and voices a
> fact like a bar of steel, a thing – that which was so nakedly the
> centre of everything that it could not even examine itself. In the
> darkness of the skull it existed, a darker dark, self-existent and
> indestructible.

As it happens, the 'fact like a bar of steel' is precisely what has to
be destroyed in Pincher as the events of the novel take their
course. But the image seeks to realise an essential and central fact
about the hero upon which all other facts we learn about him
depend. Fundamentally, this is what Pincher is. Is what he *can be*
entirely contained in the fact about what he is? The novel seeks to
illuminate this question, to provide the terms according to which
it might even be answered, by doing two things. First, it describes
Pincher's struggle for survival on what he (and we) suppose is an
isolated and inhospitable rock in the middle of the Atlantic
Ocean. Second, it records scenes from Pincher's past life that float
across his mind as he clings to the rock. And the fact about *Pincher
Martin* that everybody who has read it will agree about is that
Pincher's rock is a great deal more interesting and a great deal
more credible than anything he tells us about his life before he got
to it – whether this has to do with his performance as an actor, a
womaniser, or a naval lieutenant. The reason it is more interesting is that it isn't alive. Only in the most fanciful metaphorical
sense can it answer back. In fact it turns out in the end to have
been a part of Pincher Martin's own body – his tooth. But
Pincher's fellow actors and sailors, and above all such women as
Mary Lovell and men as Nat Walterson, are alive. He has to enter
into some sort of scenic relationship with them. And this Golding
cannot convincingly make him do.

The mythic, poetic, metaphoric passages of *Pincher Martin* are
amazingly powerful. But the straightforward scenic passages, the
passages most novels are made out of, are crude. They remained
so in his next novel, *Free Fall* (1959), where even more of the prose

was of this character – clearly a kind of writing uncongenial to a man of Golding's imaginative stamp. The best of early Golding is *The Inheritors* (1955), which is about the lives of people (Neanderthal Men) who have no language, or at least no language that performs an individuating function. Most of their actions, too, are practical or ritualistic, forms of activity expressing relationships between people at a level Golding understands and is fully (wonderfully) capable of writing about. In the best of his later novels, *The Spire* (1964) and *Rites of Passage* (1980), there is the same emphasis on practical action and ritual performance, as well as (to be fair) a developed ability to write credible dialogue. The dialogue, however, is written in a way calculated to suggest how people spoke in a particular historical period, often when they were performing a specialised function – such as building a cathedral spire or sailing a ship. Dialogue spoken by strictly contemporary characters, as well as descriptions of actions performed by them, is still unconvincing. We are no more impressed with the Stanhope girls in *Darkness Visible* (1979) than we were with Sammy and Beatrice in *Free Fall*. Their speech and their behaviour fall equally flat. Only in childhood scenes – Sammy with Evie, Mattie with Mr Pedigree – is Golding able to represent aspects of contemporary life with conviction.

Writing of this kind is not likely to be a good influence on other novelists, even when their ambitions are as lofty as Golding's. For what is strongest in Golding's work is a heightened, visionary quality that is inseparable from the use of parable, metaphor and symbol – all aspects of his writing which are strictly non-transferable. Without them, Golding's grasp of fact, of practical activity, would be insignificant. There was nothing to borrow from Golding that was not intimately bound up with his powerful, idiosyncratic view of the world. If this was where the strength of the English novel in the fifties and sixties lay, then it was a lonely, isolated strength. It was not much use to other novelists looking for ways of creating worlds more congruent with our own, more willing to write directly about those relationships between people Golding finds it so difficult to describe.

By the middle of the 1960s, then, the English novel was judged to be in poor shape. Of the three most impressive survivors from the years between the wars, Joyce Cary had died (in 1957), and his reputation was in any case in decline; Evelyn Waugh had died in 1966 having completed his *magnum opus*, the *Sword of Honour* trilogy, in 1961; and Graham Greene, though still very much alive, and prolific, was generally considered (rightly) to have finished his best work with *The Quiet American*, back in 1955. Later, large claims were to be made for the Waugh trilogy. But these were scarcely sustainable (in spite of the high comedy) in view of the absurdity of the central figure, Guy Crouchback, and his eccentric ideas of what the war is about. In the end it seems that the Greek and Yugoslavian campaigns have been fought in order to teach one sexually enfeebled and socially snobby Catholic that he should have left well alone and secured his personal honour by other means. The fact that the woman who teaches him these things is quietly shunted off to be executed by Communist partisans is used to make us feel sorry for Crouchback. For this and other reasons it is doubtful whether serious claims can be made for *Sword of Honour* as an interpretation of the English experience of war, though it is true that in 1961 there were not many other candidates in the field.

As the sixties drew to a close, however, it was possible to trace developments from the earlier post-war period that had not been at all clear at the time. Whilst most critics persisted in tracing the development of a rugged, honest provincialism from William Cooper through C. P. Snow to the younger writers of the fifties and sixties (often from working-class backgrounds, descriptions of which might be advanced as their sole claim to serious – i.e. sociological – attention), much more significant events were taking place in other quarters. By 1970 such established writers as C. P. Snow and Angus Wilson seemed to have come to the end of their imaginative tether. *Strangers and Brothers* ended in that year with publication of *Last Things*. Wilson's flagging powers of imagination, first in evidence in *Late Call* (1964), were confirmed by the enormously over-ambitious and self-defeatingly 'experimental' *No Laughing Matter* in 1967. There was no way of telling, at that time, what a new lease of life Wilson's fiction would take on with publication of *As If By Magic* six years later, and *Setting the World on Fire* four years later still. Anthony Powell's *Dance to the Music of Time* was drawing to a close with the completion of the war volumes (*The Military Philosophers*, 1968). And Iris Murdoch was floundering badly with unwittingly self-parodic novels such as *The Nice and the Good* (1968) and *Bruno's Dream* (1969). In view of these events, it might well have seemed that the English novel was stuck, with Beckett gradually managing to stop telling all those stories *The Unnamable* failed to pass the time with telling (*Imagine Dead Imagine*, 1965; *Lessness*, 1969), and Golding transparently marking time with the attractive but not over-ambitious *The Pyramid* (1967) and *The Scorpion God* (1971), mere tinkering with materials previously used in one form or another during the preceding ten to fifteen years.

But significant events of a more positive kind were also taking place. Three in particular pointed to the future, and indicated how the immediate past might be reassessed. The first event was the appearance, back in 1961, of Richard Hughes's *The Fox in the Attic*. This was in fact a collection of three novels, written during the past twenty years, and destined to become a part of a long sequence called *The Human Predicament*. The next three novels were published together as *The Wooden Shepherdess* in 1972. The second event was the publication of V. S. Naipaul's *In a Free State* in 1971. This collection of long and short stories confirmed Naipaul's command of narrative and showed that the serious political–colonial concerns for which he had failed to find a satisfactory narrative form in *The Mimic Men* (1967) had now been accommodated in a readable fiction. The novels that followed in 1975 (*Guerrillas*) and 1979 (*A Bend in the River*) showed that Naipaul had embarked on a mature phase of writing that had its roots in Conrad and its branches in a first-hand analysis of contemporary colonial and post-colonial societies. The third event was the emergence of Paul Scott as a major writer with the publication of *The Raj Quartet*, the third volume of which, *The Towers of Silence*, came out in 1971. (It was completed in 1975 with *A Division of the Spoils*.)*

By 1980 two of these writers had died – Hughes in 1976, leaving *The Human Predicament* sadly incomplete; Scott in 1978, after publishing a pendant to the *Quartet* with *Staying On* (1977), a deeply moving (and comic) story on an altogether smaller and more intimate scale than its immediate predecessors. The younger novelist who had learned most from Hughes, J. G. Farrell, died the following year, but not before completing his trilogy on colonial themes, *Troubles* (1970), *The Siege of Krishnapur* (1973) and *The Singapore Grip* (1979). All three of these novels owe to Hughes something of their relaxed unfolding of historical events; local shocks administered by the timing and grouping of

---

* For an appraisal of the novels of Paul Scott, see my *Paul Scott: Images of India* (London, 1980).

events; and, above all, an intense, often bizarre representation of visual detail. Meanwhile, a new novel by Naipaul was eagerly awaited.

What Hughes, Scott and Naipaul had achieved was a revivification of the novel of history used as a means of interpreting contemporary problems – of competing nationalisms, colonial exploitation and distress, and clashes of race, class and ideology. Hughes's vision was ultimately religious, transcending history. Scott and Naipaul are embattled humanists, believing that moral issues are ultimately tractable, and therefore not despairing; but believing that their tractability is not to be overestimated, and therefore not given either to extravagant hopes. These novelists have drawn on an indigenous tradition of sober moral inquiry. They eschewed myth and fantasy for the realities of history and contemporary or near-contemporary politics. They have persisted with habits of critical investigation often mediated through social comedy (habits equally evident in the work of non-historical writers such as Powell, Wilson and Murdoch) but they have applied them across a wider spectrum of human experience than had traditionally been the case. The English novel has always been preoccupied with establishing proper limits within which human beings can best conduct themselves. It has been concerned with the way real events press on what are possibly unrealistic aspirations, and on what are probably inappropriate flights of the imagination. Above all it has avoided simplifying human behaviour. It has always believed that the most important issues are moral issues, and that moral issues, whilst they may be difficult, are ultimately tractable. Hughes, like Golding, presses beyond the moral to engage with issues that are fundamentally religious – but he doesn't suppose this absolves either himself or his characters from inquiring into the moral character of political events. Scott and Naipaul in their different ways have enlarged the moral lens through which they look at political and racial situations, so as to take account of the changed circumstances in which, as late twentieth-century novelists, they find themselves.

Now, poised on the brink of the eighties, it may well be that the novel of social comedy in England is experiencing a new mutation. Several young writers have risen to the challenge of a wider historical perspective and have acquired a new respect for linguistic experiment. Two of the best novels of the years 1980–1, Anthony Burgess's *Earthly Powers* and D. M. Thomas's *The White*

Hotel, differ from each other in many important ways. But they have in common three things which relate them closely to the best traditions of English fiction.

The first is their interest in history. Both are apparently cavalier about this, mixing real with imagined history in a flamboyantly challenging manner that has little in common with, say, Hughes or Farrell. This is especially true of Burgess, whose anti-hero must have met and gossiped about almost everyone of any consequence in English life, letters and society during the first three quarters of the twentieth century. But it is true of Thomas also. Who else would have had the nerve to interpolate a hitherto unknown and entirely fictional study of hysteria by Freud into the collage of poems, letters, case studies and dream narrative that is *The White Hotel*; and then to (almost?) end a surrealistic expression of psychiatric disturbance in descriptions of the mass pogrom of Babi Yar?

The second is the use they make of social comedy, as a kind of launching-pad from which to take off into much wilder and more bizarre forms of comic fantasy. Burgess maintains the social comic impulse throughout, bringing it into uncomfortable proximity with his wilder flights of linguistic and quasi-autobiographical fancy. Thomas allows it to linger phantasmally, almost, within the interstices of the surrealistic force that comprises 'The Gastein Journal', his heroine's prose account of her visit to the White Hotel with Freud's son. In both cases the use of social comedy creates in the reader a confidence that certain expected ways of looking at and understanding people in society have been taken into account. Therefore whatever the reader's feelings may be about the extremity of both the experiences and the manner of presenting them that appear prominently elsewhere in these novels, they follow on a recognition of the real comic possibilities, as well as the real historical circumstances, of the events described.

Beyond all this *Earthly Powers* is an always powerful, by turns comic and tragic picaresque progress through the terrible experiences of twentieth-century Europe and America. But its intricate plot and its narrator's uncertain memory (confessed to from time to time in the retrospective design) do not have the effect of emphasising a patent and narcissistic fictionality. There is, of course, the possibility of error, of distorted vision, occluded memory, value judgements obscured by guilt and fear. Nevertheless the novel forces us to examine fundamental moral and religious issues that have exercised the minds of our best writers for the last five hundred years and more: the existence of evil, and man's propensity to sin; the parameters of moral responsibility in a world that seems to have gone mad; absolute and relative ethics in the world of Capone's Chicago, the Nazis' Buchenwald, and something very like the fanatical and ultimately suicidal Jonestown community in Guyana.

In D. M. Thomas's novel, the documents that encapsulate Lisa Erdman's frenetic emotional experiences are not assembled in order to divert our attention from the psychological substance of the novel to its evasive form. Narrative is used here not, as in Anthony Burgess, to encapsulate the meaning of the fable, but as one intermittent and valuable component in a book that is more poetic than prosaic in its manipulation of images and its descriptions of events. But what this formally secretive combination of narrative and imagery is conveying to us is once more a matter of traditional human concern. It attempts to convey to its readers an understanding of Frau Anna's experience (which, in spite of its extremity and perversity, appears more and more to be a type of twentieth-century European experience) by precisely those techniques that earlier *nouveaux romanciers* had adopted to evade any such thing – or, to be fair, to show how we cannot prevent ourselves from evading any such thing. In other words, the spirit of moral inquiry has by no means been aborted by the bizarre form in which it has been made to work. We shall find here a great deal of insight into our condition as loving and dying creatures: treated with varying degrees of kindness and cruelty by others of our species; and having our behaviour recorded and interpreted with different degrees of sensitivity by the diarists and poets, who may be ourselves, and the psychiatrists and novelists, who are almost certainly going to be other people.

It is this seriousness about man in his moral and it may be religious aspect, issuing from firm belief in his reality – as something more than the bemused creature of habit offered to us by many contemporary continental theorists and writers – that constitutes the third relation of these and other contemporary novels to earlier traditions of English humanist fiction. To quote the great French neurologist Charcot, mentor of Freud, from a passage in *The White Hotel*, 'Le théorie c'est bon, mais ça n'empêche pas d'exister.'

A closer look at D. M. Thomas's work might help to bring out the differences between older and younger generations of post-war novelists. In *The White Hotel*, Thomas describes the career of Lisa Erdman through a succession of 'imitations', one of them indeed the imitation of a poem. The letters to and from Freud in the Prologue, Lisa's journal in chapter 3, Freud's case history in chapter 4 and the documentary material about Babi Yar in chapter 5, all add up to an indirect and highly literary treatment of the subject.

But to what purpose? The introduction to Thomas's transla-tions of Pushkin provides a very general answer to the question. Here it appears that Pushkin's late narrative poem 'The Bronze Horseman' 'encompasses the essential story of the next century and a half: the hapless struggle of the individual to survive . . . against absolute power – whether of emperor or ideology'. Clearly Thomas's interest in Russian literature springs from both linguis-tic and personal sources. His earlier novel *The Flute Player* (1979), stitching into its fantastic narrative a patchwork of phrases from Pushkin and his twentieth-century successors (the novel is dedicated to their memory), tells just such a story. Elena and her poet lovers commit themselves to the struggle in a totalitarian state reminiscent at times of Hitler's Germany (Berlin), at times of Stalin's Russia (Leningrad). *The White Hotel* is an infinitely more subtle statement of the theme. For in it the emperor and the ideology have been separated out into two apparently contrasting forces. The emperor is still Stalin or Hitler or whoever can be metonymically held responsible for Babi Yar. But the ideology is Freudian. At first, therefore, it looks as if the ideology is there to resist the emperor. For who could be less totalitarian than Freud in his person and in his work? And whose investigations of the individual psyche could reveal a greater concern with the disaggregated personality, the private man or woman, which totalitarian systems seek to crush, to absorb into the mass, to reduce to the one *fascia* among many that, together, constitute the primary unit of the state, the *fascis*?

The White Hotel is a story of a person who is so reduced in the most brutal way imaginable: from a refined, highly cultured and musically gifted young woman who becomes a prima donna in the Kiev Opera, she is transformed into a broken and scattered remnant of bones and earth under the concrete base that now conceals the ravine of Babi Yar. It is also a fantasy in which her spirit survives that utterly dehumanising death to flower again in a surreal landscape of peace, tenderness and 'loving everyone' (though a sense of loss, too, survives) disturbingly present in the final chapter.

How Lisa Erdman, or Frau Anna G. as she is known to us in Freud's case history, was transformed from the one to the other, and how we are to react to the different stages of her transformation, is perplexing, mysterious and enigmatic. Of course on one level it is not mysterious at all. We know that hundreds of Jews (and it is of only novelistic relevance that Lisa isn't in fact Jewish, though with her parental background any Nazi commander would have treated her as such) disappeared into oblivion at Babi Yar, and we can guess that some of them were as gifted and as complex human beings as Lisa was. But the singular fact about Lisa is that she had been living through Babi Yar for years and years before Babi Yar came into being. When her doctor referred her to Freud she had been experiencing pains in the breast and the stomach for at least six years, ever since she separated from her husband after his call-up during the First World War. Towards the end of the novel Lisa is kicked in the breast and bayoneted in the stomach before she completely loses consciousness in the ravine at Babi Yar. In fact the anatomical details are more precise than that, with the result that there is an exact correspondence between physical symptoms, sexual anxieties and actual causes as they are recorded in the narrative. The only startling thing about them is the order in which they are experienced; for the symptoms precede the causes, and the connection between sexual experience and the experience of pain, even of dying, is consequently rendered enigmatic.

Lisa was analysed by Freud in 1920, when she was twenty-nine. The novel makes clear that this date was as much a turning-point for Freud as it was for Lisa. For it was at this date that Freud's earlier theories of the competition between the instinct of sex and instinct of self-preservation were being modified and even transformed by his discovery of the death instinct. The stage Freud had reached in the working-out of his new theory is aptly demonstrated by the half-completed form of his essay *Beyond the Pleasure Principle*: in his casebook on Frau Anna G., Freud (in the novel) refers explicitly to this fact. What Freud was impressed by was what he calls in the novel 'signs of an irrational impulse to repeat', a 'pattern of self-injuring behaviour' which highlights 'a *universal* struggle between the life instinct and the death instinct'. These words are very close to what Freud actually wrote in the completed text of *Beyond the Pleasure Principle*: 'It seems, then, that an instinct is an urge in organic life to restore an earlier state of things'; it is 'the expression of the inertia inherent in organic life'. The first instinct, Freud now believes, is 'the instinct to return to the inanimate state'.

But in Lisa's case the hysterical symptoms she exhibits are shown not so much to hark back to the restoration of an 'earlier state of things', as to look forward to the last state of things; and not as a generalised instinct towards death, but as a precise pre-enactment of the physical circumstances of her death and what preceded it. In fact she is reliving a death that has not yet occurred, just as, after she has died, in the new Jerusalem of the soul referred to at the end of the penultimate chapter, she relives the life that could never have been lived. In other words, Lisa is totally misunderstood by Freud, because his earlier conclusions from the studies in hysteria had postulated a false relationship between sex and self-preservation, and the transformation of the earlier theory into the later (post-*Beyond the Pleasure Principle*) had not yet taken place. In any event, the later theory would have been no more satisfactory than the earlier to 'explain' Lisa. In her the Life Instinct and the Death Instinct (Eros and Thanatos) simply do not relate to each other in the contradictory way Freud was to claim they did.

After her analysis, years later when she has become an opera singer, Lisa receives a letter from Freud asking her to read and comment on his case study of her. Replying, she suggests that Freud in large part *created*, through the analysis, inclinations and obsessions which he later used to justify the conclusions of the analysis. 'Frankly', she writes to him, 'I didn't always wish to talk about the past; I was more interested in what was happening to me then, and what might happen in the future. In a way you *made* me become fascinated with my mother's sin. . . . But I don't believe for one moment *that* had anything to do with my being crippled with pain.' And we know it didn't. She was crippled with pain because, living in the future as well as in the past and the present, she was already experiencing the soldier's boot and the other soldier's bayonet, touching her violently at the strategic points of her physical sex. This was what had brought together, in a way not to be contemplated by Freud, sexual hurt and apprehension of death, which can alone explain the imagery of her poem and the origin of her obsessions.

So Lisa's experience typifies not only the struggle against emperors that Thomas refers to in the Pushkin introduction, but the struggle against (in this case Freudian) ideology too. Both of them simplify and distort. Obviously the analyst's patient investigation of the private psyche is much to be preferred to the Nazi boot and the Communist's concrete. But what if their *effect* is identical: the reduction of personality to manageable and unself-contradictory proportions? In this sense a report on 'Frau Anna G.' and a clod of earth with a gold filling in it are the same. They become the same by working from the opposite ends of a spectrum of what might be called 'attention' to their human subject. On the one hand, a minute and caring observation of the individual psyche; on the other a reduction of the individual psyche to indistinguishable substance, and the merging of that substance with that of others in a mass grave.

At the beginning of Thomas's next novel, *Ararat*, a Russian writer is discovered in a bed covered with papers that include a new edition of Pushkin's stories, to be corrected by Thursday. And there is a blank sheet of paper in a typewriter on his desk. One suspects that the first words that will appear on that paper are the words that open *Ararat*: 'Sergei Rozanov had made an unnecessary journey.'

Which indeed he had – like many another character in the novel. He had travelled from Moscow to Gorky to sleep with a young blind woman, who turned out to be not so young, and had skinny legs. Contrariwise, Donna Zarifian, the American–Armenian woman Surkov meets in New York, has fat legs; but he doesn't like them, although he too dislikes skinny-legged women. A matter of small interest but for the fact that Surkov is a character made up by Rozanov, and Rozanov is a character made up by D. M. Thomas, who also, judging by the evidence of his earlier novels, seems to like women with a lot of flesh on them.

Surkov had two new American novels as well as the typewriter on his desk. Later, there are two new American novels on Donna Zarifian's coffee table. One wonders if they were the same novels. And did D. M. Thomas have two American novels on his desk next to his typewriter when he was inventing Surkov and Donna Zarifian for *Ararat*?

An idle question? I think not. For *Ararat* is a novel about improvisation. That is what Rozanov's blind girl asks him to do for her after her skinny legs have prevented him from making love to her: to improvise. And the subject? Improvisation. That is what she asked, and that is what resulted in the invention of Surkov, and the Armenian poet, and the American novelist, who form the outer frame of Rozanov's improvisation. They too improvise, though the only one of their improvisations we read is Surkov's. Yet the subject of his improvisation, Ararat, is their common theme; Ararat, the mountain in Turkish Armenia where Noah's ark finally came to rest, and which here draws to itself the imaginations of three writers of Armenian ancestry. Through Surkov and his two companions, Rozanov's improvisation carries him closer and closer to Ararat. The mountain itself appears in a single sentence, viewed by the Armenian and the American whilst Surkov is believed to be asleep in the next room. Actually he has left, without explanation: 'the *improvisatore* was gone'.

Again, like other *improvisatori* in the novel. Like Rozanov's Armenian grandfather, who perished in the Armenian massacres of 1915. But most of all like the anonymous Italian *improvisatore* in Surkov's translation of Pushkin's 'Egyptian Nights', who twice disappears from sight without warning: once after his first improvisation before an audience in Petersburg; another time to avoid a duel to which he has been challenged as a result of someone's misunderstanding the theme of his improvisation.

D. M. Thomas has disappeared, too, behind the masks of his *improvisatori*: first Rozanov, then Surkov, then the *improvisatore* of 'Egyptian Nights'. And then? Pushkin, of course. Pushkin, who, as the novel tells us, was overwhelmed by hearing an impromptu poem spoken by the Polish poet Mickiewicz. Which inspired him to write 'Egyptian Nights', a story that ends (though it is not a proper end: the story remains unfinished) with the poem about the poet weaving 'blind as a bat' (bringing to mind a blind girl with skinny legs) 'his urgent way'. Charsky, the Pushkin-type poet in the story, had asked the Italian to improvise on the theme that 'the poet himself should choose the subject of his songs; the crowd has no right to direct his inspiration'. This poem was the result. My guess is that the whole of *Ararat* is a sort of impromptu interpretation of Pushkin's poem, the central image of Ararat arising out of Pushkin's travels in the Caucasus, and the presence in this poem of his about reaching the 'heights', the duty of a true poet being to 'rise' from 'trivial themes' and 'sterile fevers' – of which numerous and familiar examples abound in Thomas's novel. Indeed, the closer to the poem we come, the closer not only Charsky, but Surkov also, comes to taking upon himself Pushkin's identity. Surkov transforms his shipboard sexual partner, Anna the Polish gymnast, into Ann Kern, the object of Pushkin's amorous attentions and recipient of one of his most celebrated poems – translated in this novel. At the same time Surkov's wife stops being called Zina and becomes Natalya (Goncharov? i.e. Pushkin's wife?). Like Pushkin, he writes whilst lying on a billiard table.

Ararat is a commentary – by means of a series of clearly interrelated 'improvisations' – on a poem by Pushkin. It examines and it exposes the relationship between craft and genius, work and luck, deliberation and improvisation in art. In the process of doing these things it weaves its urgent way through some of the more obviously pressing issues of our time, viewed metonymically on either side – the Russian and the Turkish – of Mount Ararat. As for Ararat itself, the object of Surkov's real and Rozanov's fictional quest, it issues out of and rises above all these things. 'It stood. It let the storm clouds improvise around it.' Like Pushkin. But, then, the storm clouds are also like Pushkin. It is being what he was; they are doing what he did. At the end we are still unsure whether Rozanov had made an unnecessary journey.

A reading of D. M. Thomas suggests that the more traditional forms of fiction, espoused by Snow and Taylor, modified by Green, Powell and Wilson in their different ways, may now be experiencing a new mutation, but carrying within them much of the same genetic code that made their premutated forms so distinctive. Both Thomas and Burgess make use of the comic, the surreal, the fantastic in new ways. The more analytical, more documentary method of their immediate predecessors has been in large part abandoned. But the difference in method cannot altogether conceal the fact that they have large, general aims in common. Each generation seeks to render intelligible psychological and historical events which their continentally inspired but imaginatively more enervated contemporaries (Brooke-Rose, Johnson *et al.*) refuse to believe in. Both Hughes and Burgess write novels which have the effect of enhancing the intrinsic human value of their subject. This is something that cannot be said of the fiction of Christine Brooke-Rose or Gabriel Josipovici. There the theoretical base, failing to support the more practical activity that makes novels possible (curiosity, gossip, and respect for habit and what Iris Murdoch would call the 'opacity' of the human personality) itself becomes the primary object of the reader's attention.

Perhaps I am too optimistic. Perhaps I am comparing a strong and vigorous native tradition with a feeble grafting onto the native stock which has refused to 'take'. Perhaps the traditional novel of man in society and history, having developed healthy new branches in the last fifteen years, is now close to exhaustion and decay. And indeed there is evidence from beyond these islands to suggest that what this book offers is not only a conservative but a mistaken prognostication.

The most powerful novels I have read in recent years are those of Thomas Pynchon, an American writer in the puritan tradition of Hawthorne and Emerson, but also revealing a distinctively modern interest in the conjunction of erotic fantasy and high technology. His novels – *V* (1963), *The Crying of Lot 49* (1966) and *Gravity's Rainbow* (1974) – amply demonstrate what happens when a sensibility both morally aware and willing to encourage moral awareness to issue in moral judgement and action, confronts a world which is constructed in such a way as to call into question the need to make value judgements of any kind. Writing as a literary historian of the period (the 1960s and 1970s), Malcolm Bradbury has expressed the view that, in Pynchon's work and that of other contemporary American writers (who, in my view, are vastly inferior to him),

> Fiction might indeed be drawn from the domestic back into the historical world, but its images were disquieting – images of pattern, power, process, and system, of the struggle of animate against inanimate, of diminished self against increased force. Novelists might then celebrate an unpatterned, resistant awareness to history, system and code; they might, though, point to something yet bleaker, the entry of system into the very heart of the self, rendering humanism impossible and life absurd.*

This book ends at 1980, with the novelists it discusses firmly rooted in a historical world which, though alarming in many of its

* Malcolm Bradbury, *The Modern American Novel* (Oxford, 1983) p. 157.

details, is still felt to be explicable in imaginative terms. But the strain of creating those terms, in Naipaul for example, is proving greater than it was in the earlier post-war years. The tendency to transform and fantasise, in such novels as *Earthly Powers*, *The White Hotel*, and Salman Rushdie's *Midnight's Children* (1981), as an alternative to Hughes's or Scott's recreative and imaginative *explication* of history, is growing. The heroine of Pynchon's *The Crying of Lot 49* ends her quest for a kind of historical knowledge uncertain whether she has failed to find it or gone far beyond it, whether she has received a rebuff or an illumination. 'For it was now like walking among matrices of a great digital computer, the zeroes and ones twinned above, hanging like balanced mobiles right and left, ahead, thick, maybe endless. Behind the hiero-glyphic streets there would either be a transcendent meaning, or only the earth.' All that is in between, in the histories of Hughes and Scott and V. S. Naipaul, and in the comedies of Powell and Green and Angus Wilson, is no longer an option.

In Pynchon's own novels historical events are closely observed and social comedy remains an effective instrument for defining the world his characters occupy. But there is in them also a counter-force, working against the historical and social subject, insidiously, sometimes explosively, undermining the representa-tion of such events as are conventionally deemed to be stable, objective and of demonstrable importance. The way Pynchon sees contemporary America (or, indeed, Europe in 1945) requires that this shall be the case. For his subject is the coexistence of personal and impersonal worlds. And his inability to locate the point at which these worlds coalesce creates the dilemma that renders the subject obtuse and difficult of access. Is it possible to judge which of these worlds controls the other? If it is not possible to locate the point of conjunction, is it possible that there is really *no* relationship between them, other than the untraceable origins of the two worlds in a multiplicity of individual discoveries, inventions, impositions and transformations?

Gravity's Rainbow is a subversive celebration of rocket physics, information technology, computerisation, plastics science, and the all-embracing bureaucracies that accommodate man, but not men, to the world created by these and other technologies. It is also a sustained cry of horror, transformed by art into a crazy game with words, that such a prospect must create in anyone who cannot reconcile himself to a life sustained, even reinvented, by systems that lie so far outside his own understanding. That is why *Gravity's Rainbow* is the most fascinating and the most boring novel I have read in preparation for this book. I think it is a masterpiece that only readers fifty years hence will be able to evaluate and to understand. By then, however, the cultural forces that induced Pynchon to write such a book might make the reading of it supererogatory. What then will become of *The Human Predicament, Guerrillas, A Dance to the Music of Time?* It is in the hope that these books will evince more strength and staying-power than Pynchon's novels lead me to suspect that I offer the commentary on them that follows. Whether anyone will be left outside Pynchon's zones and binary oppositions to read their successors, only time will tell.

2 Richard Hughes

How does a grasshopper look to a Coventry slum child who has never been out in the country before?

> As he crawled through the hedge to look, the quickset above him was suddenly all alive with wings; and poking his nose in the flowering weeds beyond he saw, two inches away from his streaming hay-feverish eyes, a head like a maniac horse's with disk-like eyes you couldn't tell what he was thinking and legs like enormous jointed derricks.

Or a freezing Bavarian winter morning to a young Welshman who has never till now been in Germany?

> Then came a brief flicker of shadow over everything as a cloud of snow slipped silently off the steep roof: not in one heavy lump as when it melts, but more like a slowly falling cloud of smoke. Augustine turned, and through the window saw it drifting away like smoke on the almost imperceptible breeze. Someone (he noticed) had left a bottle of beer on the sill overnight: it had frozen solid and then burst, so that the beer still stood there – an erect bottle-shape of cloudy amber ice among the shattered glass!

Or a Jamaican landscape after an earthquake, to anyone at all?

> Tropical scenery is anyhow tedious, prolific and gross: the greens more or less uniform: great tubular stems supporting thick leaves: no tree has an outline because it is crushed up against something else – no *room*. In Jamaica this profusion swarms over the very mountain ranges: and even the peaks are so numerous that on the top of one you are surrounded by others, and can see nothing. There are hundreds of flowers. Then imagine all this luxuriance smashed, as with a pestle and mortar – crushed, pulped, and already growing again!

24

For Richard Hughes, experience is almost unremittingly visual. No other writer discussed in this book, not even Henry Green, lives so much through his eyes. When Mitzi von Kessen, the heroine of *The Human Predicament*, goes blind, Augustine Penry-Herbert cannot imagine how she will be able to go on living. He is so addicted to the 'joy' of seeing that it was 'as if his whole consciousness were concentrated close behind his eyes and almost craning out of them, like someone who can't tear himself away from the window'. Seeing, in Hughes, is a more active condition of living than it is for any other contemporary writer I can think of. It is not just that his characters share with him the joy in the visual world to which Augustine refers. All their other senses are bound up with the art of seeing. Sight and touch are intimately related to each other. Mitzi's tactile discovery of the contours of her Carmelite cell closely parallels Augustine's optical discoveries of the more spacious geographies – of Bavaria, Connecticut, Morocco – in which he wanders. His eyes open on to sea marsh, mountains and wide horizons with the same physical *rapport* as Mitzi's fingers close around a basin, a towel, a crock of water with ice in its neck.

Yet Hughes's world is not confining. Its physical, and above all visual, reality doesn't so much assault the senses as provide assurance that this is how the senses really work. Perhaps we should expect this of any novelist who is worth reading. But is it in fact all that common? Long before the Romantics tried to subordinate Nature to their own metaphysical intentions, novelists had used the outside world as a storehouse of didactic *exempla*. A landscape existed to facilitate a moral argument, an interior to 'place' a person's class and material circumstances. Later, the outside world was more violently and totally appropriated, often for mythological or symbolic purposes. A stretch of Dorset heath-land became a metaphor for 'the moods of the more thinking of mankind'; three figures glimpsed through a window an ethical summons to self-forgetfulness and duty. In due process of time the natural world had been so interfered with by those who sought instruction from it that its shapes and contours did come to validate intuitions about life that were looked for in them. Landscapes accommodated themselves to the demands writers and their readers made upon them. To notice this fact, and still to see the world as 'different' – to see trees as trees, as well as material for building; to see snow as snow, as well as what the runners of sledges slide over and what you make snowmen out of – is one of Hughes's most notable and unusual achievements. He has a vision of the world. But it remains *the* world, not *his* world. It is not made over into a mere object for human consumption, the kind of thing novelists need to settle their characters in – as a place, and as a repository of psychological metaphor. We have the extraordinary sensation that the world Hughes has created was not created to satisfy his characters. On the contrary, they are there largely to respond to it, to take it in. And that is as true of the other characters and their thoughts and feelings as it is of landscapes and buildings and things. There is a space between them which rarely exists in the pages of other novelists. Perhaps that is why Hughes's world seems at the same time so casual and so hallucinatorily real.

Hughes's concentration on the details of vision, so rapt and so complete that it excludes for the moment everything else, is shared by his characters when they are deeply moved by some aspect of the world. Particularly when they fall in love. Before Augustine realises he has fallen in love with Mitzi, his mind is totally absorbed in her. His experience of her prevents him from attending to anything that exists outside her: 'As a well-made kid glove will be so exactly filled with hand that one can't even insert a bus-ticket between them, so the membrane of Augustine's mind was now exactly shaped and stretched to hold Mitzi's peerless image and nothing more: it felt stretched to bursting by it and couldn't conceivably find a hair's-breadth room for anything else.' As so often in Hughes, visual concentration is accompanied by suggestions of physical disturbance. Later Augustine's sense of Mitzi's presence in a room becomes something that determines every motion he makes, and every image of any other thing he absorbs. His movements are compared with those of a yachtsman working along a coast by taking some point on his beam to steer by, instead of what lies straight ahead (i.e. what he is actually moving towards). The blind Mitzi cannot see him at all. He sees the blind Mitzi even when he is looking somewhere quite other. The visual sense hardly requires a direct, present object. It can create one through its negotiations with other things.

Towards the end of *The Fox in the Attic* Augustine visits Schwabing, the bohemian quarter of Munich. There he meets Jacinto, a sculptor from Brazil, whose obsession with 'Significant Form' has a profound effect on his attitude to the visible world.

What Augustine claims he has discovered from Jacinto is that
' "meaning" is something that can't be intellectually expressed,
it's something essentially visual'. 'Significant Form' is 'an immanence in the perceived which the painter's eye can uncover. A
physical immanence mind you . . . a wholly physical kind of
super-reality.' Here again the exercise of the sense of sight is
described in a way that emphasises its physicality, its relationship
with other, usually more disturbing and more immediate bodily
activities. This is summed up in Jacinto's little aphorism that
'The eye is the light of the body.' The phrase, and Hughes's work
in general, leaves one with the impression that vision almost
bypasses other mental activities, relating the world as it is seen to
the body of the person who sees it without the intervention of
reason. Of course this cannot be so, and Augustine's absorption of
Jacinto's theory is made to look mildly comic. Nevertheless all of
Hughes's books suggest that the activity of the mind in making
visual experience coherent occurs at a rather later stage than we
have become used to thinking it does. They suggest that the
mind's ability to make sense of the world is more immediately and
more directly affected by what the eye sees and the body, as it
were, absorbs through the eye, than most other writers have
assumed.

This makes Hughes's response to what he sees enormously
vivid and 'new'. It also makes the way he distributes information
about the world through which his characters move seem
strangely random, even eccentric at first. It is only when we have
spent some little time seeing things as Hughes and his characters
see them that we begin to realise, perhaps, that this is the way we
see them too. But in books we saw them differently. To see in a
book as we see in real life is a disturbing, at first a foreign
experience. It is like seeing a bowl of fruit painted by Cézanne
after having spent a lifetime looking at Dutch still-lifes. At first the
proportions do not look right, the recession of the planes is odd,
the texture of the skins of the fruit not shiny enough, not polished.
Unsurprisingly, Augustine invests in Cézannes, among other
post-Impressionist paintings, after this conversion to 'Significant
Form'. But the landscapes he has been inhabiting have all along
been Cézanne landscapes, which we have hesitated to enter with
him as a result of years of living among the visual appurtenances
of the Victorians and realists. There, too often, our moral and
psychological tutelage had been undertaken at the expense of

what we had actually been able to see and, through seeing, feel and touch, in their world.

Entering the Schloss Lorienburg for the first time, Augustine looks upward from the inner courtyard to four storeys of stuccoed stone, and then four more of steep pantiled roofs, until, on the topmost roofridge, his eye alights on a wagon wheel with a tattered old stork's nest perched on top of it. Since this is all part of a completely new experience, Augustine, we are told 'took it all in at a glance, for today he was still absorbing everything with the unnaturally observant eye of first arrrival somewhere totally strange: not till tomorrow would he even begin to notice less'. Hughes is suggesting that the eye might not be naturally as observant as Augustine's eye is made to be when he enters the castle. But his strategy as a novelist is to open his eye on everything as if for the first time. It is to see everything as 'strange', and to defer tomorrow (in the sense of the time when what is seen is 'placed' in a context of more seeing and also more reflection on what has been seen) to the day-after-tomorrow. Only gradually are Hughes's characters allowed to 'notice less' of the world around them. Since their experience changes more rapidly than that of most other characters of modern fiction – both in respect of where they are and what they do – there is often insufficient time to reduce immediate physical sensation to anything like an ordered appreciation of whatever the experience is of which it is a part.

Augustine's appreciation of the world has always taken this overwhelmingly visual form, long before he heard anything about 'Significant Form' from Jacinto. One of the ways Hughes emphasises this is by referring from time to time to a telescope he was given as a present on his eleventh birthday. The intention was that he should investigate the moon and the planets, but Augustine soon got into the habit of looking at *people* close up (and upside down) through it. Viewed through the telescope they were like specimens on a microscope slide. Unaware that they were being observed, they looked different from the way they normally looked – in society, or even in the company of family and friends. 'How different people's faces do look when they think no one sees them and so they stop gesticulating at you with their features!' This gives Augustine a 'Godlike feeling', 'seeing human nature, which the human eye so rarely sees'. In fact it placed him in a position *vis à vis* other people that novelists have claimed to have occupied *vis à vis* their characters almost since the birth of the novel form. In recent years, especially, novelists have worried about this fact, and evolved a sophisticated technical apparatus for pretending that their vision is not so comprehensive, and consequently not so artificial, as some of their predecessors had claimed it was. Hughes, though, seems not to be in the slightest degree worried about occupying the same position towards his characters as Augustine occupies towards the people on whom he is spying with his telescope. He switches focus and sighting almost at random, and keeps changing which end of the instrument to look through with bewildering rapidity. Close-ups of one scene alternate sharply with long-distance views of another. Hughes betrays no embarrassment at placing himself in this God-like position. Why does he view the characters with such calm, such equanimity, when almost every other writer who essayed large-scale ambitions during the twenties and thirties (the period in which Hughes began to write), was so busy hiding away his telescope, and evolving complicated field manoeuvres to catch his characters in a 'natural' pose?

The Human Predicament is full of scenes in which characters watch one another unawares. Almost certainly the most spectacular of them is Wolff's spying on Augustine and Mitzi from the attic at Lorienburg. But there are many others: Otto watches over the sleeping Mitzi on the night she has gone blind; Augustine spies on Mitzi in the chapel at Lorienburg, then follows her secretly back to her house through the snow; Ernst Krebelmann and Hans stare through the plate-glass windows at the Dreesen Hotel, catching glimpses of Hitler and Göring in conference immediately before the 'Night of the Long Knives'; and Anne Marie Woodcock contemplates Augustine swimming naked in a pool in the Connecticut woods at the very beginning of *The Wooden Shepherdess*. These are just a few examples. Almost invariably, though, a closer look at these incidents will show that, however carefully, however concentratedly the spectator looks at what is before him, he scarcely ever understands its real nature. Wolff totally fails to realise what is going on between Mitzi and Augustine (he does not even know that Mitzi is blind); Otto has no inkling of Mitzi's religious intuitions, and neither has Augustine; Ernst and Hans do not realise that Hitler and Göring are plotting the murder of their comrades in the SA.

Ree's behaviour is more puzzling. The rôle she plays in *The*

Wooden Shepherdess is an uncertain one, although on the level of 'plot' in the conventional sense of the word there is little difficulty in seeing why she is there and what effect she has on Augustine. She offers him sex after Janis has given him the brush-off. But Ree is only twelve years old and that means she has not yet crossed the great divide between childhood and adolescence. So when she meets Augustine by the pool she accepts him as an addition to her world which calls for no moral judgements or emotional demands to be made. She wants them to behave like two animals together; rather as Polly, six years younger, wanted to behave with him – as if they were rabbits, or dogs. Six years do make a difference, though. Ree wants her decision to please Augustine to express itself through sexual contact. She scarcely knows what this means. It seems to be more a matter of bodily gestures and contortions than anything else she can imagine. But she is capable of going through the motions; and she certainly loves Augustine, wants to use a childish parody of sex to comfort him and keep him with her.

> A yawning Augustine was spreading rugs for himself in a corner when something made him turn. From the bed an almost inaudible voice had said 'I'm *not* ashamed, so you needn't put out the lamp when you come.' He looked: she lay on her back stark naked, lit by a flicker of lightning itself. 'I don't *want* you put out the lamp', she repeated: then cupped her half-apple breasts in her hands for her elbows to take her weight, and playfully ran her little feet up the wall like mice till her hips were lifted clear.

Ree is uncorrupted, also virtually amoral. Her spying on Augustine at the pool is as close as most people get to a truthful, disinterested vision of another person. Her inspection of the roughly sewn-up scar on the back of his head ends only with the words 'It's scary.' Her touching him is possessive only in the sense that it is a physical counterpart to the curiosity she shows about him in the questions she is asking at the same time. She sees Augustine as a new, fresh, interesting object in the world, about which she wants to know more. But, until she 'betrays' him to the Pack after he has scared her in the ruins of the Big Warren Place, she makes no demands on him, beyond the 'bare reassurance he liked her'.

Other 'spies' have their vision distorted by the selfish demands they try to make it satisfy. Wolff needs an object for his hate and love to coalesce in, and Mitzi is ideally suited to *be* that object – provided Wolff can fantasise around her a reciprocated passion for Augustine. So that is what he does. He spies on her, intently, from his eyrie in the Schloss Lorienburg attics. But what he *wants* to see is so rooted in his subconscious mind that the most obvious thing there *is* to see, Mitzi's blindness, he fails to notice. The fact that 'the eye altering alters all' is brilliantly represented in *Stille Nachte* when Ernst and Hans make out only an indistinct picture of Hitler, Göring and others at Bad Godesburg. This is because the light outside throws their own reflections on to the plate glass windows across which incomplete images of the Nazi leaders and the SS pass occasionally. When, during a rain storm shortly afterwards, Ernst turns his head and accidentally catches a glimpse of Hitler's face looking out, he takes in what he sees without preconceptions, with a clarity that no amount of concentrated attention has been able to produce. 'The gaze of a man half-conscious: vague, shifting, glassy, settling nowhere and seeing nothing.' The expression on Hitler's face tells us more about his state of mind before Röhm's arrest and the massacre of the SA than any amount of psychoanalysis could have done. What is dramatised in the following chapters is merely an extension of narrative of what Ernst has glimpsed on the terrace of the Dreesen Hotel.

The Human Predicament relates this activity of seeing and knowing with more inward processes of biological and psychic growth, and then embeds them both within a carefully reconstructed historical context. The characters exist in conformity with a theory of human development that places great emphasis on the interaction of public and private lives. And public lives are lived in accordance with a deep seated feeling of nationhood. In its widest sense, social life in Hughes is national life – here the English nation and the German nation. Much is made of the inability of representatives of these nations to understand one another, so vastly different is their experience. Augustine's views on Ernst Toller are not merely anathema but incomprehensible to his uncles and cousins. To Augustine he is a great dramatist; to them a 'Jewish scribbler'. The von Kessen children cannot believe that an Englishman can be trusted to keep his word, and Augustine can't believe that they can't believe it. Conversation between Augustine and the von Kessens is a tissue of embarrassment and misunderstanding.

What accounts for this complete breakdown of communication between the two nations, represented here as two branches of a single family? On a personal level it destroys trust between the men and turns Augustine's love for Mitzi to waste. But is it possible to grasp the fundamental causes of the breakdown, causes which lie underneath the bare historical facts on the one hand and abstract philosophical theories on the other? Hughes believes that if we look closely at the ways in which people relate themselves to their fellow men as individuals and in societies, this is possible. His explanation appears in chapter 26 of *Polly and Rachel* and is continued to the end of the book. Hughes is talking about the 'abiding terms of the human predicament', 'the entropy of the self'.

The point Hughes is making, and which supports the whole structure of his biophysical approach to character, is that man possesses no discrete psychological identity, totally separating him from everything and everyone around him. He is conscious of 'some overspill of self' into 'penumbral regions', which represent his perceiver's footing in the perceived. His environment is not just somewhere he happens to live. It is a part of himself, which he misuses at his peril. On the other hand the self is not capable of being extended infinitely. There is a point at which the individual psyche draws a line and says: within this line is 'me', the necessary extension of the 'I' that otherwise would be intolerably constricted and turned in on itself; outside it is 'them', something quite different, alien, inwardly incomprehensible. And what is inside the line must assert its congruity, one part with another, by asserting its incongruity with all that is outside. It follows that a measure of hostility must be present between the inner and outer circles of the psyche's relationships with the world that is a part of it, and the world that is a part of something else. So long as a balance, and a tension, is preserved between self and not-self the psyche's health is maintained. But pressures have been brought to bear by history and ideology to thrust the self back into what Hughes calls the 'ring fence' of a man's 'minimal innermost "I"', where even such words as 'we' and 'my' have no meaning. This is the Descartian road to solipsism, and to one kind of breakdown. At the same time what Hughes calls 'emergent reason' – by which I think he must have in mind variants of post-Hegelian positivist philosophy, Marxist or liberal – has sought to remove the line altogether and forced the 'I' into an intolerable co-operation with all that lies outside it, i.e. with all that is represented by the 'we' relationship on the one hand and the 'they' relationship on the other. The ideological and psychological pressure to convert 'we-as-distinct-from-they' into 'we-who-are-a-part-of-they' is the most dangerous force in the world Augustine and his friends are trying to negotiate. For

> suppose . . . the very we–they line itself within us had been deliberately so blurred and denied that the huge countervailing charges it once carried were themselves dissipated and suppressed? The normal penumbra of the self would then become a no-man's land: the whole self-conscious being is rendered unstable – it has lost its 'footing': the perceiver is left without emotional adhesion anywhere to the perceived, like a sea-anemone which has let go its rock.

Later Hughes explains how, before 1914, the 'Liberal mystique of Laissez-faire', based on a 'rational doctrine of total *separation of persons*', had deprived Englishmen of a sense of the 'we' in their experience and trapped them in their isolated egos. The outbreak of war had restored both the 'we' and the 'they' which are necessary to individuals *and* nations – but only to be sacrificed on the Western Front. He then shows how Augustine, who had just missed being called up and sent to the trenches, failed, for that reason, to participate in this restored sense of identity, and was left as we see him at the beginning of the novel. The collapse of morale after the war and the reversal of his by now accepted expectation of an early death have made him withdraw from his fellows in a retreat from the outside world broken only by his ability to get on with children, especially his niece Polly.

Looking back to Augustine in the gun-room at Newton Llantony, or forwards to the contrast between Hitler and Mitzi, we can see that aspects of the views adumbrated in the abstract in chapter 26 are embodied in all the main characters of the novel. In the gun-room Augustine, for some time now a solitary, suddenly acquires a sense of the 'we' relation: ' "he" was no longer cooped up entirely within his own skin'. This in turn produces the necessary 'they', a 'hostile, alien "world" ' outside the 'final envelope' of the room. The rest of the novel, in so far as it concerns

Augustine, traces his coming to an awarenes of a shared identity and an accompanying sense of the foreignness of his German relatives. From time to time we share his sense of the strangeness of other people – in particular of Franz and Mitzi.

The representation of Augustine's character, however, has occasioned some of the sharpest criticism of the novel. Merely to describe what he does is to underline his lack of direction, the sense we have that he is always at the mercy of events, never their master. And this provokes a feeling of unsatisfactoriness not only about Augustine's character, but about the way his character is being presented. After all, by the time the sequence closes, Augustine will be well into his thirties and has literally *done* nothing in the way of work – nothing to match even his friend Jeremy's paper-shuffling at the Admiralty, or brother-in-law Gilbert's struggles in the Liberal Party at Westminster. He has been precipitated onto the sidelines of some of the most significant events in the history of the inter-war years: the Munich putsch, Abd el Krim's campaign in Morocco, the Night of the Long Knives. But his experience of these events is at second or third hand, or is a matter of mere geographical proximity.

It has been suggested that, with the outbreak of war, Augustine was to have joined the Navy and served on one of the ships that destroyed the *Graf Spee*. But would he have been capable of making intelligent perceptions of the importance of the events in which he might have been involved? That we cannot know. Certainly up to the point Hughes reached in his story, Augustine's development is not to be assessed in terms of his analytical understanding of the nature of the world to which he belongs. Shuttling back and forth between the flashpoints of history, he preserves his political naivety intact. But at the same time his intuitive understanding of the roots of history and politics is extended. And that understanding comes, as we should expect in a novel like this, through vision, through seeing things and then making intuitive inferences from what has been seen, rather than through analysis and abstract argument. Augustine never shows any marked ability at this, though he does show an eagerness to convince others that he is rather good at it.

The freedom to do what and go where he chooses, without a family or a job to tie him to one place, rescues Augustine from several entanglements that might have tested weaknesses in his character and, we suspect, in his characterisation too. For

Augustine's lack of sustained involvement in the lives of others, his lack of responsibility for any lives apart from his own, prevents him from experiencing those moral crises, balancing cause and consequence that help to define the inner spirit of so many earlier heroes and heroines of the English novel. The sterile alternation of doubt and certainty in his feelings towards Mitzi ensures that he misses the opportunity to speak to her about his feelings until it is too late, and she is swept off to a convent in Munich. Similar uncertainties about Joan Morgan keep him away in Morocco, whilst an old friend from his days in America, Antony Fairfax, sweeps her off her feet and marries her instead. Before this happens, though, Joan has confessed her dissatisfaction with Augustine's irresponsibility to Jeremy. 'What *does* Augustine intend to do with his life?' she asks him. Jeremy's reply is unexpected: 'Perhaps it's a rarer achievement that you imagine (he says), Augustine's knack of having things happen to him without ever having to lift a finger to make them happen.'

Augustine has been described as a Welsh version of the Russian superfluous man – what Hughes's friend Richard Poole called 'this tradition of the character suspended, not knowing what to do with his life, wandering about and continuously meeting other people and exploring himself through these meetings'. The trouble with this assessment is that Augustine seems to do very little 'exploring of himself'. Change and development of character do not seem to come about in this way in Hughes. Self-analysis gives way to other-directed seeing, and it is the link between what he sees and how what he sees connects with other kinds of perception, that gradually extends the range and quality of Augustine's experience. But Augustine never learns to articulate satisfactorily what he has discovered in this way. And he rarely uses it as a spur to effective action.

There are numerous indications of Augustine's juvenility in *The Human Predicament*. His experience with Janis in *The Wooden Shepherdess* brings out his signal lack of sexual precosity (as does, presumably, his involvement with Sadie later in the same book, when they escape together to the Canadian border – but that is pushed too far into the background to count as hard evidence). And his callowly simplistic social views have been evident from the first, at least since his argument with Jeremy and Mary about the nature of political relationships, and other relationships that create terms for social involvement between people: 'Your web can't ravel because . . . there is NO web. There is no thread, even, joining man to man – nothing.' That might go some way towards explaining Augustine's strangely atomic relation to other characters, though his attachment to children points in a different direction. Indeed it is his involvement with one particular 'child', Ree, which first brings home to him the inadequacy of his social attitudes. For his 'betrayal' of Ree, immediately before leaving New Blandford, imposes on him a sense of sin which, according to views he has held hitherto, should not exist. It is only such people as Mitzi, hopelessly stuck in the past, the pre-Freud era, who can possibly experience such feelings and attribute a meaning to them. And yet 'the pain in that small terrible face as he'd seen it last was something that never could be undone – a weight that he couldn't crawl out from under . . . : somehow he somewhere got out of step'.

Again it is something intensely seen that brings home to Augustine a new feeling which complicates his existence. He is experiencing something inside himself which he has already seen outside on numerous occasions. In himself he had detected ancient, what he had supposed to be fossilised, intuitions, where he had expected to find only a vacuum, or at best a receptacle for the dumping of fragments of liberal ideology. And it is this simultaneous presence of the old and the new, the new being incompletely manufactured out of human and geographical materials which are for the most part old, or at least 'set' in their ways and their physical contours, that Augustine has witnessed over and over again in what he has seen, especially in Bavaria.

In *The White Crow* Augustine's unease in the Schloss Lorienburg is to a large extent attributable to the persistence of nineteenth-century and even medieval attitudes at the heart of the New Germany, royalist and fascist political activities functioning within the same family, and often in the middle of activities which seem appropriate to both of them: 'Everything here confused one's sense of time! There was something Victorian about Augustine's hostess, Cousin Adèle, with her lace and her chatelaine; but equally something of an earlier, sterner century too. . . .' And at the end of *The Fox in the Attic* this interlinking of time scales, charming and amusing for the most part at Lorienburg, pregnant with the most horrific developments for the future, in, for example, the Hanfstängl's Christmas scene (see below), achieves a memorable visual representation.

The ring tables of ice Augustine sees three feet up the trunks of the trees he passes on his walk through the forests around Kamstadt have been caused by savage flooding and freezing of the Danube weeks before. The river had dammed with the barrier of its own ice floes, and when the dam burst with the pressure of water behind it the unsupported ice had collapsed and splintered, creating this charming oddity of the ice tables.

But elsewhere the Danube seemed to be frozen solid in heaps. It was wild, yet utterly still. Huge blocks of ice had jostled each other like elephants rutting and then got frozen in towering lumps: or had swirled over and over before coagulating till they were curled like a Chinese sea. None of them had remained in the place where first it had frozen: each block was complete in itself but now out of place . . . .

Augustine is horrified at the sight. It makes him hate Germany. For he can see that the force that had created this meaningless jungle would be matched in ferocity and power by the force that would later melt the ice and hurl it down the river 'grinding to bits everything in its path'. The political allegory is not made explicit. But the force underlying the shapes that are seen in nature has an obvious parallel in the historical pressure operating beneath the social contours of Augustine's Bavarian experiences. The same frozen quality applies to the surface of German political life, as applies to the surface of the enchained Danube. On the personal level, Augustine's atomic individualism, his Freudian apparatus, is an icy, apparently rigid carapace hiding the shapes of guilt and sin and possible religious intuitions about life that his experiences in *The Human Predicament*, particularly visual experiences such as that of Ree's crumpled face and the frozen Danube, are ever so gradually thawing and softening – with what final result the unfinished character of the sequence does not disclose.

For Mitzi, the discovery of the boundaries of self is a religious experience. Her journey to God is a long and onerous one. It has not been completed by the time we leave her at the end of *Stille Nacht*, alone in her cell after Father Petrus has brought news of the murder of her uncle Otto. But at first she does not understand it is a journey at all. She assumes that consciousness of God is static grace, in which the barrier between herself and God, or, as she puts it, the small 'I am' and the great 'I AM', disappears; and there is no obstacle left between the human and the divine. As usual in Hughes, the experience, of the loss of self in God, is described in vividly physical terms. To speak of God holding Mitzi 'nestling in the hollow of His infinite hand' is too 'outward' an image (rather like the one George Herbert discards in his poem 'Regeneration', where it conceals an undesirably passive relationship between Creator and creature). Mitzi feels this, it is true; but she also feels that the dynamic intercorporeality of man and God is inadequately realised in the image. Instead she thinks of Him as 'running in her veins. *He* was the tongue speaking in her mind's ear and He was the mental ear which listened. He was the very mind in her which did her thinking.' Mitzi seems to be close to a mystical experience of God-in-her and she-in-God, of the kind St Teresa witnesses in her autobiography, and to which other female saints have testified. But her experience is incomplete. Still, Hughes suggests, there is a small part of Mitzi, 'which even now watched the transaction as it were from outside; and curiously that outsider was the "I" at the transaction's very heart'.

The gap between total immersion in God (giving up the soul to full acceptance of God's presence there, as everywhere), and the state Mitzi is in now (sensing God's 'finding' her but aware of herself at the centre of His discovery), seems a very small one. But it takes Mitzi years, and Hughes volumes, to close it. At the end of *Stille Nacht* the 'Immanent presence of God' is described in much the same way: 'God was an Eye; and the Eye never slept and the Eye was inside her. God was an Ear which never slept, and the Ear was inside; and the Eye never blinked nor the Ear mis-heard.' The use of the word 'immanent' will cast the reader's mind back to the incident at Schwabing, when Augustine learnt that 'Significant Form' was an 'immanence' in the perceived which he could understand only in relation to the biblical idea of 'being born again in the Spirit'. It does seem as if Mitzi's discovery of God is being paralleled throughout *The Human Predicament* with Augustine's discovery of a principle of meaning in the world that he can grasp only in terms in the visible. But Mitzi's blindness, forbidding her access to the visible, nevertheless brings her to an experience of the 'visionary'. Visionary truth, it seems, can be apprehended by ignoring the visible world altogether, although the visible world itself, so far as he can fathom, is the only place Augustine can find it.

At the heart of Mitzi's physical darkness there is a dazzling light, which is the light shining from God's Eye. God is the light of Mitzi's body, just as the human eye, for Augustine, is the light of his own body. The power of God to see through a blind girl is preceded by metaphors of sight oddly adapted to make Mitzi's blindness intelligible, before she is able to sense this complete vision of herself shining through God, and God shining through herself. When she was half blind, living in a world of strange shadows and lights and blurred movements, the beauty of this strange world she lived in was powerfully described in visual terms. But, even in complete blindness, her discovery of being 'with God' was a visual experience. The first moment of understanding God's love is like seeing 'in the likeness of a pinpoint of light' down below, the lights of an inn left behind in the valley and then revealed again by a turn in the road. But this understanding has to be moved further and further towards (though it may seem to get further and further away), if the 'visionary' is not to be thwarted, as Mitzi almost was when, at the moment of going blind, she received her first illumination. Only on such a journey towards the source of light (even, perhaps especially, in a physically blind person) can a proper and total involvement with God survive. The true climax of Mitzi's experience comes at the end of *Stille Nacht*, when the darkness of the soul which no human eye can pierce is brilliantly irradiated by the calm, unflinching gaze of God:

> No man can see his own soul clearly and live: he must hood his eyes which look inwards as if against a dazzling by light when the light is too much – though this is a dazzling by darkness, his soul is too dark to bear looking at. Yet God can look: as the eagle can stare at the brightness of the sun, so God stared at even the blackness within without blinking; and under the burning eye of that burning relentless Love she was molten metal that heaved in a crucible under its scum.

Mitzi's Catholic spirit here joins with Milton's Protestantism to celebrate the power of God to make darkness visible:

> So much the rather than Celestial Light
> Shine inward, and the mind through all her powers
> Irradiate, there plant eyes, all mist from thence
> Purge and disperse, that I may see. . . .
> *(Paradise Lost,* III, 51–3)

This is one representation of seeing as God sees, in a mystical co-identity of God with the blind nun – or the blind poet. But God's eye turns outwards, to the world, as well as inwards, to the depths of the individual soul.

In the middle of *The Fox in the Attic* (ch. 10) Mitzi is explicitly contrasted with Hitler in terms of the theory of the entropy of consciousness. With the shock of Mitzi's crisis, we are told, the central 'I' in her had become dislodged: 'It had dwindled to a cloudlet no bigger than a man's hand beneath the whole zenith of God.' The movement from individual collapse to the ensuing infinite expansion in God is described, characteristically, by a comparison with something seen. When Mitzi has probed 'to her innermost pinpoint "I am" ', she discovers 'it was like looking into a tiny familiar room through a window and finding herself instead looking out – upon landscapes of infinite width'. That is the image Hughes applies, and the blind Mitzi experiences, to make real the supersession of her little 'I am', locked up inside a finite space, by God's great 'I AM', which can be contemplated only from a position that has no definite space or location, because it has been lost in what is being looked out towards.

Though Hughes does not repeat the metaphor – the image of the room and the window is taken from a passage near the beginning of *The Meistersingers*, where the comparison between Hitler and Mitzi is not explicit – we can see how it could be used to explain Hitler's cast of mind as Hughes interprets it in *The Human Predicament*. Hitler too cannot separate himself from God's great 'I AM'; but for different reasons, and in a different way. His impulse to control and dominate the world makes him usurp the divine position long before he has experienced that dislodgement Hughes speaks about when he is tracing the early stages of Mitzi's conversion. For Hitler there is no distinction between the room looked into from outside, and the room looked out of from within. Looking through the windows he sees the same thing on either side of the glass. However spacious the house, for him it is an image of confinement. Everything inside and outside it is some aspect of himself. The largeness of the world is all contained, and suffocated, in his littleness. For, to revert to the entropic metaphor, Hitler's was an ego 'virtually without penumbra', without any foothold in a circumambient world where words like 'we' and 'ours' acquire meaning.

By contrast with Mitzi, Hitler is a 'monistic "I" '. He lives in unnatural isolation, 'designing and creating motions enormous and without curb'. His attitude to human beings is powerfully and briefly defined: 'All tools have handles – this sort was fitted with ears.' And so Hitler manipulates other people by the force of his rhetoric, the verbal expression of his diseased personality. Yet he imposes on them nothing of himself, no idea or sentiment or policy in which he believes. The point is made over and over again in *The Human Predicament*, and it is corroborated frequently by historians of the Third Reich, that Hitler almost always led from the rear, and always did so where strategy, as distinct from short-term tactical manoeuvres, was concerned. Hence the dithering that precedes the 'Night of the Long Knives', causing Göbbels in particular to reserve his position for as long as he can. In a passage from the uncollected opening chapters of the seventh book, Hughes calls this strange power Hitler possessed, of absorbing the wishes and aspirations of other people, a 'systematic empathy'. He meant that Hitler had no fixed intentions, beyond the ambition to remain in a position of supreme power. His mesmeric will absorbed and then mobilised the desires of others, but his own mind was without any settled, substantial content. It was entirely given over to the exercise of the will in what would have been a vacuum were it not for the existence of other people, other minds, as conduits to fill it. As a 'monistic "I" ', however, a supreme solipsist, Hitler simply converted the outer to the inner. Other people became merely parts of himself. So in a way he *was* God, he was the world. One has no need of a 'penumbra' of reciprocal relationships when the line that defines where they are has been rubbed out, and everything that would have been outside it, if it had been there in the first place, has been sucked into a single mind, expressing a single will.

No one else in *The Human Predicament* thinks quite like Hitler. But there are others whose penumbral environments betray a dangerous thinness, a fragile quality. As we saw, Augustine's state of mind at the very opening of the novel was in severe disequilibrium, because he had lost contact with almost every-thing that lay outside the gun-room at Newton. In *The Meister-singers* and *Stille Nacht* Brian, the butcher's boy, who cannot love people, and can love animals only as a prelude to slaughtering them, seems to be moving towards a pathological self-enclosure that bodes ill for the future. But the most spectacular example, after Hitler, of a man whose participation in life has contracted to frighteningly narrow limits is Wolff Scheidemann. Twenty years old, he is a veteran of the Baltic wars – fought with the utmost savagery by German patriots after their government had accepted the armistice and the peace terms of 1918. Wolff has identified himself with a new Germany in the struggle in the north and east, but he has failed. Now, back in Bavaria, skulking in the attic at Schloss Lorienburg, he knows that the weak, pacific Weimar republic that has replaced his dream of an aggressive nationalist state has no place for him. He is a hunted animal who despises the only friend (Franz) who has stuck by him. For almost a year he has seen no one else, except from his attic window. And during that time he has 'grown into a unity with the very timbers of those attics. . . . Look! Like the bones of Ezekiel already these beams were covering themselves with flesh, with skin – and it was *his* flesh and skin they were growing.' Imprisoned in the dark attic, hidden most of the time under a bundle of furs squeezed into a corner, and kept company by a fox, whose smell penetrates the room, Wolff owns the most shrunken the most thinly bounded personality in the novel.

In a way Wolff is the opposite of Hitler. Instead of absorbing the whole world into himself – a dark, inverted reflection – he has had the world taken away from him, and the corner he occupies in his own shrunken psyche is externally symbolised by his occupation of that small corner of the Lorienburg attics. Strangely, the one link he retains with the world outside, apart from Franz, is his romantic attachment to Mitzi. But, as we have seen, that is based on a fantastic delusion. And when something from outside the fantasy – Augustine – invades it and deprives him even of the satisfaction of an unrequited romantic love, he turns to the only final escape, 'the absolute unreality of death'. The blind Mitzi is discovered stumbling under his feet as he hangs from a beam – unaware of her 'responsibility' for what has happened, unaware, for that matter of what *has* happened.

There is something very suggestive in this ghastly tableau, the last we see of Wolff, or of Mitzi in this volume. The extremity of Wolff's self-sacrifice as a partisan, exhausted in defeat, has created in him an exorbitant demand for compensation. But his self is not strong enough to restrain the nihilistic energies that exploit it. In the end murder and sadistic fantasy have no choice but to give way to self-annihilation. Mitzi, on the other hand, has not yet advanced beyond the outer gates of self-abnegating fanaticism. She could not destroy herself to be with God, because the line that divided God from herself did not exist: by destroying herself she would have destroyed God in her. As the blind girl recoils from the dead fanatic, so the forces embodied in their persons almost meet, unknowingly, but finally withdraw from each other – one into complete death, the other into a limbo (the convent) which the incompleteness of these first six books does not allow us fully to comprehend, or even presume to be final.

The scene is the last of a whole sequence which throws Augustine, Mitzi and Wolff into an inadvertent relationship with one another. Mitzi is at the centre of the pattern, unaware of either Augustine's love or Wolff's existence. Augustine fails to understand the situation or his own involvement in it until it is too late for him to act. His position is vividly conveyed by the ballet in the snow, during which he flutters around Mitzi, invisibly guiding her from the chapel at Lorienburg back to the hall. And all the time this mimic relationship is being played out, Wolff is watching it happen. Or watching a fantasy version of it happen, since, like Augustine earlier in the story, he does not know that Mitzi is blind. The links between the characters are hardly understood by them. They occupy positions they are not aware of. Tascha on her bicycle at the Odeonsplatz, Augustine on the drive to Röttningen, even little Polly and smaller Sylvanus – in their different ways made to exist in relation to a dead girl neither of them knows ever existed – all occupy a place in a pattern of events they cannot see, but which penetrates deep into the private psyche and extends far into the world of political action.

The scene of Wolff's discovery brings together two very different characters at stages of their lives in a way that makes them cast strange, almost parodic reflections on to each other. Their physical proximity, after living so long either unconscious of one another's presence (or the one conscious of the other only as a figment of compensatory fantasy) brings to the reader's attention a psychic proximity which is 'thinkable' only at this one point in time. Mitzi's fanaticism is merely one necessary stage in her journey to God. It is not a permanent closing-out of God and his world, either in imprisonment or death – as is the case with Wolff. But characters do not have to be actually in each other's presence for Hughes to draw attention to aspects of their behaviour which are in some way comparable. Frequently the comparison is made in a very much less direct, less dramatic manner. Some trivial (it may be) attribute of character or experience is brought into conjunction with something of the same kind in someone else, somewhere else; suggesting the existence of a pattern, of a wider significance, gradually becoming visible to us through a series of repeated gestures, scenes, images and events. One example of this is the evolving comparison between Mitzi and Augustine's sister, Mary Wadamy – two characters who never meet in the novel that we have, and who have met only once in the novel's past, when Mary visited Schloss Lorienburg in the years before the war. At that time she was in her late 'teens, and Mitzi only seven.

Mary and Mitzi have in common the fact that they both undergo terrible physical suffering. Each of them loses the use of some part of her body. Mitzi goes blind. Mary breaks her neck after being thrown from a horse, and becomes paralysed from the waist down, as well as in the face and much of the upper body. She recovers the use of her arms, but apart from that and a few other muscular functions she is incapable of movement. This makes her almost a reverse copy of Mitzi; for, although Mitzi can hear, touch and taste, without the light of the eye these senses, in Hughes's world, become merely utilitarian. The *joys* of the senses are closed to her, and she is left with four out of the five as little more than automatic functions of the body. Mary, on the contrary, is deprived almost of the whole of her body. At first she cannot distinguish this incorporeality from what she has read of the condition of the soul after death. Since she is not a religious person, and does not believe in life after death, this paradoxical condition of lifelessness and deathlessness fused together throws her into deep gloom. She has 'spells of nightmare confusion which couldn't tell life and death apart'. What saves her from total breakdown and madness is, of course, her rediscovery of the world and her place in it through the exercise of the sense of sight. Just as Mitzi's dormant religious inclinations were awakened by her loss of sight, so Mary's atheism receives a check through the rediscovery of her ability to *see* that follows from her loss of almost everything else.

The re-entry of Mary into the world through a dizzying return of secular vision is as brilliantly described as Mitzi's religious journey through the dark into the light. It begins with her first day out of bed, strapped into a special chair, moving on pneumatic wheels, and moulding itself to the body with hidden padded supports and inconspicuous straps. Bodiless herself, Mary is manoeuvred into a human position – that of sitting, with head erect – within the substitute body of a mechanical contraption. Hughes's description of the way the world becomes visible again – at first all movement, with restlessly projecting and receding planes (the motionless world of a single room looked at for weeks from one fixed position accustoms the eye to seeing in two dimensions) – is one of his most remarkable passages of writing. However, when, gradually, the world slows down, and then becomes still, with new depths and projections out of a single plane, Mary is able to see it as she has never seen it before. Especially the flowers massed in front of her, from which Polly selects one exquisite tulip and holds it to Mary's face:

> She held it to Mary face-to-face so close that the petals completely covered her mother's eyes. Thus the sun shone in Mary's eyes through green veins threading translucent scarlet; and now that so little of Mary's body was 'hers' any longer it seemed as if even the trunk and legs she had lost had never been Mary the way this tulip was Mary. . . . Moreover once she had thus far broken her old corporeal bounds soon even these lawns and bushes – these gardens, as far as the eye could see. . . . In short, it wasn't so many months since every inch from the crown of Mary's head to the tips of Mary's *toes* had been Mary's limits, but now every inch from the crown of Mary's head to the tips of Mary's *trees* rejoiced at being alive.

Hughes sensibly adds, 'Of course as summer wore on this sort of ecstatic vision was doomed to fade into common day.' Even so, it has served to bring Mary back into the world again. She is saved from *spiritual* paralysis by the access she gains to the visible world. It is significant, I think, that her need for activity was to have been satisfied in the seventh book by Norah's being brought from Coventry to teach her embroidery. The sense of sight realising itself through the work of the hands, an interplay of visual and tactile sensations, is a prerequisite for spiritual satisfaction in the secular world among most of Hughes's people. Only saints, such as Mitzi, or madmen, such as Hitler, can exist without sharing in those pleasures of the senses.

So far as I can recall, at no point in the narrative does Hughes make an explicit comparison between Mary and Mitzi. Indeed Mitzi's last appearance in the book in which Mary has her riding accident (*The Meistersingers*, ch. 22) is more than fifty pages back (ch. 6), and she does not appear again until the end of *Stille Nacht*. This is consistent with Hughes's method as I understand it. Links between events are sometimes made explicit, sometimes not. But in general Hughes has not gone out of his way to emphasise the dense network of connective threads and tissues that weave their way through his plots. Thematic reverberations do not echo and re-echo loudly along the narrative. Though the connections are there to be discovered, one does not feel that Hughes has set out to impress by his invention, his display of them. They have the appearance of being accidental. Take the little dog in the plaid waistcoat. He plays a totally insignificant role in the scene at the Odeonsplatz when the Nazis are dispersed by von Kahr's police. Nevertheless he is sufficiently important to be there again, equally inconsequentially, on the day Augustine spends in Munich with Dr Reinhold, the day he meets Jacinto sitting on a lamp-post outside the *Drei Katzen*. The little dog wanders in and out of public and private history with the purposelessness, the lack of necessity, that only the expendably real possesses. His reappearance, like that of so many other contingent people and things, vouches for other reappearances, which may be of much greater consequence to our understanding of the themes and psychological continuities of the novel.

These accidental reappearances and repetitions strengthen our belief not only in the physical world Hughes has created, but in the philosophical and historical world too. For on some occasions what at first seems merely accidental betrays more than a hint of something purposive, even 'significant'. What could be more innocent, for example, than the brief retrospective episode in *Polly and Rachel* where Wantage, the Wadamys' butler, recalls a romp he enjoyed with Maggie Winter in the Tower room at Stumford Castle, during which the featherbed Maggie was refilling fell apart and half drowned the pair of them in feathers? Or Wantage's difficulty 'picking hundreds of downy little feathers off his livery against time before going on duty at the Front Hall, swearing he'd miss some and they'd find him out'? It seems like a fully self-contained and merely private, otherwise insignificant, incident. Two hundred pages later, however, near the beginning of *The Fox in the Attic*, another incident takes place that involves feathers floating about a room in a castle. This time, though, the castle is in Bavaria; and the feathers have floated out of a cushion that has been slashed apart by massive sharp-bladed swords wielded by two little German children, 'acting out some legend of their race'. The children, too, are playing a game. But the game is different, and strangely appropriate to the circumstances in which it is being enacted. On the one hand, the gaiety of life in the servants' quarters of an aristocratic English household some time before the outbreak of the Great War; on the other, the delight in games of violence in a Bavarian castle on the eve of Hitler's trial on charges relating to the abortive putsch of 1923 — a castle, moreover, in which at least four of its inhabitants were working secretly for the violent overthrow of the elected government.

Describing the dining-room in which little Rudi and Heinz are slashing at the feather cushion, Hughes casually mentions a stove: 'There was white down everywhere, swirling in the currents of hot air the stove set up.' On my count this is the sixth reference to the stove in the von Kessens' castle, and there are to be several more, and passing mentions of other stoves elsewhere in the German scenes. This particular stove first appeared at the beginning of *The White Crow* — 'the hot air over the huge blue porcelain stove quivered visibly'. When Mary reflects on her visit to Lorienburg much earlier (*Polly and Rachel*, ch. 22) one of the things she remembers about the castle was 'those gigantic porcelain stoves', and later Mitzi, Otto and Augustine are all to be related in some way to the presence of these objects. They seem innocuous, comforting even — to Mary, who remembers how they kept out the cold of a bitter Bavarian winter. Even so, we are not entirely taken by surprise, I think, when Wolff, searching below his lair to discover the whereabouts of Augustine's and Mitzi's rooms, recognises Augustine, asleep on his bed, by the light emanating from one of the Schloss Lorienburg stoves. Seeing Augustine, and seeing the stove, Wolff immediately connects the two of them in a murderous waking dream: 'he must drag this young man out of bed . . . and kill him by holding his head against the red hot stove'. He has done this once before, actually done it, to a police spy at Aachen and he remembers what happened then and transfers the memory to what will happen in the future to Augustine — 'Wolff heard the sizzle, smelt cooking bone and hair'. Finally, in a chapter (14) in *The Meistersingers*, when Hitler is visiting the Hanfstängls on Christmas Eve, the image of the stove surfaces again. Hitler (Uncle Dorf) has brought Putzi's four-year-old son two presents – a sabre, which he uses to slash open the sofa (bringing back memories of the von Kessen twins, though without the feathers); and a 'tiny stove you could really-and-truly cook on'. Nothing more is said about the stove until little Egon unwraps it in his room upstairs. 'But then, in his dream, that cooking-stove grew and grew till its chimneys hid the whole horizon in smoke. . . .' Somehow, Dachau and Auschwitz have grown out of that comfortable old blue porcelain stove Mary remembered back in her toy Bavarian castle. History has become visible. Social and political processes are exactly located in vividly visualised descriptions of things.

By a system of visual cross-reference gently submerged beneath the level of anything it would be appropriate to call 'symbolic', Hughes shows how psychological impulses, released in action, come to form a pattern – a pattern which gradually clarifies and reveals itself as history. Augustine's puzzlement at finding Walther von Kessen's desperate farewell to his wife Adèle inscribed on the wall of his hotel room in Munich gives way in the course of time to Walther's own memories of the events of February 1919, when he was almost executed by the Communists: Augustine's hotel bedroom was used as a prison cell only four years ago. In another retrospective passage dealing with the events of 1919, Franz accidentally fires his rifle and may have shot a young child during his search for Toller after the Communists had been routed by the Berlin government. We are likely to remember Augustine, almost the same age as Franz, returning from shooting wildfowl out on the marshes near Newton, his man bringing in the shot-guns and himself carrying a dead child. A year later, in Connecticut, Augustine still cannot forget the child: his visions of a white ghost in the lake there bring back memories of the dead Rachel, whom he has not killed, but whose death has nevertheless reawakened in him a sense of guilt, he has been brought back to life and relationships. Under the skin of the narrative these connections are persistently being made – sometimes in the form of coincidental meetings and reacquaintances; sometimes in the form of images and objects related in different ways to different characters. But the characters are seldom aware of the patterns to which their presence in the story is contributing.

At best they will grasp a single, apparently random connection – as Wolff hits on the connection between the oven at Aachen and the oven in Augustine's room; or as Augustine is dimly aware of a sinister 'meaning' in the straight rows of pine trees in the Bavarian forests – long before Otto is murdered in the middle of the plantation (*Stille Nacht*, ch. 32), or Hitler picks pine needles out of Sophie's yellow hair on the Obersalzberg (Book 7).

Unlike the characters, we can see the pattern. It is not complete, because these were intended to be parts of a larger novel. But the details of it are felt to be gradually falling into place as characters occupy new positions, or cross positions previously occupied by others. Hughes's refusal to *occupy* his characters' minds and feelings is remarkably at variance with contemporary practice. Readers are usually invited to live in the consciousness of a limited number of interesting characters. There is a close, continuous involvement of the reader in the characters' lives; and so there is a fairly straightforward equation between the way characters and the way readers react to the situations described. That is why many of Hughes's critics feel that Augustine, the hero, seems to be overwhelmed by events. The point-of-view technique has been used so thoroughly in any but the most barely documentary modern fiction that its absence in Hughes leaves many readers baffled. We never stay in Augustine's consciousness for long enough to acquire a sense of familiarity with it. We never settle in it. We do not in any sense of the word belong to it. The same is true of Mary, Mitzi, Hitler, any of the other characters. Once we have got used to what at first feels like wanton jerkiness – the rapid substitution of long-shot for close-up, the conflation of past and present activities for purposes of comparison, the use of mimetically inappropriate imagery to explain what a character feels like in a new situation – we become aware of a spaciousness, a freedom from confinement in specifically 'novelistic' devices, which confounds our expectations of what can and cannot happen in prose fiction.

The White Crow ends with the Munich putsch, a startlingly vivid presentation of events that it is difficult to believe is only ten pages long. All the more so when we see that Hughes is doing full justice to the putsch on two levels – as a chaotic jumble of present actions, and as a historical event presaging other events of much greater consequence. The putsch as a fact of history is conveyed in three ways. First, by the unavoidable associations of the names of the principal actors – Hitler, von Kahr, Ludendorff, Göring. Then by the 'setting' of events in a historical context by both the author and the characters. The description opens with a contrast between the cold weather of November 1923 and the warm weather of the same month in 1918, when Kurt Eisner came to power in much the same way that the Nazis are attempting five years later. And, throughout the four chapters that deal directly with the putsch, Ludendorff ('the fabulous, the Army's idol') is viewed as a historical figure rather than a private individual. He sees himself in this light, confident that because of his historic identity he will not be shot at by the troops on the Odeonsplatz. At the same time as he stands upright for the troops, who are firing into the marchers, his mind broods almost mystically on the fact that both 1-9-1-4 and 1-9-2-3, the two dates of triumph for Germany's enemies, add up to 1-5, ten and five; and that the tenth and fifth letters of the alphabet are J and E, signifying Germany's greatest enemies, the Jews and the Jesuits. Later, when he is taken to the police station, the sergeant professes not to know how to spell 'Ludendorff', even though he claims he lost an eye in the Ludendorff offensive of 1918. Finally, a historical context has been created for the putsch by Dr Reinhold, who has returned from the *Bierkeller* in Munich to attend a party given by his brother, a friend of the von Kessens, at Röttningen. His description of what happened there (before we see for ourselves, and through Franz's friend Lothar's eyes, the events that followed) places Göring, Hitler and the rest in a dramatically historic perspective, almost as though it were a description of one of those stilted German realist historical pictures of the 1930s.

Superimposed on the historical event, recollected and made rhetorical and heroic, is the patchwork of actions and non-actions out of which the historical event has been created. The illusion of reality is remarkably powerful. It is produced in large part by Hughes's technique of rapid engagement and disengagement, a brisk movement from event to event, or from the inside to the outside of the same event, which does not allow the reader to settle in any one controlling position for longer than a few seconds of reading time. A death is not prepared for by placing the reader suspiciously close to the intended victim. Max-Erwin von Scheubner-Richter lies on the ground with his lungs bursting from his chest before we have ever heard his name. He is noticed because Mitzi's *émigrée* Russian penfriend, Tascha, happens to have got into the Odenosplatz by chance just when the soldiers open fire. As she glances down at Max-Erwin it flashes through her mind: 'She'd met him at parties: he'd had so much charm.' Between Göring dragging himself behind one of the stone lions in front of the Residenz palace and Hitler limping to the yellow car that is waiting for him on the Max-Josefs-Platz, the historically insignificant, indeed historically non-existent, Tascha is riding wildly down the street on her bicycle, hoping to get plenty of splashes of blood on the wheels. She fails to get any of Hitler's: Lothar has seen him getting into the yellow car. 'So Tascha had to be content with quite anonymous blood: it was mostly Willi's, as it happened.' Willi is a friend of Lothar and Franz. To us he is not anonymous, though it is true we do not know much about him. Only later do we discover, far from all the muddle and excitement, that he is not dead, only wounded in the leg. Through all the confusion a little dog in a plaid waistcoat, 'looking important', has been trotting aimlessly through the streets. At the end of it all we find he has rejoined his master, 'an elderly, frock-coated, elegant citizen with so neat a spade beard it deserved a prize (he slept with it in a net)'. These abrupt transitions from Hitler and Ludendorff to the yellow car, Tascha on her bicycle, the dog in the plaid waistcoat, are the mechanisms by which we are convinced of the reality of the situation. From where we are standing, on a clear view of events, Hitler and the little dog are of equal importance. They both occupy defined positions within a field of vision. The present picture is excitingly chaotic. The historical perspective, set back from the present, controls the chaos and explains the significance of what is happening, or did happen. The two ways of looking meet in a historic present (though written in the past tense) which has all the clarity of epic, rather than contemporary novelistic narrative.

The point of view, I have suggested, is much more mobile than nineteenth and twentieth-century narrative usually encourages us to expect. It is not only the rapid cutting from scene to scene that conveys the feeling of extraordinary speed and momentum characteristic of Hughes's prose; but also the sheer amount of retrospect, anticipation, comparison and reflection that his description of a single incident so often causes to rush through the reader's mind. As an example of this, let us look at the way

Augustine's search for Mitzi in the chapel at Schloss Lorienburg
is handled (*The Fox in the Attic*, ch. 7). In the previous chapter
Mitzi's experience of blindness had been traced entirely within
the recesses of her own mind, and what we discovered there had
been her first intense communion with God: 'Mitzi believed
herself quite lost in God.' But that word 'believed', coming more
than half-way through the chapter, alerts us to the fact that
Hughes's own all-seeing, God-like eye has detected a residue of
detachment in Mitzi. There is an 'outside watcher' in her that, in
a beautiful comparison, is described as being 'as faint as the
piping of a gnat dancing in the spray of a roaring waterfall'.
Through this detachment from Mitzi (in observing her own slight
detachment from what is otherwise for her an overwhelming
experience), Hughes moves outward to 'No one saw Mitzi cross
the hall', and then upwards to Augustine's window. There we find
ourselves, in the final paragraph, alongside Augustine looking
down on Mitzi in the courtyard. Unlike ourselves, however, he
does not know anything about her recent religious illumination.
He still thinks that her religion is skin deep. The opening of the
next chapter will explain why.

For at the opening of chapter 7 we find Augustine following
Mitzi's steps to the chapel. We enter with him, first the vestry,
then the chapel itself. Therefore we see the baroque interior
through Augustine's eyes, which means that at first our attention
is drawn to everything about it that is 'extravagant', 'painted
trompe d'oeil', 'silver soap-suds' and 'peeping angels' – 'the very
last word in decadence and bad taste'. The visual outrage merely
confirms his suspicions about the meretriciousness of Mitzi's
beliefs, the ease with which she will be able to discard them: 'Mitzi
must know now there is no one else in heaven or earth to love her –
only him.' He is puzzled, though, why she should have come here.
The first phase of Augustine's search concludes with his surprise
at this, and his uneasiness at not having found her yet.

The second phase opens with a new perception of Augustine's
into what the chapel's interior looks like. Having got used to the
'general effect' of chaos and vulgarity, his eye can't help but be
drawn to the details of the painting, especially above the altar.
There he sees that colour and glitter come together to produce an
enormous storm cloud with the rays of God spreading over the top
of it. Then he notices the miniature heads of child-angels 'peeping'
from every cranny and interstice of the cloud – each one of them

lovingly painted from life. A whole generation of children from Dorf Lorienburg has been preserved in the chapel, all of them immortalised and singing. Or that is what Augustine thinks at first. For of course the angels are not singing. The singing is coming from elsewhere – in fact from Mitzi, who has just completed a Latin chant. Echoes of that chant have drifted into the chapel round the altar and made it seem 'inconceivable one couldn't *hear* that singing: the eye filled the lagged ear with visionary sweet sound'. At present Mitzi is praying at the foot of a wooden Gothic deposition. The direction from which the echoes come leads Augustine to her. So Augustine's 'supernatural' experience came to him through a sort of 'sleight of voice'; the immortality of the children, in the forms of angels, has been achieved by the accidental way a blind girl's voice and a dead sculptor's eye have joined to create the illusion of life in dead painted wood. In other words Mitzi's blindness has already promoted a religious experience in another person and, paradoxically, it has done so by making him suppose that his own eye has filled him with (crucial paradox) 'visionary sweet sound'. The way the senses of sight and hearing contribute to a religious experience that is real and lasting in the one person, deceptive and fleeting in the other, is wonderfully suggestive. The simple movement from the girl's to the man's point of view has coincided with an equally simple falling out of events (Augustine's looking and Mitzi's singing) to produce a complex poetic description.

This poetic manipulation of the point of view runs throughout *The Human Predicament*. One thinks of Otto von Kessen entering Mitzi's room at Lorienburg, and so pitying her that he wishes she were dead. Though he does not know it, at this very moment he is protecting her from death. For Wolff Scheidemann has come down from his attic lair to butcher her, and Otto is standing between him and his intended victim. Or one thinks of the way Wolff's brother Lothar is used for us to gain access to the scene at the monastery, and in Göring's room in Munich, just before the 1923 putsch; and of the execution of the SA men in the yard of the Stadelheim prison during the 'Night of the Long Knives'. On both occasions the fact that he is wearing borrowed clothes is entirely comprehensible to the reader, but a source of confusion and misunderstanding to the people he had to deal with. His death in a general's overcoat, thrust before a firing-squad in place of his master, Kettner, is symptomatic of the disastrous combination of spiritual conviction and practical misunderstanding that has typified his career, and that of many others in the lower echelons of the Nazi party.

At other times the searchlight of Hughes's prose flashes over a single object for a few seconds only, brilliantly summarising, as it were in a snapshot, the real significance of events which, in their historical and political character, seem complex, uncertain. One sentence, describing the movements of a cat that had been sleeping in a room full of dead partisans deep in the Livonian countryside, encapsulates the terror and savagery of Wolff's experience in the Baltic wars: 'But now she took refuge on the top of that ornate mantelpiece clock, arched and spitting, her drawn claws slipping as she scrabbled to keep her balance on the smooth marble.' When the clock suddenly chimes the cat jumps from it, and Wolff, who has just entered the room tears the animal to pieces with his bare hands. Another brief image of violence, hidden beneath sentimental evasions, now exposed in its true horror, appears when Hitler is spending Christmas with the Hanfstängls. Little Egon has just finished diving into the sofa and slashing away at it with his new sabre: the seasonal decorations have been upset, and 'From the tree a tilting candle dripped hot wax on the face of the china doll in the crib.' These images have the intensity and brilliance of those luminous deep-focus camera shots in *Citizen Kane*. Their containment in frames of rapid narrative is also reminiscent of Welles – though the effect of the whole narrative of which they are a part is more classical than Gothic, I think.

Classical, because finally Hughes's vision is so composed, and so complete. He himself has suggested that *The Human Predicament* is less like a conventional novel than an epic, or a medieval romance. Details of several incidents described in the novel suggest that he had something of this sort in mind. For one thing, it is filled with portents and dreams (no other novelist I can think of spends so long recounting the dreams of his characters). Elaborately developed comparisons (financiers during the Great Inflation like skaters on melting ice; Mitzi's journey to God like that of a traveller gazing behind him at the lights twinkling in the valley below; etc.) play the same part in Hughes's narrative as epic similes do in Vergil and Milton. References to classical and biblical mythology embroider the text, often in the form of simile and metaphor: Ludendorff is like Achilles in his tent; Franz like

Agamemnon at Aulis (prepared to sacrifice Mitzi/Iphigenia);
Norah and the Coventry slum-children (on an outing to the
countryside) like Agag barefoot on the turf. And what happens
often takes place in settings, even costumes, that are as medieval
as they are modern. In Dorset the Hermitage, where Nellie brings
her tubercular husband Gwilym to die, is an eighteenth-century
Gothic folly; the castle at Lorienburg looks, and much of it feels,
medieval; the roofs of the Coventry slums look like a scene from
Tennyson's 'Morte d'Arthur'. The German children (Franz, for
example, dressed up for the sleigh ride to Röttningen; or the twins
chained together 'in durance vile' as a punishment for their
misbehaviour on the battlements) frequently look medieval.
Walther would like to be one of the poets 'with winged words
hooded on their fists'. Over and over again characters, especially
in the Bavarian and Moroccan scenes, behave as if history were
telescoped – as if, to quote Augustine on his Bavarian cousins,
'King George V had been wounded at Bannockburn'.

These are minor details of Hughes's assimilation within his
modern, novelistic method of some of the techniques of epic and
romance-writing. Some of them have been fabricated with a very
particular purpose in mind; to contrast the 'long perspectives and
slow changes' natural to Englishmen, with the rapid evolution of
historical processes experienced by the Germans. More important realignments of the contemporary and the more ancient
forms of narrative are built into the very structure of *The Human
Predicament*. They have more to do with the transformation of ideas
and attitudes into sequences of clear visual imagery, and with the
mobility of the narrator's eye as it plays over the vast continuum
of the story, than with the absorption into a contemporary fiction
of distinctive features of classical epic or medieval romance.

As Wolff looks down on Mitzi from his attic, we are reminded of
Chaucer's *Knight's Tale*, of Palamon in his Athenian tower
catching sight of Emily in the garden below. Mitzi's yellow hair
was also 'broyed in a tresse / Behinde hir back, a yerde long I
gesse'; and like Palamon (Hughes tells us) the moment he saw it
Wolff too had 'bleynte, and cryde "A!"' / As if he stongen were
unto the herte'. Wolff is the least likely person to summon these
lines to mind. Hughes has put them there to expand the
possibilities of the situation. Like so much of the imagery –
including the epic similes and the descriptive set pieces – the lines
from Chaucer have the effect not of concentration, of bearing

down ever more heavily on one pressing point of consciousness, but of an airy expansion, a sense of the continuity of the action with the vast continuum of human life which stretches out beyond the interlocking action of this one book. Hughes's preoccupation with forces lying beneath the level of differentiated character does not involve his readers either in the toils of passion or the thin air of an abstracted argument. Instead, there is something Chaucerian in the effect of the novel as a whole. As in the *Troilus*, all is referred to a dominating metaphysical schema, and then back again to the teeming and patterned multiplicity of the world at large.

3 Henry Green

No English novelist of the last fifty years has been more scrupulous in his craft, and more reticent about its character, than Henry Green. His novels and his views about them are equally enigmatic. The expression of these views is rare and occasional, to say the least. Even so, from time to time he has made a comment or two on the writing of fiction: his autobiography *Pack my Bag* (1940) secretes a few cryptic suggestions, and there are two fascinating broadcast talks he gave in 1950 and 1951 which, though brief, contain some provocatively intelligent comment on the writing of dialogue. These occasional glimpses into the mind of the author are unsupported by any reference to the subject in the novels themselves, since none of them contains a single character whom one could believe capable of discussing anything in intellectual or analytical terms. Apart from Sebastian Birt, an unassertive economics tutor employed by Misses Edge and Baker at their school for young ladies in *Concluding*, no one makes the effort to do this, and he does so only on one occasion. Also Green himself, whilst obviously an eclectic and sophisticated reader, tends to use literary references uncertainly in his novels. A scrap of dialogue in *Nothing* (1950), where Mrs Weatherby mistakes her son's quotation of 'To be or not to be' for a line from *Richard II*, is one of the few implausible events in a novel where dialogue is a sharply accurate register of the characters' states of mind.

Outside the novels, Green's observations about writing are unusual but consistent with the unusual novels he has written – and of which he must be presumed to be speaking. Prose, we learn from *Pack my Bag*, is 'a gathering web of insinuations . . . a long intimacy between strangers with no direct appeal to what both may have known. It should slowly appeal to feelings unexpressed . . . .' The title of his first broadcast talk in November 1950 is 'A Novelist to his Readers: Communication without Speech'. It emphasises the intimate quality of his writing by insisting on the private character of *unspoken* prose. Green deprecates the reading-aloud of his novels, preferring that they should be read silently in order to make that 'slow appeal to feelings unexpressed' which would go unnoticed in a voiced reading, even to oneself. Little attention is given to the knowledge of the world which we should usually expect a novelist to provide. Instead Green talks of his prose as a direct appeal to feelings through a 'non-representational' art: 'if you want to create life the one way not to set about it is by explanation'. And Green is as good as his word. His novels avoid explanation. They offer 'a gathering web of insinuations' rather than a straightforward representation of how we think we live.

This fact about Green's work, supported as it is by his own few, brief critical pronouncements, has resulted in a peculiarity about the way his novels have been written about. There is a surprisingly large amount of intelligent criticism of Green, especially prolific in the middle fifties, when he had written his last novel, *Doting* (1952), and before it was realised that in fact he would write no more. But its emphasis tends to fall on two very different and, one might suppose, irreconcilable aspects of the novels. On the one hand there is the kind of appreciation represented by Giorgio Melchiori in his book *The Tightrope Walkers* (1956). This emphasises the stylistically pure, 'unattached', 'non-representational' character of Green's achievement. Melchiori's essay is entitled 'The Abstract Art of Henry Green'. He admires the way Green's work is based on 'a consistent vision of life as an inconclusive sequence of episodes to which the only order we can impose is of an aesthetic kind'. On the other hand Edward Stokes's *The Novels of Henry Green* (1959) emphasises the humanity of the novels. Stokes is impressed by their close attention to the minutiae of human behaviour and their representation of characters who possess a reality and vitality rarely achieved in modern fiction.

Neither of these critics is wholly mistaken in his assessment of Green's eccentric art. The novels are highly patterned artefacts, aspiring to an aesthetic abstraction which might have been appreciated by Flaubert in the nineteenth century, and might make some appeal to experimental novelists of the *nouveau roman* persuasion today. But at the same time they produce an impression of unerring accuracy in their observations of how people feel, how they speak and what they do, which seems to be at variance with those non-representational functions. I should like to tease out the connections between these two apparently contradictory, but actually complementary, novelistic qualities.

However convincing one might find the world Henry Green has created, it has to be admitted that they are built out of a highly artificial prose style which seems to make no attempt at 'naturalness'. This style doesn't *try* to satisfy the normal expectations of an intelligent reader. Green forms his sentences as if in accordance with a manual of English grammar which is an imperfect twin of the standard text. The opening half page of his first mature novel, *Living* (1929), is a well-known example of Green's English at its most peculiar:

> Bridesley, Birmingham.
> Two o'clock. Thousands came back from dinner along streets. 'What we want is go, push', said works manager to son of Mr Dupret. 'What I say to them is – let's get on with it, let's get the stuff out.'
> Thousands came back to factories they worked in from their dinners. 'I'm always at them but they know me. They know I'm a father and mother to them. If they're in trouble they've but to come to me. And they turn out beautiful work, beautiful work. I'd do anything for 'em and they know it.'
> Noise of lathes working began again in this factory. Hundreds went along road outside, men and girls. Some turned in to Dupret factory.

The most obvious idiosyncrasy of the prose is the omission of the definite article or substitution for it of the demonstrative adjective ('Noise of lathes working began again in this factory'); and the (less unconventional by 1929) omission of the verb from short 'sentences' establishing place and time of day. But this is only a continuously highlighted instance of Green's deliberate mismanagement of conventional sentence formation, which elsewhere takes less dramatic forms. The sentence 'Thousands came back to factories they worked in from their dinners' sounds almost conventional, but it is not quite conventional in its *written* context. We might speak a sentence like that, but in writing we should almost certainly alter the position of 'from their dinners' to prevent the ungainly proximity of the two prepositions 'in' and 'from'. We should probably *write* that 'Thousands came back *from their dinners* to *the* factories they worked in.' Over the page there is another good example of Green's manipulation of the expected grammatical pattern of a sentence. In the engineer's shop, he writes, 'Sparrows flew by belts that ran from lathes on floor up to shafting above by skylights.' Again the slight oddity is created by a combination of dropped articles and bunched prepositions. The result is a certain arhythmical flaccidness, a feeling that the pitch of the prose is all proceeding on one level. It is the opposite effect from the one Hopkins produced by what at first appear to be similar habits of compression and distortion, and a different one, too, from the one Auden achieved in his early poems (written at the same time as *Living*). What Green has produced is a language which has been deprived of the expected music of English speech rhythms and consequently drained of timbre, expressiveness and spoken density.

In Green's later novels the staple narrative style I have tried to characterise as voiceless; transparent, lacking in expected rhythmic cadence, persists. But Green takes fewer liberties with conventional grammar to achieve it. The separation of styles is therefore less noticeable in these books than it was in *Living*. There is an almost imperceptible modulation from dialogue, through interior monologue, of deliberate and involuntary kinds, to objective narrative and description. The same kind of thing is happening as happened in *Living*, but less obtrusively, with far less recourse to startling distortions of sentence structure. *Party Going* was completed ten years after publication of *Living*, in 1939. It begins with the sentence 'Fog was so dense, bird that had been disturbed went flat into a balustrade and slowly fell, dead, at her feet.' One definite and one indefinite article, and a relative pronoun that might have been expected, have been omitted. Thereafter, this throwback to *Living* is not repeated. The omissions are less regular and less spectacular. The other dislocations of syntax are more furtive; hidden, as it were, under the skin of the prose. This surreptitious distortion of normal English usage, discreet, but giving a just perceptible air of foreignness and strangeness to the prose, persists in the novels that follow. Relative clauses are prefaced with a redundant conjunction ('and which . . .'). Half-expected relative pronouns do not appear ('So it was Albert received . . .'). Relative clauses are slightly misplaced ('So it was Albert received Michael Mathewson at the entrance, who took this man's business card . . .'). These and other slight grammatical peculiarities are responsible for most of that sense

we have when we read a novel by Henry Green that the
expression, and perhaps the world it is there to create, have
shifted from their expected positions. They appear to be somewhat at a tangent from the grammar we have learnt and the world
we have got into the habit of describing with it.

By the time he completed *Party Going* Green had created a
medium of expression which appears to be slightly to the side of
expected patterns of English prose. There is a continuous
departure from standard usage, a series of minute deflections from
the norm. And this grammatical dislocation is paralleled by
dislocations of other kinds – in the organisation of the phases of
the narrative, in the timing of the representation of events, in the
behaviour of the characters and in the varying forms of the
descriptive prose. It is as if the world has shifted a tiny degree on
its axis, and the novelist, having remained in his accustomed
place, sees both less and more of it than novelists usually see. For
the most part the things that go on in this world are the same
things that go on in the world we live in. But, like the language that is
used to describe them, they pass by at a tilt, ever so slightly
elongated or compressed, magnified or diminished. The most
noticeable effect of this is that we have a fresh vision of
commonplace events as our attention is drawn to facets of them
that normal vision tends to pass over or absorbs unthinkingly.

To attend to something, however, is not to receive an explanation of it. As we have seen, Green deplores explanations in novels
because explanations get in the way of the novelist's primary duty
to create life. Possibly the novel which explains least of all in
Green's work, the one where a rapt attention to events puts out of
our minds the requirement for an explanation of them, is
Concluding. Here the principal event in the plot is the disappearance of two young girls from a state academy and the effect this
has on various people connected with the academy on the day of
its annual dance. But 'plot', in the usual sense of the word, is
conspicuously absent from the novel. Little that is conclusive
happens in *Concluding*. One of the girls is found, and one of them is
not found. The principal and her assistant exercise their authority
in different ways – over the girls and over each other – but nothing
that is in any sense final, or definitive, comes out of the way they
behave. For a variety of reasons, few of which are connected with
his personal conduct over the affair, the future of Mr Rock, a
retired scientist who occupies a cottage in the grounds of the

school, may be affected by the girls' disappearance. Some of the
girls at the school are influenced in one way or another by the
disappearances, though there is no sign that such influence will
make much difference to the way they behave in the future, let
alone in the short time span covered by the novel.

What happens in *Concluding* happens in a context of inconclusive shifts in relationships between people. Events that go largely
unexplained exert for a while some influence over the way other
events seem to fall into patterns during a brief space of time. Such
an event is the discovery of Merode, one of the missing girls, quite
early on in the narrative. Sebastian Birt, a teacher from the
school, and Elizabeth, Mr Rock's granddaughter, find her in
the middle of a fallen beech tree while they are out walking in the
school grounds. At first the presence of the tree, glowing in the
early morning sunlight, has a vitalising effect on the two lovers.
Their physical movement from shade to sunlight (which penetrates from the space left open by the fallen tree) corresponds with
an emotional movement from a pleasant dreaminess to a more
conscious awareness of each other's presence and the sexual
contact this brings with it:

> A world through which the young man and his girl had been
> meandering, in dreaming shade through which sticks of
> sunlight slanted to spill upon the ground, had at this point been
> struck to a blaze, and where their way had been dim, on a sea
> bed past grave trunks, was now this dying, brilliant mass which
> lay exposed, a hidden world of spiders working its gold, the
> webs these made a field of wheels and spokes of wet silver.

But the beauty of the fallen beech lodges within itself another
beauty, in the person of Merode, which evokes a more complicated response – in keeping with the uncertain reasons for her
being there, the awkward mystery of her presence. After Merode's
call for help, Sebastian moves towards the tree. This is Green's
description of what he sees:

> By this time both had gathered its direction, which was
> lefthanded to the deepest of the stricken beech. Sebastian began
> to force his way through and, as Elizabeth cried out, 'Now do
> mind, take care, it's your best suit', he had parted a screen of
> leaves that hung before him bent to the tide, like seaweed in the

ocean, and his pale face, washed, shaved, hair cut and brushed, in this sun a bandit, he looked down on a girl stretched out, whom he did not know to be Merode, whose red hair was streaked across a white face and matted by salt tears, who was in pyjamas and had one leg torn to the knee. A knee which, brilliantly polished over bone beneath, shone in this sort of pool she had made for herself in the fallen world of birds, burned there like a piece of tusk burnished by shifting sands, or else a wheel, revolving at such speed that it had no edges and was white, thus communicating life to ivory, a heart to the still, and the sensation of a crash to this girl who lay quiet, reposed.

As in the earlier description of the fallen beech, the prose here combines an impression of sensuous luxuriance with a certain distancing effect achieved by that customary Greenian angularity, that slight deflection from expected grammatical patterns already noted. The 'direction' of the voice being 'lefthanded *to*' the 'deepest of the stricken beech' represents a minute departure from normal English word order with its unemphatic mismatching of noun, participle, and preposition. It is a scarcely noticeable departure. But in consort with minor oddities of usage elsewhere in the passage it does something to check the immediacy of our response to the picture. Equally disconcerting is the way Sebastian had parted a screen of leaves 'that hung before him bent to the tide'. The referent of 'bent to the tide' is uncertainly Sebastian or the leaves. Uncertain, that is, until we look back at the earlier descriptions of Sebastian among the trees and notice the continuous play of water imagery they contain. The sudden sunlight made by the gap in the tree canopy clothes Sebastian and Elizabeth 'like a depth of warm water that turned the man's brown city outfit to a drowned man's clothes'. So Elizabeth's warning to Sebastian to take care (as he forces his way through the branches) – 'it's your best suit' – carries us back to the 'drowned man's clothes' and prepares us for the otherwise abrupt and incomprehensible 'bent to the tide', immediately followed by 'like seaweed in the ocean'. The sudden appearance of the fanciful image of the sea is made right, in the context of the whole passage, outside this particular paragraph, by the minute filaments of connective metaphor floating back to the half page or page before.

An important effect of our observation of this connective tissue or thread is that, although what Sebastian sees has a sensuously powerful effect on him, we, as readers, are removed from his immediate experience of it. The imagery which tracks him into the heart of the fallen tree does not occur to him. He does not call it to mind. It has been imposed on his experience from outside. He responds to the sunlight playing on the leaves of the tree. It is our response to his doing so that brings the sea imagery into the description. It has been constructed around him, and he is quite unaware of it. With the same effect, we are told that the girl in the beech tree is Merode at the same time as we are told that Sebastian didn't know this: 'he looked down on a girl stretched out, whom he did not know to be Merode'. The main effect of this combination of devices is to keep us at a remove from Sebastian's consciousness. It places us in a position from which we can contemplate his experience within a framework that includes more than that experience alone.

What follows is a celebrated passage describing Merode's knee, which has been exposed by a tear in the leg of her pyjama trousers. Green's attention to this object is mesmeric, insisting on its stasis at the centre of activities about to erupt around it. It is impossible to decide whether the long sentence which describes the knee makes it actually do anything (by inserting an active verb of which it is the subject) or deactivates it beneath the swirling metaphors that adorn it. Green's odd little comma after 'which', strictly speaking, turns 'burned' (three lines down) into a subordinate verb with the same function as 'shone', i.e. extending the long adjectival clause, which would then persist to the end of the sentence. But 'or else' seems to detach itself from the long unwinding spool of the adjectival clause. With the result that for a while the description seems to have floated away from Sebastian and from the 'event' in which he is involved.

After a brief exchange of words between Sebastian and Merode the descriptive prose takes over again, at first apparently as an expression of Sebastian's point of view. He is confused by the beauty of her body stretched out in the bark of the tree, and his response to that beauty is shared by the reader: 'and *he* saw, so that it interrupted his breathing'. But what follows again detaches the image of Merode from Sebastian's perception of it, this time by hindsight, since the last sentence of the description is followed by the at first quite inexplicable: 'Then he was reprieved, now that he was so at her side.' Inexplicable, that is, until we read what comes immediately after: 'For she reached behind and brought out some nondescript overcoat which she pushed over her middle.' As Green then interpolates, 'A schoolmaster mind knew she must have put this away at the back before she called. Thus he was saved because she had made him suspicious.' We are never sure whether Sebastian's suspicions are justified or whether his prudent transformation from voyeur into schoolmaster produces a comforting explanation of Merode's behaviour that to others remains mysterious and irrational. In any case, her motives seem to be completely detached from the impression she. makes as the subject of a delightful linguistic confection. Not only the knee but the whole of Merode's body has been converted into a work of art, with its 'enamelled' toes and pointilliste colouring – the sun 'spotting the cotton with drips as of wet paint, and making small candle lamps of flesh'.

When Sebastian tells Merode that there must be some explanation for her being where she is, she walks out of the tree and runs off. He climbs out of it too, and tears his trouser leg. 'He found a vent in his own trouser leg and scowled.' The mysterious image of the girl in the tree has given way to a parody of it that descends again into plain narrative. The girl's overcoat and the vent in Sebastian's trousers become inconsequential properties in the 'plot' of the novel. The memory of Merode's discovery fades into speculations about the other girl, Mary, who remains, presumably, somewhere in the grounds.

These two to three pages of Henry Green's mature writing bring out many of its peculiarities and suggest some of the reasons for the difference between it and more conventional narrative prose. Discussing Green's style, Melchiori writes that it is 'characterised by asymmetry, by the lack of precise focus and, when successful, by the capacity to achieve a new precarious balance in fleeting moments in spite of, or even *through*, the absence of a predetermined equilibrium'. Certainly the description of Merode's discovery lacks precise focus. The prose settles on a random detail at the expense of everything one expects to be going on around it. Our aesthetic experience of what the object and Green's linguistic concentration on it combine to produce halts the narrative and obscures the activities of the characters whose behaviour brought them into existence. Out of a moment of aesthetic stasis, a linguistic tracing around the object, developments in the plot struggle forward to produce complications at a later stage. But these complications fail to produce any significant activity in which issues can be resolved and actions concluded. They too are drawn into aesthetic patterns which are created out of an eccentric combination of the events described and a language that does more than merely describe them.

So Melchiori's 'precarious balance' is not only a balance between the asymmetrical shapes of events in the narrative. It is also a balance between events as constituents of the novel's plot, and events as opportunities for a display of style. Green's dislocated language gathers to itself and disengages itself from the story in an almost random way. It leaves a double impression in the mind – of events occurring in almost plotless inconsequence, and a queer elegance of style which uses incidents thrown up by the narrative as opportunities for displays of linguistic celebration.

Party Going is at the opposite end of the spectrum from *Concluding*. It inaugurates what *Concluding* concludes, and in so doing carries with it a 'cruder', and less abstracted picture of the world. Both the sensuousness and the abstraction of *Concluding* are less in evidence. In spite of the condition of stasis which both circumstance (the fog) and character contrive to bring about, more seems to have happened at the end of this novel than at the end of the later one. There are more tangible relationships and intimacies waiting to be left unresolved.

Stokes has remarked on Green's talent for 'creating an effect of livingness through incongruities'. He was referring to incongruities of events rather than of language. Particularly to the way these are assembled to produce the strange atmosphere of frivolousness and threat that permeates *Party Going*. Miss Fellowes's peculiar behaviour over a dead pigeon she finds near the Departure area of the station is just one of those 'intrusions of the abnormal on the normal' mentioned by Stokes. It is not restricted to the opening pages, but winds its way in and out of the events and conversations of the whole novel. Initially there is no explanation why the pigeon should have fallen dead at Miss Fellowes's feet at that particular time. Or why Miss Fellowes should have behaved as she did towards it. Green's description of what she does, after bending down and lifting the pigeon by its wing, indicates clearly what his attitude to the event will be:

No one paid attention, all were intent and everyone hurried, nobody looked back. Her dead pigeon then lay sideways, wings outspread as she held it, its dead head down towards the ground. She turned and she went back to where it had fallen and again looked up to where it must have died for it was still warm and, everything unexplained, she turned once more into the tunnel back to the station.

Miss Fellowes's behaviour is not strictly rational. It is not altogether peculiar either. Having suddenly been brought into such immediate contact with the dead bird, Miss Fellowes does not behave strangely when she picks it up by the tip of the wing. And, having done that, as the prose confirms, it becomes '*her* dead pigeon', her responsibility. Also, the return from the Departure tunnel to the place where the bird had fallen is unconstructive but not irrational. The bird still warm in her hand, she might well look up into the fog where it must have just died. The brief authorial parenthesis, 'everything unexplained', is a comment not only reproducing Miss Fellowes's thought processes, but mirroring our own. From this point on, with Miss Fellowes's decision to wash the bird so as to get rid of any fleas that might be lodged in its feathers, the old lady's behaviour does become more odd. Even so, it is a natural consequence, given her background and experience of dead animals in more appropriate rural surroundings, of her decision to *notice* the pigeon. The description of her in the ladies' washroom, drawing up her sleeves and plunging her fingers in the hot dirty water where the pigeon drowns in 'a thin wreath or two of blood', is grotesque. She is observed by two threatening 'granite' nannies and an attendant who is described as the 'guardian of this place' as she does 'what she felt must be done with hot water, turning her fingers to the colour of its legs and blood'. Miss Fellowes cannot get rid of the pigeon. She has the attendant wrap it up in brown paper. Later, feeling faint, she allows one of the hangers-on of the party to deposit it in a wastepaper basket. Still feeling unwell but having come out of her fainting-fit, she retrieves the parcel. That is the last we hear of her for the time being. Members of the party have begun to assemble on the platform, forcing her to withdraw into a subordinate position. The next section opens in the fog outside, with Julia Wray, one of the principal females of the party, leaving her uncle's house to make her way to the station.

Thereafter Miss Fellowes and her dead pigeon move to the side of the story. They will not go away altogether, though. In the tea-room she reflects on the correctness of her action in attending to the bird. But she is badly shaken and, after ordering a whisky and enduring the rudeness of the girls who are serving the drinks, she falls ill again. As a result she has to be taken into one of the rooms at the station hotel booked by Max Adey, the host. There she remains as a constant reminder of the vulnerability of human beings in the face of death (if she is as ill as some of them think she is) or of some spiritual infirmity which has been expressed through her behaviour with the pigeon. The nannies, attending in the sick-room, have 'an unfailing instrument for disaster'. They ruminate on the signs of mortality in comic–grotesque terms which later, in *Nothing*, are found to be absurdly appropriate to the way one of the minor characters, Arthur Morris, actually dies. From time to time we are invited to share Miss Fellowes's interior monologue, in which a frightening death is dreamed into being through images of crushing and drowning. Claire Hignam, her niece, and Evelyn Henderson, another member of the party, feel weighed down by their responsibility for this sick woman, separated from the frivolity and carelessness of the party by a single flight of stairs. Meanwhile Miss Fellowes mentally transfers her argument with the girl in the tea-room into an argument with death. A trivial social inconvenience takes on the character of a desperate struggle for health and life. And all the time the dead pigeon in its brown-paper parcel exerts an indefinable but powerful influence over everyone in the room:

'I think what we are both afraid of', said Evelyn, 'is that parcel she had and what was inside it. You know I have absolute faith in searching out whatever it is that is really worrying one underneath what seems on the surface to be the matter with anything . . . and I know in my case it was her having picked that pigeon up somewhere and then seeming so ill.'

Evelyn concludes, however, that 'it isn't anything to worry about'. Other characters in the novel don't worry about it. Julia, who is also related to Miss Fellowes, takes only a perfunctory interest in the old lady. The others are happy to accept the diagnosis of a doctor they are able to secure for a cursory examination, that nothing is seriously wrong. Again Green has

largely separated the feelings of his characters from the feelings of
his readers. We share some of the anxiety of Claire and Evelyn,
not the purposeful ignorance of the rest of the party, and the
presence of the sick woman and the dead pigeon colour our
picture of everything else that happens. The sexual games of the
principal characters are played against a background of sudden
death (of the pigeon), 'natural' behaviour leading to hysteria, and
inadequately diagnosed illness. The fact that these things are
sealed away from Max, Amabel, Julia and Angela Crevy, busy
with their own sexual and social activities in the rooms down-
stairs, does not mean that they are put out of our minds as they are
out of theirs.

The mixture of the odd and the threatening, that which
provokes unease and anxiety in the midst of a light-hearted
upper-class frolic, is by no means restricted to the incident
involving Miss Fellowes and her pigeon. What is concentrated
there spills out into the general situation in which Max and his
party are discovered. One small example of this is the presence of
the 'mystery man' who speaks to Miss Fellowes in the tea-room
and follows her as she is carried into the station hotel. He is
convinced of the seriousness of her illness and is recognised by the
party-goers as a possible threat to their enjoyment of whatever
facilities the hotel offers. He appears several times at unexpected
moments, sometimes abashed, sometimes vaguely threatening.
His dialect slips in and out of Yorkshire, Brumagem and standard
English. His role also changes from scene to scene. At first it is
rumoured he is the hotel detective, anxious to ensure that a
seriously ill person does not remain on the premises. At other
times he is made use of by the party-goers to (unsuccessfully)
bring up Julia's servant, Thomson, with her luggage. In the
process of performing this service for Julia, the man moves
through a station platform which has been metaphorically
transformed into a graveyard. Abandoned commuters stand like
mourners over tombstones, which are their cases: 'they were like
the dead resurrected in their clothes under this cold veiled light'.
And the man 'dodged about asking any man he saw if he was Miss
Julia Wray's so much as to say, "I be the gravedigger, would I
bury you again?".'

It might be argued that this Pinteresque figure is unsuccessfully
imported into the novel, adding to it a deposit of dramatic fantasy
that is foreign to its essential character. Apart from Miss

Fellowes's disturbing presence in the hotel, a more potent and mysterious threat issues from general properties of the scene: the fog itself; the huge vault of glass under which everyone in the station is trapped; the steel shutter, forming a trap within a trap, that separates the hotel foyer from the crowds outside on the platform; and those milling crowds themselves, appearing ever more threatening and rebellious as the evening, and the fog, wear on.

The imagery of the fog is especially striking. One of the finest descriptions appears immediately after the affair of Miss Fellowes and the pigeon, during Julia Wray's walk to the station. Here the movement of human beings along the pavement is experienced as a 'dark flood' passing beneath a 'pall' of fog that renders traffic motionless and blocked. The lamps seem to be great distances away, making it 'like night', with fog as a 'ceiling shutting out the sky'. At any moment Julia expects the fog to 'drop suddenly down to the ground', enveloping her in a palpable gloom. After a movement onto more open ground she is 'reassured to see leaves brilliantly green veined like marble with wet dirt and these veins reflecting each light back'. The lights, from car headlamps, come 'like thoughts in darkness, in a story' until Julia is able to leave them and join the crowds disappearing down tunnels into the station and under that great vault of glass.

The fog has precipitated Julia and the others into a region of death where those tombstones and mourners on the platform are appropriately assembled. The emphasis falls almost continually on a claustrophobic sealing in of the people. 'Palls', 'marble' and 'vault' suggest a burial. The tunnels and dark floods summon up a picture of some pagan Underworld strangely infiltrated, as in a surrealistic fantasy, by the modern appurtenances of street-lamps, conduits and heavy suitcases.

It is in this land of the dead, of claustrophobic restraint, that the party-goers are prevented from travelling to their destination in the South of France. But the urge to escape, to free themselves from whatever restraint is represented by the fog, strangely and vitally crystallises out of the very heart of the fog. Julia, having decided to return home for her 'charms' – a wooden revolver, an egg with toy elephants inside it, and a top – crosses a footbridge and then, 'struck by misery', feels she has to stand still and look down at the stagnant water beneath her. 'Then three seagulls flew through that span on which she stood and that is what had happened one of the times she first met him [Max], doves had flown under a bridge where she had been standing when she had stayed away last summer. She thought those gulls were for the sea they were to cross that evening.' As her charms suggest, Julia is one of the most empty-headed and selfish of all the party-goers, competing first with Angela Crevy, then with the more formidable Amabel, for Max Adey's attentions. And yet this image of the birds flying under the bridge, through the fog into clear skies, has a potent effect on her. It brings her superficial self-concern into contact with more general feelings of release and freedom. At the end of the novel, where she had renewed hopes of engaging Max's interest, her mind reverts to birds – perhaps these birds, which have changed from swallows to doves already, and might therefore have produced the image of pigeons in her thoughts now. Then, also, it is hinted that Julia's ambition might be less frivolous than she has ways of expressing it. She hopes 'it would be as though she could take him back into her life from where it had started and show it to him for them to share in a much more exciting thing of their own'.

Most of the rest of her story, and Amabel's, throw out few suggestions that their feelings for Max or for anyone else spring from such deep-seated psychic need. For the most part they are competitive, shallow and manipulating young women. They have little to do with their lives but impress suitable members of the opposite sex with their sophisticated manners and provocative sexuality. Also the men in the party are self-indulgent and charmingly predatory. They appear to have no sense of the seriousness of living, because their lives have never brought home to them that anything could happen differently from the kinds of things that were happening to them now. A minor inconvenience – fog delaying the boat train – can be made the opportunity for any number of sexual and social diversions. In any case, Max has so much money that he insists on their taking over half of the rooms for the evening. Then the competition between Julia and Angela can provide a welcome *divertissement*, with Julia in the stronger position, and Angela something of an outsider forcing her personality onto the other members of the party with the ultimate ambition of detaching Max from Julia. Further complications arise with the arrival half-way through the book of the beautiful, wealthy Amabel. Now the focus changes to Max's uncertainty as to whether he will drop Julia in favour of his

uninvited mistress, or find a diversion for Amabel. Such a
diversion eventually materialises in the form of a hitherto much
discussed, but not actually present, young man called Embassy
Richard. When the fog lifts, the exchanges of partners and
confidences in the hotel are seen to have acted as an amusing
prelude to further potential complications.

The competition for Max among the three unattached young
women is almost entirely frivolous. Each of them directs her
ambitions and her feminine guile to the single aim of securing this
rich and glamorous individual for herself. But there is beauty, too,
in the physical presence of these women, and Green is very
susceptible to it. Nowhere is this more seductively charming than
in the description of Amabel's bath. It is interesting to trace the
way Green shares this susceptibility with his readers by carefully
distributing impressions of it from a variety of points of view – to
all of which every reader, but none of the characters, is privy.

Amabel proposes that she will take a bath after a brief
conversation with Angela Crevy, whom she has just met and
doesn't appear to care for. Alex Alexander rings down to order it
and telephones Amabel's maid to bring her crystals. This
involvement with Alex, coupled with his use of Max's name to
secure another room with a bath, establishes Amabel's sense of
her own pre-eminence. It also establishes a propensity to tease
Miss Crevy, which dominates the later description of the actual
bathing. When her maid finally arrives with the crystals, Amabel
repels Angela's bid for intimacy (she has asked if she should come
and watch her have her bath) by inviting Alex to come into the
room with her. Angela is left wondering whether Alex is actually
watching Amabel in her bath. She weaves erotic fantasies around
the situation by wondering whether it will be expected of her that
Max shall play a similar rôle *vis à vis* herself.

This mixture of anxiety and excitement is accompanied by
speculations about Alex and the maid being in the bath-room
together: 'But surely not in front of her maid, she thought, without
noticing how this would make it better in one sense, even if it could
not make it right.' She decides that, even if Amabel does call, she
will not enter the room if Alex is there: 'she could not be by the
bath in front of Alex, looking into his eyes . . . it would be to look
into his eyes laid upon the woman's nakedness'. Amabel is
perfectly aware of Angela's discomfort and manoeuvres Alex into
sharing it – in an imaginatively voyeuristic sense. For Alex is

firmly placed behind the bath-room door, forced to imagine Amabel's nakedness after being told, with a giggle, that 'She thinks we are in here together.' Alex asks if she takes her rings off when she has her bath. On being asked why, he confesses 'I was wondering what you looked like.' Meanwhile next door Claire is telling Evelyn that Amabel is keeping Alex hanging on. She tells her that, incongruously (and improbably – since it is Embassy Richard's gossip), Amabel allows no one, not even those who go to bed with her, to see her without clothes on, 'because someone quite early in life had carved his initials low on her back with an electric-light wire'. This absurd Firbankian allegation closes the incident for the time being.

Green has placed Amabel at the centre of several outer rings of voyeurs, or would-be voyeurs. First there is the maid, who plays a potent part in Alex's erotic picture of Amabel: he thinks of her as a negress, dark against the pink of Amabel's skin, with eyes that 'might have shone like two humming birds in the tropic airs she glistened in'. Alex converts Amabel into a pink-skinned Olympia, a healthy complement to Manet's pale-bodied courtesan. One circle further from the centre of Amabel's luxuriant immersion is Angela Crevy. She is calculating what kind of erotic exposure might follow her own displacement of Amabel from the position Amabel (or is it still Julia?) at present occupies in Max Adey's scheme of sexual gratification. Then, to import an additional air of ridicule into the situation, and particularly Angela's position in it, there is the gossip between Claire and Evelyn in the adjoining room.

What the description of the positions occupied by members of the cast in relation to Amabel excludes is our own position, what we ourselves are privileged to see. As it happens, we are in a position of the greatest privilege. Before Alex asked his question about the rings, we had seen them from an observation point even closer to the adorable nude than even her maid has occupied; 'She kicked her legs and splashed and sent fountains of water up among the wreaths of sweet steam, and her hands with rings still on her fingers were water-lilies done in rubies.' When Amabel gets out of the bath, with Alex and the others still at various removes from the inner sanctum of her self-exposure and self-adoration, we are still present. It is for our benefit as well as for her own that Amabel's body is allowed slowly to emerge from the wreaths of steam:

The walls were made of looking-glass, and were clouded over with steam; from them her body was reflected in a faint pink mass. She leaned over and traced her name Amabel in that steam and that pink mass loomed up to meet her in the flesh and looked through bright at her through the letters of her name. She bent down to look at her eyes in the A her name began with, and as she gazed at them steam or her breath dulled her reflection and the blue her eyes were went out or faded. . . .

As she went over herself with her towel it was plain that she loved her own shape and skin. When she dried her breasts she wiped them with as much care as she would puppies after she had given them their bath, smiling all the time. But her stomach she wiped unsmiling upwards to make it thin. When she came to dry her legs she hissed like grooms do. And as she got herself dry that steam began to go off the mirror walls so that as she got white again more and more of herself began to be reflected.

She stood out as though so much health, such abundance and happiness should have never clothes to hide it. Indeed she looked as though she were alone in the world she was so good, and so good that she looked mild, which she was not.

This loving and witty celebration of the woman's body comes to an appropriate climax with that stinging little comment 'so good that she looked mild, which she was not'. But in the description of her drying we see her as she sees herself – with narcissistic delight at the changing colours of her skin and at the slow emergence of her body as the steam evaporates from those provocatively misted mirrors. We are at the core of Amabel's charm, her delight in herself, which is inseparable from her occupation of that splendidly exposed but still private flesh. Her drying and polishing of herself is an erotic act, the towel descending from face and neck and shoulders down to breast and stomach and legs. Every feature emerges doubly from the ever more luminously reflecting mirrors in which she delights to view herself.

The astringent framework of rumour, embarrassment and sublimated desire encloses ourselves as well as Amabel: we are an unseen presence, an appreciative mirror before which she stands and enjoys herself. We have to go back to Donne and Carew, or at least to Keats in 'The Eve of St Agnes', to come anywhere close to the calm, aestheticised eroticism of this passage. It is not, however, so very unusual in Green. Merode, too, in *Concluding*, takes us into her bathroom – though for considerably less time. And there is the climax to Charley Summers's discovery of his dead Rose in the living body of her half sister Nancy, on the last page of *Back*.

In *Party Going*, as in most of Green's other work, a frank appeal to the reader's sensuality is made through images which are erotic but not pornographic. They are not pornographic because they relate back and forward to the changing lives of women who become them, and because they are placed in the setting of a physical awareness of the world which exists quite apart from them. But Green's awareness of the desirability of women and the constant undercurrent of sexual attraction and disturbance he knows this gives rise to does not always create the kind of sensuous epiphany we have enjoyed in the descriptions of Amabel's bath or Nancy Whitmore's bed. More often it is responsible for an undercurrent of physical awareness that coexists with other activities, desires, and often trivial worries and anxieties. Two of Green's novels where this is conspicuously the case are *Caught* and *Loving*. To my mind these two novels represent the apex of Green's achievement, bringing together more satisfyingly than any of the others do the intricate patterning and the insight into human psychology which are the hallmarks of his art.

All of Green's best work is marked by his experience of the war years. Usually it takes as its subject some aspect of civilian life during that time. The threatening atmosphere of the fog-bound station in *Party Going* suggests some imminent catastrophe, though the nature of that catastrophe is muffled by an eccentric symbolism. Charley Summers's mental disturbance in *Back* has been caused by the death of his mistress while he has been separated from her in a POW camp in Germany. What happens in it happens in London during the last half of 1944, the period of the 'flying bombs', which play an important part in the plot. *Caught* is set in the period of the 'phoney' war and the first air raids of May 1940; *Loving* at some unspecified time during the middle of the war.

Of all Green's novels *Caught* is the most closely involved with the war. The private fantasies of the characters are seen against a

backdrop of historic events, from the declaration of war, through
the invasion of Norway, to the London blitz. Stokes has dealt in
great detail with the dependence of the events recorded in the
story on the wider public events which determine their shape.
However, the link between the private foreground and the public
background is only of superficial importance. The real substance
of the novel lies in the relationship between two men in an
auxiliary fire service sub-station; a relationship which would
never have come into being were it not for the urgencies of war,
but which is unaffected by anything which has intrinsically to do
with the war.

The two men, Richard Roe and Albert Pye, are different from
each other in almost every way. Roe is a country gentleman. He
has joined the auxiliary fire service as a patriotic duty, as well as
for other, more personal reasons. Pye is a member of the
professional fire service. He has been promoted to Instructor,
and, later, head of a London sub-station. This would not have
happened had it not been for the increased work load of the fire
service during the bombing-raids of August 1940. Roe appears to
have no politics, accepting society as it is and not reflecting on the
peculiarity of his position in it. Pye has left-wing leanings, in so far
as a vague and often embittered grievance against the bosses can
be defined as left-wing. Part of the antagonism Pye feels towards
Roe, his subordinate, probably has to do with his recognition of
their different class backgrounds. This provides Green with
innumerable opportunities for sketching in situations where
status and class don't quite synchronise, and an odd mixture of
comedy, tension, and uncertainty in human relationships ensues.
Much of Green's best writing springs from his ability to show the
cumulative effect of petty confusions springing from circumstances of this kind. In *Caught*, these circumstances involve almost
everyone in the sub-station at one time or another.

But beneath the antagonism of class runs a much more
powerful and individual antagonism between the two men. This is
caused by Pye, whose life has been severely damaged by
circumstances involving Roe during the period when Pye was his
Instructor, and some time before Roe discovered that he had been
sent to the sub-station Pye happened to be in command of. Roe
bears no direct responsibility for this. What has happened is that
Pye's sister has abducted a little boy from a toy shop, and the little
boy turns out to be Roe's son, Christopher. This event, which is

described very early in the novel, illuminates aspects of Pye which are in large part responsible for the deterioration of his character. It also draws attention to Roe's own predicament, widowed and estranged from life in spite of the responsibility for his son which he shares with his sister-in-law, Dy.

It is typical of Green's oblique style that the scene in which Christopher is abducted from the toy-shop is described in a lengthy parenthesis that is bracketed off from the main narrative. In fact it is at two removes from the main narrative, since the description of what happened to Christopher follows Roe's memory of his own visit to the toy-shop after Christopher's return. The present circumstances in which Roe remembers the later event take the form of a journey by train from his home in the country to London and the fire station. It is now December 1939, two or three months after mobilisation and Roe's discovery that Pye is his sub-station officer. So we and Roe are looking back beyond the as-yet-undescribed awkwardness of his position under Pye, to an event that occurred whilst Roe was under instruction by Pye and other senior fire officers.

Coming back to London, Roe sees a picture of the fire station in his mind's eye. Imagining in particular its tower, with five open platforms one on top of the other, he recalls his fear of heights. In particular he recalls one occasion, unconnected with the fire service, when he had to walk on a ledge forty feet off the ground under the windows of the choir of Tewkesbury Abbey. The point of comparison in the two experiences – Roe's fear of heights – gives way to another comparison between the abbey and something else which the sight of the fire station has brought to mind, but which it does not itself have in common with the other two experiences. Nevertheless, in the person of Bert Pye it *does* contain the reason why Roe fixes on an aspect of the abbey which suggests a complementary aspect of a quite different experience. The experience is that of Roe's visit to the toy-shop, and the point of comparison with what happened at the abbey is the mysterious play of colours in each place: light from the stained glass of the abbey windows throws colours onto the stone flags of the church below; light from the stained glass of the toy-shop windows spills over on to the display cabinets and the rest of the shop's interior. There follows a description of Roe's experience in the toy shop as he remembers it in the context of the previous memories of the fire station and the abbey; and, after it, the bracketed, third-person

description of what actually happened to Christopher there some
weeks before his father's visit.

When, from curiosity, he went to see for himself the store out of
which Christopher had been abducted, he stopped, unknow-
ing, by that very counter with the toy display which had so
struck his son as to make him lost. Fire engines attracted the
father, but deer, then sailboats, had bewitched the son. For
both it was the deep colour spilled over these objects that, by
evoking memories they would not name, and which they could
not place, held them, and then led both to a loch-deep
unconsciousness of all else.

The walls of this store being covered with stained glass
windows which depicted trading scenes, that is of merchandise
being loaded on to galleons, the leaving port, of incidents on the
voyage, and then the unloading, all brilliantly lit from without,
it follows that the body of the shop was inundated with colour,
brimming, and this colour, as the sea was a predominant part of
each window, was a permanence of sapphire in shopping hours.
Pink neon lights on the high ceiling wore down this blue to some
extent, made customers' faces less aggressively steeped in the
body of the store, but enhanced, or deepened that fire brigade
scarlet to carmine, and, in so doing, drugged Richard's
consciousness.

He then saw the heraldic deer, the light that caught red in
their bead eyes. And the sails, motionless, might have been
stretched above a deeper patch of fathomless sea in the shade of
foothills as though covered with hyacinths in that imagined
light of evening, and round which, laden, was to come the wind
that would give them power to move the purple shade they cast
beside the painted boat they were to drive.

In remembering his stand at the counter he supposed he had
been trying to see what his son had seen. He imagined that, his
pink cheeks grape dark in the glow, Christopher had leant his
face forward, held to ransom by the cupidity of boys, and had
been lost in feelings that this colour, reflected in such a way on
so much that he wanted, could not have failed to bring him who
could have visited no flower-locked sea on the Aegean, and yet,
with every other child, or boy at school, with any man in the
mood, who knew and always would that stretch of water, those
sails from the past, those boats fishing in the senses.

We have no difficulty in understanding why Roe was attracted to the fire engines on display. Christopher's interest in boats is clarified later when we discover that he had been carrying one of the toy boats when he was brought back from Pye's sister by the police. What the prose does, though, is to superimpose Roe's vision of things in the present on his son's vision of very similar things in the past. The writing has been described as hallucinatory, and I think this is true. Like so many images of past events which play just under the surface of consciousness, these images possess a vivid, mesmeric power that influences, sometimes in a very direct way, the behaviour of the characters who experience them. Here the colours of blue, of the marine images reflected from the windows, and of pink, from the neon light on the ceiling, pick out and fuse together the colours of the fire engine (deepened from scarlet to carmine) and the boat (in a purple shade, with Christopher's cheeks, bending over it, changing from pink to 'grape dark' in the glow). Words such as 'bewitched', 'inundated', 'steeped' and 'drugged' emphasise this shared vision. At the same time the complicated periodic sentences of the second and fourth paragraphs, holding the descriptive passages suspended in a linguistic net, tend to merge the primary subjects, actual or imagined. The result is that it is difficult to disentangle Roe's perception of the objects in the toy-shop from his son's.

After the first passage of narrative, describing Christopher's abduction, we are reminded that Roe is remembering the scene as he saw it in retrospect. There, he had already commented on the 'heraldic deer'. *They* must be intended to cast our minds back three or four pages to the 'heraldic cattle' that Roe and Christopher had seen in the park before Roe took the train back to London. Now he thinks of the light in the shop 'as though he had been seeing the toys through Christmas cracker paper'. This image takes us forwards a hundred pages to a scene in which Roe and his girl, Hilly, are dining in a Soho club. When the lights go out a 'steep purple' is left behind by the presence of a single blue line, and Roe feels that he is 'looking through Christmas cracker paper' at the negro singer who has begun to perform. Immediately after this simile, another comparison is made, this time of Roe watching the singer 'as though in stained glass window light'.

In each of these incidents the centre of perception is Roe. Somewhere in his mind are linked together what seem to be the separate elements of experience represented by his relationship with Christopher at home, his absence from him during his visit to the toy-shop, and the way he makes use of him in his conversation with Hilly. The last point requires further explanation: the conversation between Roe and Hilly (from pp. 100–5 in the Hogarth edition) is an extraordinarily complex and subtle piece of writing in which Hilly is shown as being interested in Roe's mysterious background as a widower and father. Roe is partly deliberately, partly unknowingly, using the idea of Christopher as a bait to get Hilly to go to bed with him. This strategy and counter-strategy gets mixed up with conversation about other issues involving Roe's relationship with the men at the fire station. But the idea of Christopher, the motherless boy, as a common point of reference for the promotion of what are, superficially at least, different intentions on the part of Roe and Hilly, is very strongly felt. And so the imagery associated with Christopher's relationship with his father weaves its way in and out of descriptions of incidents in which the boy himself plays no part, but where whatever emotionally attaches Roe to him emerges from his subconscious mind either directly – in his passages of reminiscence and imagination; or indirectly – in the author's third-person narrative.

At other times the use of images or colour words to suggest links between events in the narrative that at first glance appear to be quite unrelated to one another does not involve the appropriation of them by a single presiding consciousness. In showing how Roe's and Christopher's responses to the display cabinet are overlaid in Roe's re-creation of his visit to the toy-shop, I was suggesting that images and events might parallel one another in ways that cannot be explained by a claim made upon them by the mind of any one of the characters. Instead the author himself or (since Green is nowhere present in the prose he writes) the style and language in the novel seem to be teasing out apparently random connections between events. For example, in a rather vague and general sense the colours of blue and pink, which dominate the picture of the interior of the toy-shop, recur in other, unrelated contexts. These often involve people quite separate from Roe, Christopher, or other members of their family. In particular, Pye's sister is described by these colour words more than by any others. When she abducts Christopher she keeps him in the dark of her room, lit only by a fire 'which as it was disturbed to flame, sent her shadow reeling, gyrating round sprawling rosy walls'. At the toy-shop, a little earlier the 'rose diamonds in her eyes' are shaded, 'and so had gone an even deeper blue'. The colours of rose and pink, which represent elsewhere in Green whatever is sensuously desirable or comforting (think of the end of *Back*, again, with the figure of Rose bathed in the gentle rose-lighting of the lamp by her bed) have been sinister illuminations, parodying their usual functions in a perverse and distorted way.

In another hallucinatory incident described early in the novel the emphasis on blue also brings with it sinister and perverse connotations. I am referring to Pye's memory of his return home after his first sexual experience many years ago ('with Mrs Lowe's little girl'). In the moonlit night he catches a glimpse of his sister also creeping back from some illicit affair: 'In the grass lane . . . that winding lane between high banks, in moonlight, in colour blue . . . .' The black-out brings the scene back to Pye's mind, 'with the moon, this blue colour, and with the creeping home'. When we have discovered why these images keep returning to Pye's mind – he had forced his sister into having sex with him, and then squeezed the knowledge of it out of his mind – we understand why the colour images associated with her are now associated with him. Pye leaves the station at night to find out how clearly he can make out the faces of the girls who pass by him in the darkness. He walks into a world of electric blue, where shadows are 'sapphire' or 'indigo', and even the mucus pulsating from the nostrils of a boy passing by is 'Eton blue'. More suggestively still, 'The milk moon stripped deep gentian cracker paper shadows off his uniform.' Pye, whose imagination has not made use of the cracker-paper image and who has not been described by it up to this point, suddenly becomes enveloped in it, like the scene at the toy-shop or at the night club – as they were viewed by Roe. Green has developed the image in relation to Roe, Christopher and Pye's sister to the point at which its cumulative suggestions now attach themselves to Pye. They suggest the sinister ambience of dislocation and breakdown into which he is moving.

The deterioration of Pye has been anticipated slightly earlier, when his affair with Prudence (who has been caught up in the frenetic admiration of the fire-fighters that was fashionable during the blitz) for a moment coincides with a half-erotic memory of himself and his sister. Pye covets the soft touch of Prudence's fingers, which, in the daytime, are milk white, 'not chalky, as they would now be under the violet-hooded lamps'. Now the imagined touch of the fingers, combined with the violet colourings, brings to mind his sister's fingers, 'so long ago . . . the time his sister put her hand inside his boy's coat because he was cold, to warm his heart'.

At other points in the narrative the memory of Pye's seduction of his sister is, as it were, transposed from Pye's sensibility to that of another person – who doesn't, of course, *remember* it himself, but who allows the reader to remember it on Pye's behalf. A good example of this kind of thing is where Roe, in the middle of an air raid, finds a couple embracing in the dark corner of a surface shelter. The description of them, the girl with trembling hair, both of them 'motionless, forgotten, as though they had been *drugged* in order to forget' (emphasis added), cannot help but carry our minds back to the scene in the lane thirty years ago, when Pye must have behaved with his sister in just such a drugged and trembling state. This sort of transposition of memories occurs among the other characters too. For example, Roe's absent-minded supposition that his wife, who is dead, is going for a stroll with him on the morning of his return to London is mirrored in Piper's (he is one of the older men in Pye's sub-station) muttered addresses to his absent wife when he is doing any mundane job at the station: 'Well, mother,' he cried, 'I think I'll take me boots off now.'

These memory images, looping backwards and forwards across the linear time scheme, weave into a distinctive style the deeply rooted obsessions and anxieties of the principal characters. On the surface Green captures with intense fidelity the atmosphere of gossip, misunderstanding and rumour that are bound to get mixed into the social relationships of groups of men and women under stress. But to open up depths of private misery and despair, of spiritual vacuity and nameless guilt (that in their different ways Roe and Pye share), Green has used a different method, one that cuts across the forward movement of the story. At the end of the novel Roe has emerged from his severe withdrawal from reality to find new possibilities and new hopes in the work he has performed as a fire-fighter and the human relations he has forged during the bombings. Pye has not been able to live with the knowledge that has been forced upon him by his sister's illness, his loss of command at the sub-station, and his realisation of what happened between himself and his sister thirty years ago. Ironically his end was foreshadowed when his sister abducted Christopher from the toy-shop, before the 'main' events of the novel get under way. For, when it comes, it comes as a direct result of what might be described as his own 'Christopher-substitute', a starving London boy he discovered during one of his moonlight walks through the city. At the moment he picks him up, to take back to the sub-station, Pye is thinking of Christopher. At the same time he is trying to prove that he must have been mistaken about his sister. The moonlight walks are not only attempts to prove to himself that he couldn't have recognised his sister in the darkness. They are also expeditious in search of sexual gratification and release. The urgency of the search derives from feelings for his sister, feelings which he still experiences when he brings back the past and which are undoubtedly incestuous. It is the acknowledgement of this last fact that must have caused Pye to put his head in a gas oven and kill himself.

The setting of Green's next novel, *Loving*, is Kinalty Castle, a large country house somewhere in Ireland, at some time during the Second World War. The meticulous documentation of historical events, which played so large a part in providing a wider context for the action of *Caught*, has here given way to rumours and melodramatic hypotheses about the general conduct of the war. The atmosphere of the novel is far removed from anything Green had achieved, or sought to achieve so far. It is an atmosphere of fairy-tale enchantment. We feel this from the very first sentence: 'Once upon a day an old butler called Eldon lay dying in his room . . . .' For good measure the novel ends with the traditional phrase, describing the married happiness of the two main characters: 'Over in England they were married and lived happily ever after.' Between these two statements the action of the novel is always set against the background of the castle and its decor. The servants' quarters are separated from the rest of the house by a green baize door. The pantry and the servants' hall are connected by a long high stone passage with a vaulted ceiling. The hall itself is dominated by a mahogany sideboard decorated with a swan at either end and with gold Worcester vases at the centre. In these rooms and in the kitchen, attic bedroom and butler's room we meet the servants, and discover their possessions lying cheek by jowl with the treasures of the big house. Paddy O'Conor, in the lamp-room among the outbuildings, is separated from the estate's peacocks by nothing more than a glass-fronted cupboard. The ruined Greek temple and tower-of-Pisa dovecote are used as if they were the common property of the children, servants and (usually absent) masters. The rooms beyond the servants' quarters are even more reminiscent of fairy-tale palaces. The walls of the Red Library are covered in green silk, its armchairs in purple leather, and the desk top in rhinoceros hide supported on pillars of gold-coloured wood. The bed in Mrs Jack's bedroom is shaped like a boat in black and gold, with a gold oar at the foot. Most enchanting of all is the Blue Drawing Room, which also has a vaulted roof, this time painted to represent the evening sky at dusk. But the crowning glory of the Blue Room is an imitation of a cow byre – Marie Antoinette style – with milking stools, pails, clogs and gilded wood furniture. Kinalty is 'the most celebrated eighteenth century folly in Eire'.

The dovecote is the setting for a fairy story within a fairy story, for it is here that Miss Swift, the old deaf nanny, tells the children a story about a court of doves. The interruptions of the children – Evelyn and Moira, and the cook's son Albert – prevent the story from being concluded, and we don't hear much of it. There is enough, though, to apply what happens in it to what is going to happen to Edith and Kate, the under housemaids, who pass by, as the story is being told, like fairy-tale characters themselves: 'They saw Edith and Kate in long purple uniforms bow swaying towards them in soft sunlight through the white budding branches . . . .' The silence is broken by the girls' arrival. 'All five [children] began soundlessly giggling in the face of beauty' as Miss Swift presses on with the story, regardless. While she does so the real doves in the dovecote are mating and fighting. They are seen to be doing so by the children. Only Nanny Swift remains oblivious to everything that is not a part of her story.

The scene at the dovecote is typical of the novel as a whole. It allows different kinds of 'story material' to float together, creating suggestive shapes and patterns. Nanny Swift's fairy story is told in idyllic surroundings. But the surroundings embrace the passion and violence of the real doves as well as the sedate good breeding of the fictive ones. Edith's and Kate's appearance on the scene suggests emotional propensities that are concealed by their graceful entry. But they will burgeon later when Edith and Raunce fall in love, and Kate, in desperation, gives herself to Paddy, the lampman. Towards the end of *Loving* Edith and

Raunce conduct their lovemaking at the very place where Nanny
Swift told her story: 'Charley and Edith slipped out after supper
that same day to be with each other on the very seat by the
dovecote where Miss Swift that first afternoon of spring had told
her charges a fairy story while they watched the birds lovemaking.'

The feelings of the characters drift and settle into unforeseen
relationships as the artificial conditions of the 'castle' – cut off
from the mainland by the war and more or less cut off from the rest
of Ireland by its inhabitants' fears of the IRA – act as a
forcing-house of the emotions, and of the nervous system. The
oddity of this baroque environment rubs off on the sensibilities of
the characters who inhabit it. Also, it affects the kind of contact
that we, as readers, feel we can establish with them. Perhaps this
contact, which makes us respond to the servants in particular with
a mixture of comic enjoyment and aesthetic delight, is affected by
our knowledge that the house and its contents will soon be
destroyed. We know that it is a charming anomaly in the middle of
a world of warfare, violence and threat. This is not simply a
hypothesis based on our present knowledge of the destruction of
the Anglo-Irish castles and big houses during the war. Green
mentions, *sotto voce*, on two occasions, that Kinalty *will* be
destroyed. Quite early in the story, before Raunce finds Edith and
Kate dancing in the ball-room, we are told that this house, 'a
shadowless castle of treasures, . . . had yet to be burned down'.
And near the end, during a description of the Blue Drawing
Room, Green slips in the information that Kinalty 'had still to be
burned down'. The phrasing is almost the same on each occasion.
And it surrounds a picture of aristocratic, fairy-tale splendours
with portents of imminent tragedy and destruction. The effect is
rather like those poems of Tennyson – 'Ulysses', 'The Lotus
Eaters', 'Oenone' – where the shadow of what is likely to happen
falls on the description of what is happening, and which Tennyson
to all intents and purposes has cut off from what we feel we know
must be its final issue.

But Green's fairy-tale is made extraordinarily real by the
presence of the below-stairs servants in it. The owner of the castle
is away in the war in Europe, and his mother and wife, Mrs
Tennant and Mrs Jack, are absent for much of the time. Whilst
the owners of Kinalty make important contributions to the plot of
the novel, it is how the servants react to those contributions and

how they create plots of their own that attracts our attention. We find ourselves attending to the ordinary goings-on of the servants, from the head butler to the under housemaids. But these are disrupted by the war conditions and the absence of the master. They are further disrupted by apparently unimportant incidents which cumulatively, especially in the context of this highly artificial environment, transform the ordinary into the extraordinary. The background of the house and its contents – a broken weathervane, peacocks' eggs, a jar of waterglass in Mrs Welch's pantry – provide an appropriately exotic ambience for the development of relationships between the characters. Or it may be that this same environment comes to seem utilitarian, something to be accepted as a matter of course. The characters make use of their familiar surroundings in the same way as characters in a novel by Alan Sillitoe would make use of the surroundings of a Midlands factory or a back street in Nottingham.

A good example of this prosaic response to poetic surroundings occurs not much more than five pages from the beginning of the novel. Raunce, the head footman, has persuaded Mrs Tennant to accept him as butler in place of the late Mr Eldon. Although he will collect no extra wages, his rôle as butler enhances his status among both servants and masters. He has already experienced something of the change by having Mrs Tennant address him by his real name instead of 'Arthur', as she has called all her previous head footmen. Raunce's new prospects and his fresh sense of self-importance issue in an uncharacteristic display of high spirits as he approaches the green baize door:

he stopped. In one of the malachite vases, filled with daffodils, which stood on tall pedestals of gold naked male children without wings, he had seen a withered trumpet. He cut the head off with a pair of nail clippers. He carried this head away in cupped hand from above thick pile carpet in black and white squares through onto linoleum which was bordered with a purple key pattern on white until, when he had shut that green door to open his kingdom, he punted the daffodil head ahead like a rugger ball. It fell limp on the oiled parquet a yard beyond his pointed shoes.

Raunce removes one kind of poetry from the malachite vase and substitutes for it another, more comic and humanly acceptable

one – as he punts the daffodil over the parquet with his pointed
shoes.

This impractical, self-expressive behaviour is just one of the
things that brings into being a poetic environment which has little
to do with fantasy, much to do with the way human beings
actually do respond to each other. Even in the first fifty pages we
are constantly coming across short phrases, sentences, or paragraphs which brighten the physical image at the same time as they
deepened our emotional response to whatever the image is
expressive of. When Raunce sees Edith in the pantry, some time
before he has consciously fallen in love with her, he appraises 'the
dark eyes she sported which were warm and yet caught the light
like plums dipped in cold water'. After his talk with her there, she
retreats down the corridor: 'The tap of her shoes faded. He walked
on. He appeared to be thinking. He went so soft he might have
been a ghost without a head.' Mrs Burch, the head housemaid, is
having one of her bad days. Her face looked 'pale and blotchy as a
shrimp before boiling'. Mrs Welch, the cook, examines her
waterglass' with arms upraised in the gesture of a woman hanging
out smalls'. Accurate physical detail, yes. But also there is an
undercurrent of feeling passing beneath the still surface of the
prose in which these apparently simple observations are made.
Raunce doesn't know he is falling in love with Edith, but we sense
it. Also we sense his disturbance at finding her there. (He is
disturbed about other things as well. Much of the interest of
Green's prose here lies in the way it allows us to wonder about
what kind of disturbance is uppermost in the mind of whichever of
the characters is present at any given time.) Miss Burch is likely to
have one of her bad days every day from now on, because Eldon,
the butler who has just died, was her lover and she is having
difficulty reconciling herself to the fact of his death. Mrs Welch is
poised between guilt and suspicion, because she knows that her
nephew Albert has wrung one of the peacocks' necks (the carcase
is hidden by a cheese cloth on the pantry shelf, next door to the
waterglass) and she suspects that Kate or Edith or one of the
maids has been stealing peacocks' eggs from the waterglass to use
as a love potion. All these brilliantly but unfussily observed details
carry in their train a wealth of psychological possibilities,
emotional predilections, and nervous uncertainties.

None of these feelings manages to produce a strong narrative
line which rises to a climactic point at a particular stage in the

development of the plot and then moves on to a carefully positioned dénouement, resolution, or settled determination. As James Hall put it in his useful essay on Green in the *Kenyon Review*,* 'He [Green] sees experience as an hour-to-hour, day-to-day shift in the ratio of pleasure and pain.' He might have gone on to say that, though pleasure and pain are important constituents in the experience of Green's characters, ratios of other distinctive human feelings and aspirations also shift over short periods and consequently, usually, with little perceptible influence on the general unfolding of the action. The stress, anxiety, sexual urgency and irresponsibility, among other things, that eventually lead Raunce and Edith to elope from the castle, do not crystallise in any one act of overwhelming significance. Raunce manages to convince the older women in the household of his new authority as butler. But he also makes a number of decisions (such as insisting Edith bring him his breakfast in bed, as she did for Eldon when he was alive) which rebound on him when circumstances alter and his feelings change. Edith finds Mrs Jack in bed with Captain Davenport, and this brings about some sort of bond between herself and Raunce. So does the discovery of a live mouse trapped in the machinery of an ornamental weathervane. When Raunce discovers Kate and Edith dancing together in the ball-room, and when he interrupts a game of blind man's buff (in which Edith has been wearing one of Mrs Jack's silk scarves over her eyes with 'I love you' written over it), his interest in the girls subtly changes. Circumstances have been created in which he will betray his sexual awareness of Edith more and more. Developments in the relationship between Raunce and Edith affect the behaviour of the other servants. Kate is forced into the arms of Paddy O'Conor, the unprepossessing lampman. Raunce's Albert is made desperate in his frustrated calf love for Edith. The changes of feelings among the younger characters produce several minor complications which turn out to be very difficult to resolve. For example, there is the matter of the stolen peacocks' eggs (Edith and Kate had taken them and now Raunce must protect the girls, especially Edith, from Mrs Welch's discovery). Or the missing peacock (killed by Mrs Welch's Albert and hidden by Mrs Welch in a variety of places, all discovered by Raunce as useful counter-ammunition in the event of Mrs Welch making difficulties over

* James Hall, 'The Fiction of Henry Green: Paradoxes of Pleasure-and-Pain', *Kenyon Review*, 19 (Winter 1957) 76–88.

the eggs). Above all, there is the sapphire cluster ring Mrs Tennant has lost and which keeps turning up and disappearing again as one or other of the servants or the children finds it and appropriates it to his or her own use.

All of these trivial and irritating little things have their effect, but none of them, not even Edith's discovery of Mrs Jack and Captain Davenport, or Raunce's Albert's confession to the insurance agent that he stole Mrs Tennant's ring (he didn't; he is protecting Edith – who also didn't steal it – which creates further complications), brings to a head all the most important aspects of the plot. In Green, plots don't work like that. Instead they insinuate possibilities. The little details of the plot are nudged back and forth, first affecting one group of characters, then another – but never doing anything *effectively* dramatic. Nothing, that is, until the combination of all of them drives Raunce and Edith into elopement. Afterwards Kinalty must have been burnt to the ground. But this has nothing at all to do with any of the characters, who may or may not have been inside it at the time. Since the novel ends before that happens, we have no way of knowing whether the characters we have been living among will be affected by it. In any case the self-contained quality of *Loving*, in spite of its tragic prolepses, makes this kind of speculation inappropriate, strangely irrelevant to the novel we have read.

Hall was right to say that Green is 'superb at showing dogged devotion to "small" personal concerns in a world of "large" events which seem to be passing the principals by and engaging their interest only as by-products of their personal problems'. But these 'small' concerns are rendered luminously important by the subtle artifices of Green's prose. The surface of *Loving* is dominated by an accumulation of worry and sexual frustration. (Incidentally, a good example of this and an excellent demonstration of Green's skill with the dialogue in this book is the scene of the picnic where Raunce's Albert is teased by Kate and Edith – an effective preparation for Albert's confession to the insurance agent, and, eventually, his escape to England to join the war effort.) But there are depths too, and these have a habit of pushing against the surface, showing how thin and precarious it is. By this I mean that the highly wrought passages of description that interrupt the dialogue from time to time emerge very unspectacularly, unpretentiously, from the rest of the prose. We find we have been drawn into experiences that ought to lie very much at a tangent to the main story, but which have strangely combined to get themselves deflected towards the centre.

The most celebrated example of this sort of thing is the scene in which Edith and Kate are discovered by Raunce in the ball-room. In fact it is a very brief passage – disappointingly so when one tries to pull it out of its context. There is only one paragraph describing the girls dancing, as follows:

> They were wheeling wheeling in each other's arms heedless at the far end where they had drawn up one of the white blinds. Above from a rather low ceiling five great chandeliers swept one after the other almost to the waxed parquet floor reflecting in their hundred thousand drops the single sparkle of distant day, again and again red velvet panelled walls, and two girls, minute in purple, dancing multiplied to eternity in these trembling pears of glass.

That in its way is beautiful, but to be fully appreciated it needs to be read in the context of *both* girls' feeling for Raunce; its setting in the doomed castle, the greater part of which (including this) remains closed; and Raunce's half practical, half mesmerised search for them through the castle, following the music, dipping his fingers into a potpourri whose rose petals have dried up long ago, so that when he sniffs at his fingers he recognises that he had 'dabbled in the dry bones of roses'. It is the close contact of light and vitality, and death and dust, with Raunce poised between them in quest of Edith, which gives this scene its extraordinary power, its appeal to a mysterious poetry of the emotions. In a similar way, the success of the beautiful image of Paddy O'Conor asleep in the saddle-room, with golden cobwebs strung from his hair to the sill above, depends on his having been discovered there by Kate and Edith – at a time when Kate has caught her first intimations of Raunce's attraction to Edith, but, before she has shown anything but a kindly, comic interest in Paddy as a man.

Like the images of *Caught*, these images of Kate and Edith in the ball-room; of Edith playing blind man's buff with Albert, Kate and children; of Nanny Swift at the dovecote; and Paddy the lampman in the saddle-room, intensify our response to feelings that usually lie beneath the surface of the characters' conscious minds. Since they are usually witnessed by one or more of the other characters, they have a similar effect on their minds too. The image of Paddy lightly enchained in gold awakens Kate to possibilities she had not looked for in his direction. Raunce's journey to the ball-room shows him, as well as us, how the faded beauties of the house contrast with the activity and liveliness of the girls who inhabit it. Other, less evocative and more humdrum events, push Kate and Edith further in the direction these 'scenes' have pointed. However, the way the scenes themselves impress, disturb and mobilise the inner consciousness of the characters who participate in them remains mysterious and irrational. We feel the effect of it, on their conduct, but they never explain to themselves or to each other how the effect has been produced or how their sense of themselves has changed. In *Caught*, Pye tries to come to terms with situations which are 'held' in memory images from the past. On the other hand, Roe's memory images (of the toy-shop and the abbey, also of the frozen winter in his country home and, later, of the fires he fought against in the Blitz) never do present themselves as soluble, enforcing a single special meaning. In this respect Green's manipulation of imagery has changed considerably since *Living*. There the 'meaning' of the birds, the homing pigeons, grew clearer and clearer to the characters and ourselves as the narrative concentrated more and more heavily on the activities of Lily Gates and her guardian Mr Craigan. And as the themes of the novel become more and more emphatically those of escape and return, freedom and security.

Caught and *Loving* are Green's finest achievements. They were written by him when his attention to patterning-devices which are fundamentally poetic did not exclude a profound interest in character, motive and plot. Albert Pye, Richard Roe, Edith, and Charley Raunce, are all vividly conceived characters whose personalities and feelings could have dominated the plots in which we found them. They have not been allowed to do so because Green's prose has shaped their destinies into a form which is aesthetically desirable as well as psychologically convincing. The deflection of the grammatical form of the sentences from the expected pattern is less noticeable here, especially in *Loving*, than it was in *Living* or even *Party Going*. But the prose has not yet been released into the descriptive luxuriance of *Concluding* or the bathetic dialogue of *Nothing* and *Doting*.

In a brief newspaper article on Green, Frank Kermode has written that 'he valued in fiction the tangential and the inconsequent. . . . He would use his story as a ground against which all manner of unexpected and gorgeous figurations stand out, figurations lacking any of the relevance we have been taught to expect by novels which . . . "hug the shores of the real?".'* I have tried to show that these figurations, whilst appearing arbitrary and actually being unexpected, contribute to the depth of our understanding of the states of mind represented in the novels. At the same time they disengage those novels from too close a contact with the world at large. They are worlds of their own, conscious and deliberate artefacts existing half-way between the author's and the reader's creative and receptive imaginations. We are aware of the configurations of the author's imagination, patterning events and formalising situations. At the same time we cannot help noticing that the patterns these events and situations are sucked into are remarkably like the ones we too use to make sense of the world. Green's artifice is always evident in his writing, but in his middle novels – in *Caught*, in *Loving* especially – it corresponds in a remarkably faithful way to what goes on in the world that we rarely consider to be artificial or moulded into special forms and patterns. An idiosyncratic style has become so transparent that, whilst we are reading, it seems like no style. This transparency is difficult to achieve. Often, as in Green, it is the result of the most extreme experiments in the application of artifice.

* For a more extensive discussion by Kermode of Henry Green's fiction, especially *Party Going*, see ch. 1 of his *The Genesis of Secrecy* (Cambridge, Mass., 1979) pp. 5–14.

4 Anthony Powell

It is by a happy combination of accident and design that the narrator of Anthony Powell's *A Dance to the Music of Time* and his favourite painter bear the same Christian name. For Nicholas Jenkins and Nicolas Poussin share a preference for large canvases, intricate designs, and a classical coolness of expression. Also, in the work of both writer and painter mythological themes are present – for Poussin, in a direct representation of classical and Christian myth; for Jenkins, in Greek and Roman mythological parallels to the contemporary scene, usually made explicit, sometimes suggested by prolonged description of a painting of a subject taken from Ovid or the Greek mythographers. On the surface, the intentions of the two artists could hardly be more different. Poussin's motives were didactic and antiquarian, Jenkins's mock heroic. Yet the rich luxuriance of Powell's descriptions – of Poussin's 'Dance' itself for example, or of Tiepolo's (fictional) 'Candaules and Gyges' (in *Temporary Kings*, 4), seems to belie a merely mock heroic intention.

The twelve volumes of *A Dance to the Music of Time* open and close with a reference to the painting by Poussin from which the sequence takes its name. In Poussin's scene, Jenkins says, 'the Seasons, hand in hand and facing outward, tread in rhythm to the notes of the lyre that the winged and naked greybeard plays'. That is what has been happening too in the novel Powell has written. The wintry spectacle of the opening paragraphs is completed only at the close of the whole *Dance*. It is the same season and the same scene, one of workmen gathered round a fire bucket: at the beginning of the novel, descending into a trench they have dug, or retiring into their tarpaulin shelter; at the close, turning back to the fire bucket, or preparing to knock off work. Scarcely a minute has passed, perhaps not a second. Yet a vast span of time has been traversed in memory, from Nicholas's schooldays at Eton in the winter of 1921, to the moment, in Barnabas Henderson's picture gallery in the autumn of 1971, when Nicholas hears the news of

Kenneth Widmerpool's death. Only at the close is that scene around the fire bucket located in space and time: 'The men taking up the road *in front of the gallery* were preparing to knock off work. Some of them were gathering round their fire-bucket' (emphasis added). The slightly later time during which the scene is recalled, and with it all the earlier 'scenes' it brought to mind, follows in the description of Jenkins himself lighting a fire, in the grounds of his country house – an event with which *Hearing Secret Harmonies* itself had opened. There follows a passage from Burton's *Anatomy of Melancholy*, summarising the themes of the *Dance*. Then a last reference to Poussin's canvas: 'Even the formal measure of the Seasons seemed suspended in the wintry silence.'

Forty years have passed. Yet the events of those years, recollected as they occurred and as they were interpreted at successive stages in Nicholas's career, are framed in the present consciousness of the narrator, held at either end by the 'scene' at Jenkins's bonfire, and converted into the stasis of a Poussin canvas, the edges of which occupy the opening and closing pages of the sequence. Life, finally, has been frozen into art. Into a painting, in fact. A painting composed of many paintings; for the device which dictates the form of the *Dance* as a whole also dictates the form of each of its separate movements – its 'parts', 'volumes', and collections of volumes into units of three. At every stage in the *Dance* the reader is referred back to a presiding consciousness which sees the whole pattern, or whatever of pattern there is. But the details of the pattern are painted in for the reader roughly in chronological sequence, as one figure in the dance takes hands with another. It is as if the movement of the eye around the circle of dancers, occurring in space, were to correspond with the move-ment of the speculative, questioning, even nosy intelligence along the life-span of the characters, occurring in time. Frequently, though, Jenkins's retrospective consciousness suggests the linking of other hands, steps taken by other feet, the directing of our attention to other parts of the canvas. This corresponds with the release of information, for purposes of comparison or anecdote, having to do with later, or earlier, events of which we have not yet heard, or which we had heard and, perhaps, forgotten some time ago. The superimposition of painterly (spatial) techniques over literary (temporal) ones, is a notable characteristic of Powell's art. It is a feature of *A Dance to the Music of Time* he is very much aware of, as Jenkins tells us elsewhere in the sequence – again with reference to Poussin's canvas.

Near the beginning of *Hearing Secret Harmonies* Jenkins confesses how much he admires Sir John Harington's translation of Ariosto, and describes a passage in the *Orlando Furioso* in which the English knight, Astolpho, visits the moon and watches Time at work. This is also one of Powell's own favourite texts: he entitles one of the chapters of his memoirs 'Astolpho's Horn', and prefixed to his first novel, *Afternoon Men*, a passage from the Astolpho sequence in Harington, as glossed by Burton in the *Anatomy*. The quotation from Burton is interesting when placed alongside Jenkins's commentary on Harington/Ariosto, especially since, as I have already mentioned, another passage from Burton, providing a similar description of chaos, almost closes the last volume of the *Dance*.

The preface to *Afternoon Men* reads as follows: 'as if they had heard that enchanted horn of Astolpho, that English duke in Ariosto, which never sounded but all his auditors were mad, and for fear ready to make away with themselves . . . they are a company of giddy-heads, afternoon men'. In *Hearing Secret Harmonies* Time, as viewed by Astolpho, is a 'naked ancient . . . in an eternally breathless scramble with himself'. He is collecting small metal tablets (representing the reputations and fortunes of men) from the Fates, and 'dumping' them in the waters of Oblivion. This, says Jenkins, is the writer's Time, less relaxed than the painter's, in fact 'appallingly restless'. It has to be, because it attends to human life as a shapeless blur of occurrence, not the formal pattern of a graceful arrest. Poussin's Time is, by contrast, undisturbed and undisturbing. As he plucks his lyre to provide music for the dance, he is shown 'in a sufficiently unhurried frame of mind to be sitting down while he strums his instrument. The smile might be thought a trifle sinister, nevertheless the mood is genial, composed.'

In fact the mood and, one surmises, the smile are not unlike Anthony Powell's, as he creates his own version of 'A Dance to the Music of Time'. For a writer, life is for the most part disorganised and shapeless. The representation of life in fiction must take account of this fact, and the novelist must spend much of his time in the rôle of Ariosto's greybeard, keeping his characters on the move, and finally shoving them into the waters of Oblivion. On the other hand the painterly alternative is seductive. At times, after all, we do sense the existence of some sort of pattern; brief, fleeting glimpses of design which tantalise before they disappoint, and fade. Hence Powell's shifting occupation of the ground between the greybeard and the lyrist, his habit of trying to superimpose the one on the other and, with a triumph of *trompe l'oeil*, make their gestures appear the same. As he suggests in his earliest description of Poussin's 'Dance', when the fall of snow on the workmen's fire calls to mind those classical shapes, 'infinitely removed from life' ('Infinitely remote' at the end of *Hearing Secret Harmonies*),

> The image of Time brought thoughts of mortality: of human beings, facing outward like the Seasons, moving hand in hand in intricate measure: stepping slowly, methodically, sometimes a trifle awkwardly, in evolutions that take recognisable shape: or breaking into seemingly meaningless gyrations, while partners disappear only to reappear again, once more giving pattern to the spectacle: unable, perhaps, to control the steps of the dance.

Here the dance is measured, shapely, patterned, melodic; at the same time as it is awkward, meaningless, uncontrolled. Or it *might* be these things, 'seemingly', 'perhaps', 'a trifle' this or that.

Conversely the pedestrian image of the workmen outside the gallery seems to want to transform itself into a significant myth, a ritual with classical, and painterly, reverberations. The men are at work not in a 'hole' but in an 'abyss' in the road. The drain pipes are not 'underground' but 'subterranean'. Later, with Dantesque gravity, the men are discovered to be 'lowering themselves laboriously into the pit, or withdrawing to the shadows' of their tarpaulin shelter. Little wonder Jenkins describes their throwing kipper skins and bones into the fire, as if in the performance of a rite, the subsequent movements of the workmen being 'required observances'. It is all in simile, of course, an admittedly strained comparison, an irresponsible fancy. On the other hand, the kippers were only 'apparently' kippers. 'Some substance' was thrown onto the fire, but Jenkins will not commit himself to kippers any more than he will commit himself to Infernal rites. We know that behind it all there is merely a group of workmen packing in work for the day, in spite of the (mock?) heroic tendencies of the prose. The tone makes it clear that Jenkins is more apologetic about the 'rite' than he is about the kippers. Yet it will not do to describe this prose as merely mock heroic. At this early stage Jenkins does seem to be suggesting that in an ordinary event such as the one he is describing here, and which he will describe again at the end of the *Dance*, there may be present, however faint, the outline of a pattern, or at least of a part of a pattern.

There are many indications in all the subsequent volumes that random lives may be connected in ways that hint at a point, a purpose, some underlying design. Sceptical though he may be of any theory that approximates human life to the life of a painting, Jenkins does from time to time entertain the notion that there might be a pattern deeply hidden in the texture of living, which surfaces in the minds of individuals on infrequent occasions during the course of their separate journeys to oblivion. It is a notion he shares with his creator, who, in the second volume of his memoirs (*Messengers of Day*), reflecting on his life in London during the war years, tells an anecdote about Rosa Lewis, the eccentric proprietor of the Cavendish Hotel. Powell had known Rosa Lewis in the twenties. But when he visited her twenty or more years later she failed to recognise him, introducing him to her guests as Bimbash Stewart (someone Powell had never heard of, but whom later he discovered was a captain in the British Army who had served with the Egyptian forces some time in the late nineteenth century). Powell speculates about Rosa Lewis's mistake, one of those arbitrary failures of recognition which often occurred in her memories of the past: 'Nevertheless, it was pleasant to feel that one had found some sort of niche, even if an incongruously shared one, in Rosa Lewis's vast tapestry of memory; rather like becoming an element in that larger con-sciousness, which some think awaits us when individual existence fades.' The careful placing at arm's length ('which some think') of any such belief in the 'larger consciousness' has something in common with Jenkins's qualified dismissal of the same sort of thing; his willingness to entertain, but not subscribe to, metaphys-ical or even mystical notions of the kind referred to here.

The character in *A Dance to the Music of Time* who most closely resembles Rosa Lewis as an avatar of mysterious knowledge is probably Myrah Erdleigh. Mrs Erdleigh, it will be remembered, is a longstanding and not quite respectable acquaintance of

Nicholas's Uncle Giles. Nicholas first meets her in his uncle's room at the Ufford, not far from the beginning of *The Acceptance World*. Appearing both mysterious and ridiculous on this occasion, she impresses Nick with her 'huge liquid eyes', which seem to penetrate deep into his soul 'and far, far beyond towards nameless, unexplored vistas of the infinite'. Mention of the 'infinite' in Powell usually brings with it both grand philosophical meanings, and a tincture of affectation and exaggeration imported from its adverbial, social usage (as in the opening passage from *A Question of Upbringing* already referred to: 'infinitely removed from life'; or a character in a novel who is referred to as 'infinitely tedious' or 'infinitely amusing').

This indecision whether to be serious or facetious is typical of the way Mrs Erdleigh is presented. Our general impression of her is almost certainly one of suspicion and distaste, and her association with Giles is not the only thing that accounts for this. All the same, it is surprising how often her prognostications about the future prove to be correct. Jenkins invariably pooh-poohs her claim to paranormal psychic powers. Typical observations of his are that 'Such trivial comments, mixed with a few home truths of a personal nature, provide, I had already learnt, the commonplace of fortune telling.' Or 'Mrs Erdleigh was probably speaking no more than the truth, voicing an analysis that did not require much occult skill to arrive at.' But in fact the predictions in response to which Jenkins makes each of these observations are surprisingly accurate.

In the first (*The Acceptance World*, 1) Mrs Erdleigh has foreseen Nicholas's affair with a girl who, I think, we are intended to identify with Jean Templer: Jenkins will describe how he became involved again with Jean in the next chapter of this same novel. She also foresees that he will have difficulties with an elderly man and two young men connected with him in some way. Nicholas feels sure that she has got it wrong, and that she should have said one young man (Mark Members) and two elderly men – i.e. St John Clarke, the novelist, and Horace Isbister, the painter. Nicholas is supervising publication of a book entitled *The Art of Horace Isbister* with an introduction by St John Clarke. And Members is St John Clarke's secretary. However, Nicholas is thinking of the present situation. In the future, also described in the next chapter, Members's rival J. G. Quiggin will supplant him as Clarke's secretary, and Nicholas will suffer an inconvenience in his business life, which *will* involve one old man and two young ones. So Mrs Erdleigh has got it right; and Powell has Jenkins point up this fact by making him stress his doubts about the prediction, doubts which we are to see in the next chapter are entirely without foundation. Mrs Erdleigh is equally correct in her predictions about the outcome of Pamela Flitton's relationship with Odo Stevens (*The Military Philosophers*, 3), which produce the occasion for the second of Jenkins's dismissive comments about her. In this case Mrs Erdleigh prophesies that Pamela and Odo will soon break off their relationship; that Pamela will marry a man in an important position, a little older than herself, and who will prove to be a jealous husband; and that Odo will soon be going overseas, there will be danger, but he will survive. Sure enough Pamela leaves Stevens soon after this prediction has been made; she marries Widmerpool, who is the sort of person Mrs Erdleigh has described; and Stevens survives an operation with Communist partisans in the Balkans – incidentally the same operation in which Peter Templer is killed. All these events are narrated in the next chapter but one to the one in which Mrs Erdleigh makes her predictions. To be fair, Powell inserts, by implication, minor qualifications to the complete accuracy of her powers of prophecy in all of these cases. On the occasion at the Ufford she tells Nicholas that she and he will meet again in about a year's time. In fact the next time they meet is at the Templers' house about fifteen months later. Is fifteen months 'about a year from now'? On the occasion of the flying-bomb raid, her prediction about Stevens is completely accurate, but her assessment of Pamela's future husband's age as 'a little older than yourself' must be an underestimate: Widmerpool is at least a year older than Nicholas, who is almost the same age as Charles Stringham. At Stringham's wedding Pamela was a bridesmaid of six or seven. So Widmerpool must be about fifteen years older than Pamela. But, even allowing for this, Mrs Erdleigh's foreknowledge of the future is uncannily correct on most counts; far more so than Jenkins's dismissive attitude to her would have led us to believe.

Mrs Erdleigh is not alone in her prophetic powers, her access to the 'larger consciousness' to which Powell animadverts in his comments on Rosa Lewis. Other characters, often of a dubious, unrespectable kind, also seem to possess powers of divination which make human lives look a great deal more patterned and purposeful than common sense suggests they are. Dr Trelawney, for example, the reprobate *mage* of Aldershot, and later of Albert Creech's boarding-house on the south coast, makes accurate, if fancifully expressed, predictions about the outbreak of world war: 'The sword of Mithras, who each year immolates the sacred bull, will ere long now flash from its scabbard' (spoken some time during the summer of 1939). This prophecy follows Trelawney's release from the lavatory at the Bellevue. He has locked himself in and shortly afterwards suffered an attack of asthma. Strangely, he manages to force his way out after Nicholas has responded correctly to his ritual asseveration that 'The Essence of the All is the Godhead of the True' with the words, recalled from his childhood days at Aldershot, 'The Vision of Visions heals the Blindness of Sight' – another queer little piece of evidence in support of the view that parapsychic powers do exist, and can affect the relationships people enter into with one another. In the same chapter of *The Kindly Ones* (3), Uncle Giles's horoscope, found among his belongings after his death at the Bellevue, is not at all wide of the mark. 'It had to be admitted', says Jenkins, 'that all gave a pretty good, if rough-and-ready, account of my uncle and his habits.' Even so, he adds, Giles's financial affairs were a great deal more arcane than anything to be found in his horoscope, 'far more mysterious than anything revealed about him astrologically'.

Because of the way astrological and necromantic practices bulk large in the later volumes of *A Dance to the Music of Time*, especially in the last one, it is helpful, I think, to have available these facts about the way Powell uses magic and divination in the earlier books – at once incredulously and with great deliberation. Through Jenkins's disbelief in most of the evidence, and through the suspect nature of the characters who lay claim to supernatural powers, Powell gives us the impression that he does not take these matters at all seriously. But he goes out of his way to show how well, by and large, the predictions fit the facts – as they later became established. Powell seems to want to shuffle off anything but an amused interest in the occult. At the same time he seems to want to use the occult to suggest things, perhaps metaphorically, about the way human lives are connected and how life in general occasionally reveals secret harmonies. Something must explain the network of coincidence, 'chance' meetings and oddly connected events that comprise so much of Nicholas's experience and

Powell's fiction. Most of the time it appears to be nothing more than an unlooked-for consequence of the social ambience within which Nicholas and his acquaintances live their lives. But sometimes Powell tentatively makes other suggestions, which the tone of his narrative then goes on to imply are ridiculous. Yet we might infer that the harmonies Powell seeks to impose on life, by overlaying his writer's scepticism with a painter's conviction (about pattern, in a different relationship between art and life), he would like instead to find *in* life – in no more than sufficient quantity to justify the patterns created by his retrospective narrative. *Hearing Secret Harmonies* is what such novelists as Jenkins and Powell are expected to do, in some deeply responsible way. It is not supposed to be merely a pseudo-activity performed by such people as Scorpio Murtlock to instil fear and exercise power over other people.

Harmonies in the first phase of this last *Dance to the Music of Time* are so secret as to be almost inaudible. In the grounds of the Jenkins's country house, Nicholas's niece, Fiona Cutts, is observed with three other members of a commune angling for crayfish in a brook that flows through their camp site. Fiona's presence went unremarked in earlier volumes, though her parents, Roddy and Susan Cutts, had contributed to some of the best scenes of *Books Do Furnish a Room* and *Temporary Kings*. Rusty, a surnameless girl 'with the look of a young prostitute', remains stolidly featureless, one of those blank characters who convincingly reproduce the forgettability of so much of what falls within the outer reaches of our social acquaintance. The two men, Scorpio Murtlock and Barnabas Henderson, are also new characters, carrying with them no echoes from the past.

Yet the past presses on the present with a notable persistence. The scene is mediated through Jenkins's unobtrusive but tirelessly retrospective consciousness. The quarry in the distance reminds him of Edgar Deacon's painting 'The Boyhood of Cyrus', a ubiquitous presence in the early and middle volumes. Echoes of blasting combined with a flight of duck over the landscape call to mind an argument between General Brobowski and General Philidor back in *The Military Philosophers* (not actually reproduced there). Fiona's presence on the estate is explained through further retrospect, involving her aunts Blanche and Norah Tolland, and

touching the later careers of their brother Hugo and their friend
Eleanor Walpole-Wilson.

This retrospective propinquity, even where the figures *en scène*
are new, does not surprise. In *A Buyer's Market*, almost at the
beginning of the sequence, Jenkins had expressed the belief

> that existence fans out indefinitely into new areas of experience,
> and that almost every additional acquaintance offers some
> supplementary world with its own hazards and enchantments.
> As time goes on, of course, these supposedly different worlds, in
> fact, draw closer, if not to each other, then to some pattern
> common to all.

We have seen that the word 'enchantment' carries more force
than might have been assumed if it had been taken out of context.
We have seen also that, though Powell makes a great deal of
'enchantments', with their occult and magical association, he
attends to them more as metaphors (and opportunities for comic
entertainment) than as matters calling for serious consideration.
At any rate that is what he seems to be doing for most of the time. I
want to go on to discuss what they are metaphors of, and to
emphasise as I do so what a large, perhaps too large, gap exists
between the metaphor and whatever it is that it imports.

From the middle of the *Dance* onwards, the supplementary
worlds Jenkins refers to in the passage quoted above have
proliferated in an increasing abundance. After the worlds of
school and university traversed in the first volume (*A Question of
Upbringing*), Jenkins's set remains fairly homogeneous and inter-
connected at numerous points (from *A Buyer's Market* to *Casanova's
Chinese Restaurant*). The progress from the Walpole-Wilson establishment at Eaton Square to the raffish Bohemian quarters of
painters and musicians such as Ralph Barnby and Hugh
Moreland (punctuated by weekends in the country, at Sir
Magnus Donners' Stourwater or Erridge's Thrubworth, for
example) is a progress that establishes marked, if sometimes
tenuous, relationships within a clearly defined social milieu. It is
not easy to put a name to this milieu. Phrases such as 'upper-
middle-class' are not precise enough. In some ways the juxtaposi-
tion of a time and a place, or places, comes nearer to providing a
satisfactory definition. Critics have referred to a world at which
Mayfair and Soho meet, at some time during the twenties and

thirties. Perhaps this milieu is defined more accurately by aspects of its life style: comings-out, debutante balls, dinners presided over by titled hostesses; but also such pubs as the Mortimer, and the film studios (never visited by the reader) at which Nicholas and Chips Lovell work as script-writers; also interests its members share in respect of certain writers, painters, political causes; and buildings they entertain in, sometimes live in, which are considered half-way between examples of architectural styles and insecurely maintained family possessions.

Above all it is characterised by the language its members use: inflections of tone; choice of slang; ways of responding to questions without answering them, because they are recognised as not being questions but polite forms of self-assertion, or protection. Jenkins is referring to it early in the pages of *At Lady Molly's* when he reflects on Chips Lovell's comment that 'Realism goes with good birth.' The statement, he says, might be hard to substantiate universally,

> but, by recognising laws of behaviour operating within the microcosm of a large consanguineous network of families, however loosely connected, individuals born into such a world often gain an unsentimental grasp of human conduct: a grasp something superior to that of apparently more perceptive persons whose minds are unattuned by early association to the constant give and take of an ancient and tenacious social organism.

Nicholas appears to have been born into just such a world. His ability to move at ease in it over the span of those first six volumes contrasts with the awkwardness of some others among the characters – notably Widmerpool. Most of the *élan* of the narrative depends on Jenkins's movements within a social world to which he is so acclimatised as to be invisible. His lack of visibility, and his assimilation to the habits of mind, manner of expressing himself, and indeed the biographical history of his creator, are fundamental properties of Powell's narrative technique.

If it were not obvious before, then it has become unmistakable with the publication of the first three volumes of Powell's memoirs, *To Keep the Ball Rolling*, that in nearly all important respects Nicholas Jenkins's career mirrors Anthony Powell's very closely indeed. An Army background, including residence in a bungalow near Aldershot that Powell calls 'Stonehurst' in *Infants of the Spring* as well as in *The Kindly Ones*; Eton and Oxford (neither of them named in the novels, but clearly identifiable through descriptions vouchsafed by Jenkins); lodgings in Shepherd Market, work at a publisher's offices, work at a film studio; dances, dinners, novels, marriage, war service, a book on Robert Burton (instead of John Aubrey), more novels, retirement to the country. The two lives parallel each other year by year, book by book. But, as every reader soon discovers, Jenkins does not provide us with any information about his personal life which is remotely interesting. Mention of events that concern Nicholas directly are immediately followed by a description of a similar situation experienced by some other person, usually in the form of an anecdote; or by generalised introspection, where 'my' love or envy or ambition is converted in a trice to the nature of love or envy or ambition in its general aspect; then as it tends to affect such and such a class of people or member of such and such a profession; then as it is written about in such and such a (real or imagined) writer's memoirs, poems, novels; and then as such and such a person confessed to Nicholas about it, or his mistress had a friend who experienced such and such a sensation which another woman she had known had also experienced – but at a different time and in different circumstances. Soon, the remotest memory of what happened to Nicholas has faded, giving way to a mere frame of mind, a habit of reminiscence, comparison, incomplete speculation and uncompletable definition. Jenkins has become a tone of voice occupying a certain space at a certain time; an absence of personality strangely coexisting with the presence of a physical position, an ear for confidences, a memory for scandal and gossip, and a tendency to refer, to compare, to fancy and to hypothesise.

This aspect of Jenkins's character is so pronounced that it is something of a shock to find him actually at the centre of his own story, even where what he is recalling is an event of little consequence. Such events occur most frequently in the earlier volumes, when Jenkins is describing himself as he was before he matured into the curious but imperturbably reflective individual he has become by the time he marries Isobel Tolland, in *At Lady Molly's*. There are a number of them in *A Question of Upbringing*. Some, such as Nicholas's first experience of sexual attraction, when he dances with Gwen Macreath at the Templers', mark important stages in the development of his personality. Others carry less emotional freight: their content is rather like that of the anecdotes Jenkins scatters so liberally in his conversations about other people. A good example of such an occurrence is Nicholas's approach to Mme Dubuisson, having mistaken her for Suzette in the summer house at La Grenadière. The event is unimportant, but the fact that Nicholas is made to look ridiculous, that he is caught in an ungeneralisable experience, makes him startlingly real. The transparency of his emotional existence is for the moment rendered opaque. A temperament has become uncomfortable, and therefore been made part of a personal experience. This will not happen often. If it did, we should have an introspective comic novel very different from the comic novel we actually have. The success of *A Dance to the Music of Time* depends on the imperturbability of its narrator. Jenkins's experience is hidden away behind the farthest recesses of the novel. It exists only to support the play of his temperament over the lives of others.

A distinctive tone of voice, a capacity to appreciate the oddities and absurdities of life, have to belong to a *person*; a person who has done, felt and thought about something. But the doing and the feeling might be taken for granted, mentioned only in passing, where the subject of that person's narrative is not himself but what he sees, hears and speculates about other people. The most pronounced features of Nicholas's character that we are likely to take away from the book are, I think, his frustrated ambition to acquire a reputation as a writer; and his unsuccessful but prolonged love affair with Jean Duport. Jenkins often refers to these things. At one stage Powell tries to get him to look more closely at his affair with Jean. But Jenkins's introspection soon carries him away from his actual feelings about her, into previously occupied territory of generalised analysis and tentative classification.

Jenkins as a narrator, then, occupies a position at some considerable distance from his experience as a character. But this does not matter very much, because Powell is using him to reflect on life in general terms, where what has happened to him is taken on trust and used as a basis for his perceptions into the behaviour of others. What might matter rather more, though, is that Jenkins's distance from experience does not end with himself. When he is describing what has happened to other people he maintains his habit of indirect representation, filtering their behaviour through the opinions, anecdotes and conversation of friends and acquaintances. Sometimes, even, he relies on hypothetical suppositions about how some other character – for instance, Uncle Giles – might have responded to something that has happened if he had been present at the time. Or he describes crucially significant events by means of gossip, which may be quite unreliable. Some strands in it are almost certainly mere fiction; others of doubtful authenticity; others probably true, but conflicting with alternative versions of the same event which also have the ring of probability.

A good example of this sort of thing is the description of Pamela Widmerpool's nude appearance in Bagshaw's father's house (*Temporary Kings*, 4). Bagshaw claims that Pamela appeared, undressed, on the landing of the first floor of the building, during a period when Russell Gwinnett, whom she had been pursuing for some time, was a lodger there. But *was* it on the first-floor landing she appeared? Or wasn't it perhaps in the hall? How many people actually saw her? Bagshaw himself, in spite of the fact that he is telling the story (or rather Jenkins is recollecting Bagshaw's telling the story), was not present on the occasion. His father, in Bagshaw's words, was 'the man on the spot' and therefore 'the only human being who really knew the facts'; but, as Bagshaw agrees, he himself knew only some of them. 'To express how things fell out', then, 'is to lean heavily on hearsay.' And that is what Jenkins does, filling out Bagshaw's account with doubts, uncertainties, alternative explanations and circumstantial details in support or denial of the other characters' testimony. Some of his speculations are concerned with important aspects of the affair. Had Pamela spent any time with Gwinnett in his bedroom before she appeared on the landing? Why did she remain utterly motionless, as if in a trance, before Gwinnett himself appeared and she suddenly left the house? Others are concerned with trivialities: to ascertain the time and place when and where the incident occurred proves impossible, involving prolonged and ridiculous emphasis on the presence of Christmas decorations (the holly having fallen down in the middle of Bagshaw senior's vigil). As more and more information is produced to authenticate Bagshaw's story, the story itself becomes more and more speculative, hypothetical, fictional. Jenkins prefaces his account by referring to its subject as an 'alleged' happening. The more

credible the description of the event becomes, the less 'event' one
suspects there really is to be credible about.

This kind of thing happens very often in Jenkins's narrative.
Events which punctuate the account he offers of whatever period
in his life he is describing grow ever more diffuse as they sound
ever more credible. We are often left firmly believing that
something happened, and that it had to do with somebody. But
exactly *what* it was becomes increasingly unimportant, compared
with Jenkins's belief, which we share, that it *was* something.
Hypothesis and a proliferation of alternative explanations drive
under cover any simple, straightforward account of events.

James Tucker, in his very sensible book about Powell,*
comments on 'the general atmosphere of manufactured impreci-
sion' that this scene shares with many others in *A Dance to the Music
of Time*, and claims that 'We do accept the episode of the naked
visitor as credible.' It is true, I think, that we believe something of
the kind Bagshaw has described must have taken place at his
father's house some time around Christmas. But the details are so
blurred, the precise nature of the event so uncertain, that, in the
absence of more positive information about the two protagonists,
Pamela and Gwinnett, at other stages of the narrative, it really
tells us very little. What were Pamela's motives? How far was
Gwinnett her accomplice? Why did she behave in the strange way
she seems to have done? Incidents both before and after this one,
involving one or both of these characters, tend to be equally
anecdotal, equally fuzzy both at the edges and at the centre. What
really lay behind Pamela's previous adulterous relationship with
X. Trapnel is never made clear, beyond her obvious wish to
incense Widmerpool to further fits of jealousy. The dark deeds she
is reported to have performed on the deathbed of Ferrand-
Seneschal, with Widmerpool some sort of accomplice, are never
fully illuminated. They could be the grossly exaggerated figments
of a scandalmonger's imagination, or they might constitute
evidence of an extreme sexual perversity which must also have
affected Pamela's relationships with men throughout the whole of
her life. Tucker shows how Jenkins withholds what he takes to be
hard information about Pamela (her sexual frigidity: see Trapnel's confession in *Books Do Furnish a Room*, 4) in order to allow

---

* *The Novels of Anthony Powell* (London, 1976).

himself to speculate more freely about her love life with Odo Stevens in an earlier volume (*The Military Philosophers*, 3). But Trapnel's verdict on Pamela does not seem to me to be at all final. Furthermore, even if it were, it would not explain very much about Pamela's character in general, or the intensity of her affair with Trapnel in particular. To discover that the reason a woman has been behaving as she has is because she is sexually frigid tells one very little. Why is she frigid? What link is there, in this case, between Pamela's offensive self-advertisement – in evidence as long ago as Stringham's wedding, when she was six or seven and was sick in the font – and her present (supposed) frigidity? Powell's representation of her character does not allow us to answer these questions. Or, rather, the uncertainty about what she has done, the gossip that surrounds all her relationships with other people, allows for so many varied and contradictory interpretations that we are at liberty to create in our minds almost any picture of the sort of person she is. That is taking relative interpretation too far. Really, a character you can do that with is scarcely a character at all.

One aspect of Jenkins's tendency to set back 'real' events at a distance from himself reinforces that other tendency of his, which I discussed at the beginning of this chapter. I mean the placing of events that occur in time within the spatial form of retrospective memory. As I tried to show, the result is that the narrative to which we are at any given moment attending looks like a picture inset within a much larger picture; and this larger picture comprises all Jenkins remembers of his life and times, finally framed in the scene at the bonfire with which *A Dance to the Music of Time* begins and ends. There is always an appeal open from Nicholas the character, doing what he is doing in whatever circumstances he finds himself, to Jenkins the narrator, reflecting on his previous experience, and only too willing to grant the appeal and subsume past events in present reminiscence and speculation. Speculating is what Nicholas has spent most of his time doing. And so the presence of Jenkins, always ready and able to rescue him from the possibility of too close an involvement or too private a confession, is felt as an extra layer of protection against embarrassing self-exposure. Indeed the appeal is made, and granted, so frequently that for much of the time Nicholas seems to have no present tense. His own life and the lives of his acquaintances are being lived somewhere out of time, in some pocket of timelessness that Jenkins has slipped in between the recessive planes of his time scheme.

Just as the whole of *A Dance to the Music of Time* is set in the frame of Jenkins's bonfire, his observation of the men round the fire bucket, and his memories of Poussin's painting, so the separate volumes create a still deeper recession by placing the 'present tense' of Jenkins's recollections in a context of other tenses, reaching back to different periods in the past. Only gradually does the actual time of which Jenkins is going to speak free itself from these overlapping periods of time, and then never completely. The openings of *A Buyer's Market*, *Casanova's Chinese Restaurant* and *The Soldier's Art* provide elaborate variations of this process. If we take *Casanova's Chinese Restaurant* as our example, we shall find that Jenkins opens his narrative with an account of how he visited the site of a pub called the Mortimer, some time after the war, when the building was bombed out and it lay in ruins. The song of a crippled woman reminds him of the last time he heard it, 'years before, when Moreland and I had listened in Gerrard Street, the afternoon he had talked of getting married'. Jenkins goes on to elaborate a little about what happened on that afternoon. But we know that this cannot be the 'time' at which the events of this part of the novel are going to take place, because we have not met Moreland before and so we are not in a position to appreciate the importance or otherwise of his announcement. The cripple's song, 'Pale hands I loved beside the Shalimar', carries Jenkins's mind back to several occasions in the past when he and Moreland had discussed the whereabouts of the Shalimar, the past tense of the novel now taking on the function, though not the form, of the imperfect or past continuous. A passage of dialogue is inserted, which could have come down from any one of several occasions in the past. Then we return to the announcement of Moreland's marriage, with the further inset of a conversation between Nicholas and Barnby about the identity of the fiancée. This creates an opportunity for Jenkins to shuffle into the already numerous time sequences another one, in which Moreland discusses Barnby's attitude to women. Jenkins, from the security of the retrospective present, muses on Barnby's and Moreland's attitude to women in general terms; not, so far, as they manifested themselves at any one time or in any one conversation. And this leads him to the occasion we have been waiting for: 'Their different methods were, as it happened, displayed in high relief on the occasion of my first meeting with Moreland.' But we have to wait a long time before we are allowed to witness this display. For the next paragraph opens with a parenthesis on the Mortimer as it now stands, rebuilt since the day Jenkins visited its ruins after the war, when, we recall, these memories of what had occurred earlier within its walls first came into Jenkins's mind – or so he supposes in his present speculations at the bonfire. Even now, when the scene is at last set in the Mortimer as it was in 1929, when Nicholas did indeed first meet Moreland, description of the meeting is delayed whilst preliminaries involving Edgar Deacon and his friends take up a great deal of narrative time. It is some while after this that Barnby enters, they all leave, and the incident at Casanova's Chinese Restaurant occurs at which Barnby and Moreland reveal their different approaches towards women (Barnby picks up a waitress who has previously been Moreland's mistress).

The effect of this stalking of the present 'tense' of the narrative is to weaken its hold on the reader's confidence once it has been caught. At any time, we feel, the present will slip away and we shall be caught up in some quite separate reminiscence by Jenkins – of Moreland, or Barnby, or love, or the Mortimer. In Powell's fiction, continuity of events in the present is always provisional. There is never any guarantee that the activities we are reading about comprise the principal subject of the novel at this point. Again, the recessions of retrospect have taken away any feeling of purposeful movement or narrative drive. At each stage in the exchange of times and the substitutions of events, time itself is flattened out. It is incorporated in the spatial design for which Jenkins the narrator entertains so marked a preference.

A very welcome and unusually distant retrospect opens the sixth volume of *A Dance to the Music of Time*, *The Kindly Ones*. Here, intimations of the Nazi war bring with them a fine and unexpected flashback to Jenkins's childhood near an army camp outside Aldershot in 1914. The description of the lives of domestic servants during that period, the muted pathos and comedy of Billson the parlourmaid's unrequited love for Albert the cook, and the melancholia of Bracey, Captain Jenkins's manservant, are consummately achieved, and represent a high point in the development of English social comedy. Much of what follows in

The Kindly Ones comes close to the perfection of these early scenes, especially the occurrences in Albert's seaside hotel involving Dr Trelawney, and Jenkins's erstwhile rival (for the favours of Jean Templer), Bob Duport. Here the comedy shifts to a different key. The pathos is gone, but the restrained articulation of social absurdities is not harsh or critical. Trelawney in the lavatory, muttering mystical inanities through the locked door as he tries to pick his way out, is as funny as but less moving than Billson's nude appearance at the Jenkins dinner table – crazed out of her wits by Albert's announcement of his engagement to another woman.

Thereafter the 'supplementary worlds' in which Jenkins moves become less and less closely interrelated, less homogeneous. The army brings him into contact first with a battalion full of Welsh bank clerks, then with eccentric foreigners of the Intelligence Corps (Polish Liaison). In the post-war volumes he mixes with writers and editors of uncertain provenance. Bagshaw, Trapnel, Gwinnett and, in *Hearing Secret Harmonies*, Scorpio Murtlock are much less firmly identified in their social ambience than, say, Maclintick or Ted Jeavons in earlier novels. Some of them, Trapnel in particular, possess pasts shrouded in mystery. Others, such as Gwinnett or Bagshaw, have ascertainable origins in the English (in the first case American) class system, but Powell is not as alive as he was in the past to the details of the social station from which they have emerged. Moving into Jenkins's own social circle they carry with them little convincing testimony to the social contexts of their previous lives.

There is a provocative passage near the beginning of *The Acceptance World* that throws some light on Powell's difficulties. Nicholas is sitting at a table in the Ritz, casting his eye over a party of South Americans who are chatting excitedly to one another at a little distance from him. He begins to brood on the complexity of writing a novel about English life, somewhat in the Jamesian manner – I mean in the life of Hawthorne. He feels that 'Intricacies of social life make English habits unyielding to simplification, while understatement and irony – in which all classes of this island converse – upset the normal emphasis of reported speech.' We have to remember Nicholas is living in the late twenties, early thirties, at this time. Even so, the statement strikes me as being only half true. Not all classes of this island have at all times conversed in understatement and irony. And, though it may be true that understatement and irony were not, and are not, the monopoly of the upper and professional classes, the verbal understatement practised by people who might be considered models for the 'unassimilated' characters of *A Dance to the Music of Time* is different from that available to the 'assimilated' ones.

Powell nicely evades the problem in the army volumes by setting his scene first of all in Wales (and tactfully underplaying the Welsh accents) and then by making good use of the fact that army life, particularly among officers, possesses a language of its own, cutting across class barriers for the most part, or at any rate muffling the point of contact between class and class. This deflects attention from the unassimilated languages Powell cannot manage in their pure, or neat, forms. As a result his comic touch here is as sure as it was in the earlier volumes, but it is rather more emphatic.

The difference can be illustrated by comparing the way Powell handles two comic incidents, from *A Question of Upbringing* and *The Valley of Bones*. It is generally agreed that among the finest scenes in *A Question of Upbringing* is the one in which Jimmy Stripling tries to substitute a chamber pot for the top hat in Sunny Farebrother's hat box – the box being perched on top of his luggage the night before he is about to leave the Templers' house. As in the later passage from *The Valley of Bones*, Nicholas is a personal witness to this incident. So it is not essentially enigmatic, like the one in *Temporary Kings* where Pamela Widmerpool was found in Bagshaw's house. Also, Stripling's motives are not in doubt: he envies Farebrother his war record, and he has just been made a fool of by him in the affair of the mechanical collar-presser. But, in spite of these differences, Powell's comic method here has a great deal in common with the way he is going to handle the Bagshaw incident later in the sequence.

As in the Bagshaw affair, what happens is hedged about with hypotheses and expressions of incredulity. Before Stripling gets hold of the idea for his practical joke, Jean Templer has referred to Farebrother's luggage in a way that has caused Jenkins to wonder whether it were 'not impossible that she was the true cause of the events that followed'. Even if it were not, it gave her sister Babs the opportunity to comment that it might give Stripling an idea for one of his jokes. So from the beginning Jenkins expresses doubt as to who was initially responsible for what happened. There is nothing funny, however, about this characteristic uncertainty.

What is funny is the trail of speculation laid in Nicholas's mind by the sight of Jimmy Stripling advancing along the passage towards the hat box, with the chamber pot in his hand:

> My immediate thought was that relative size might prevent this plan from being put successfully into execution; though I had not examined the inside of the hat-box, obviously itself larger than normal (no doubt built to house more commodious hats of an earlier generation), the cardboard interior of which might have been removed to make room for odds and ends. Such economy of space would not have been out of keeping with the character of its owner. In any case it was a point upon which Stripling had evidently satisfied himself, because the slight smile on his face indicated that he was absolutely certain of his ground.

Jenkins's speculations here are similar to his speculations about the exact position Pamela Widmerpool must have occupied in Bagshaw's house on the night of her nude appearance. There is the same earnest weighing of the pros and cons: 'immediate though . . . though I had not examined . . . obviously larger . . . no doubt . . . would not have been out of keeping'. We are expected to feel that the activity described is scarcely worth the trouble of being made the subject of so elaborate a series of hypotheses. What does it matter whether the pot fits into the hat box anyway? What will have been achieved, what rib-tickling *coup de grâce* will have been delivered, if the plan actually comes off, and Farebrother opens his hat box at the office next day and finds a jerry instead of a hat in it? The discrepancy between Nicholas's anxiety (blandly and unexcitedly recalled) and the object in respect of which it has arisen (the relative sizes of a hat and a chamber pot) is enormous; as is the discrepancy in linguistic terms between calling a pot a pot and calling it a 'china receptacle', which is what Jenkins does later in the same paragraph: Stripling holds it in front of him 'as if it were a sacrificial urn'. As Stripling advances on the luggage, Farebrother unexpectedly opens his door and comes out into the passage. Stripling, unable to think of what else to do, or how to explain himself, continues past the door and round the corner into the far wing of the house:

> When he strode past me, I could see the sweat shining on his

forehead, and at the roots of his rather curly hair. For a moment Farebrother continued to gaze after him down the passage, as if he expected Sunny's return. Then, with an air of being hurt, or worried, he shut his door very quietly.

The success of Powell's treatment of this incident depends on something close to, but not quite the same as, understatement. The false note is struck by the mock heroic references to the 'china receptacle' and the 'sacrificial urn'. Both of these phrases lend the passage an air of facetiousness, a suspicion that the novelist is patting himself on the back for being clever, which is at variance with the professions of utter seriousness with which he treats the incident elsewhere. Discussing the passage, Tucker refers to the way Powell 'loads a negligible incident with all the pernickety shifts and queries of intense moral debate', and approves V. S. Pritchett's phrase about the 'brutal thoroughness' with which Powell treats his ludicrous material. This seems to catch very well the tone of the prose here. Jenkins is made to ignore altogether the (mutedly) farcical character of what is happening. He knows it is a joke, but he is fascinated by the mechanics of the operation, so much so that the banality of its intended, let alone its actual, consequences, seems to have escaped him. The comedy, there-fore, is not only in the discrepancy between what Nicholas sees and how he describes it. It is also in the unthinking way he separates the machinery of the joke from those of its attributes which actually make it a joke. Since it is such a poor joke, there are at least three phases of comic deflation: the joke is not anything like as funny as Stripling thinks it is; Nicholas's speculations about it remove the 'joke' element and leave behind merely a technical operation of doubtful success (i.e. the pot might not fit inside the box); and these speculations are couched in such a bland, matter-of-fact prose that Nicholas's anxiety dissolves into a flat succession of inappropriate qualifications. The comic effect depends on an extremely depressurised (and depressurising) manipulation of language. The prose gives the impression of having deliberately reduced what might otherwise have been the too strident tones of farce to a level just a fraction of an inch above sheer banality. With the exception of the inflated diction of these two odd phrases about the chamber pot (which I think were a mistake) there is nothing in the slightest degree emphatic about the comedy here.

In *The Valley of Bones*, as elsewhere in the war novels, the extent
to which Powell has been prepared to allow his prose to rise above
the merely banal has increased markedly. Take for example
Captain Gwatkin's interview with the reprobate Private Sayce.
With characteristic indeterminacy Powell informs us that Sayce's
affairs 'had reached some sort of climax' and Gwatkin, his CO,
decides to have a 'straight talk' with him. This turns out to be a
sentimental heart to heart about everybody in the company doing
his bit towards the war effort, with Sayce conspicuously letting the
side down. Sayce's incomprehension (whilst saying the right
things and feeling momentarily abashed when, later in the day,
the light begins to dawn) and Gwatkin's self-satisfaction and
genuine, though absurd, feeling are accurately observed. Part of
the comic effect is unpatronisingly achieved by the way the
public-school ethos of Gwatkin the bank clerk's sentiments, and
even his phraseology, are brought to our attention. The Army has
provided an opportunity for what would otherwise have been
considered an alien form of address. Sayce, 'that bugger Sayce' as
Sergeant Pendry refers to him, is, of course, quite untouched,
ethically and linguistically, by this pep talk. He sniffs 'frantically'
towards the end, and 'seemed moved almost to tears by the
thought of all his own hitherto unrevealed goodness' (everybody
is fundamentally a good chap according to Gwatkin). But this is
clearly an irrational reaction to the strangeness of the situation.
The comedy lies in the mutual incomprehension between the two
men, disguised from one of them by the fragile bridge of words,
conventional feelings, one-sidedly good intentions, that he has
thrown across the cultural abyss. And the success of the comedy
lies in the fact that the cultural separation does not correspond to
a class separation; or if it does (we are not told what Sayce's
civilian occupation is) neither of the classes we are concerned with
falls into the categories within which Powell has up to this point
(with the exception of the Stonehurst domestics) concentrated his
attention. Linguistically the comedy is expressed through man-
nerisms of speech we associate with the Army; and, though these
probably have their origins in upper-class *mores* and speech
habits, they are not the same speech habits as the ones we got used
to in the civilian scenes in earlier volumes.

Unlike the incident of Jimmy Stripling and the chamber pot,
this scene between Gwatkin and Sayce is couched mainly in
dialogue. But the difference does not end there. Powell is amused

at the spectacle of two human beings having wandered so far away from their real characters that neither of them has any idea of the artificiality of the situation that has been created. For Sayce this is only a temporary lapse. He will be mesmerised by the unfamiliar identity Gwatkin has forced on him only for the length of time it takes him to get out of the room. But Gwatkin's illusions about himself are so deeply rooted in his imagination, the expression of such a deep psychological and emotional need, that he will never be able to settle for a life that is appropriate to his real, and in many respects limited and inadequate, character. This adds an extra dimension of humour to the interview with Sayce. The comic touch may be more emphatic and less delicate than it was in *A Question of Upbringing*, but it achieves a great deal more that is not merely comic. It tells us more about Gwatkin than the chamber pot told us about Stripling. Or, rather, it convinces us that there is more to know about the one than the chamber pot convinced us there was to know about the other. And maybe there *is* more to know about Gwatkin. Maybe the fact that he is not one of the 'assimilated' characters of *A Dance to the Music of Time* tells in his favour here. For Powell's access to the language of Army life protects him from an unmuffled confrontation with members of classes other than his own – something he is going to have some difficulty with, linguistically speaking, from *Books Do Furnish a Room* onwards.

Elsewhere Powell's comedy is expressed through dialogue that is unambiguously the creation of a particular class. Within this class there is an almost infinitesmal accumulation of sub-strata, ranging from Widmerpool to Erridge, or from Frederica Budd to Rosie Manasch. Much of the fascination of *The Music of Time* evolves out of shifts in station, fashionableness and success, as the fortunes of individuals change through marriage or accumulation of wealth; or as times change and different accommodations are made with classes above or below. Lady Molly Sleaford's marriage to Ted Jeavons in the 1930s has an altogether different social complexion from Rosie Manasch's marriage to Odo Stevens in the 1950s. Through all this, though, the language the characters speak remains startlingly uniform, and the dialogue tends to confine them in a linguistic quarantine where only the bland, the suave, the standard English is spoken. Even J. G. Quiggin, who is supposed to hail from the Midlands and to speak with a pronounced 'North country' accent, betrays no hint that he has ever spoken a dialect that hales from anywhere north of Potter's Bar. What can only be taken, so far as the characters are concerned, as a widening of the class waveband in later volumes, is accompanied by no significant variation in the language spoken. This is true also of other things we would have expected to modify the character of speech affected by different persons in age, profession, style of life. There is none of, say, Angus Wilson's ear for the idiosyncrasies of speech and what they can be made to reveal of social position, among other things. And so Powell's comedy owes very little to those clashes of idiom, dialect or linguistic tone that had played such an important part in earlier comic dialogue, in the novel or on the stage. On the contrary, the levelness of speech forms and the uniformity of pitch and tone throw the responsibility for the success of the comedy onto the information each separate part of the dialogue transmits – as well as on the timing of the release of each of those parts.

Many of the most celebrated scenes in the later work, though, owe nothing to dialogue at all. The linguistic devices which have been described as the expression of a class, each member of which manipulates them in order to project and dramatise himself in the company of his peers, re-emerge in Jenkins's own descriptive prose. I am referring to those habits of understatement and irony, appropriate in the forms they take here (in spite of Powell's suggestion to the contrary) to a particular class and milieu, which Jenkins referred to in the passage quoted from *A Lady Molly's* (at p. 103 above). They take the form of diffident qualification, muted insistence, indirect and circuitous stalking of a point, an opinion, a pronouncement. The muffling effect achieved by this prose is reproduced in the situations it is so often used to describe. Powell's situations and his style combine to put some considerable distance between his readers and what they are reading about. The result is that the comedy is established somewhere in between what the events suggest, and what is done to them by Jenkins's apologetic mode of presentation. It is the opposite technique to that of Evelyn Waugh, a writer with whom Powell has often, for the most part mistakenly, been compared. The sports day at Llanabba Castle in *Decline and Fall* or Apthorpe's peregrinations with his thunder box in *Men at Arms* succeed by virtue of the emphasis Waugh places on the ever-increasing absurdity and incongruity of what happens. Having set events in motion he gets out of the way, or appears to do, which novelistically speaking is the same thing. Powell, by contrast, interposes not merely Nicholas (and therefore, as we have seen, someone very like himself), but, as often as not, at least one anonymous and usually unreliable third party in whom the story originated.

Powell knows that 'When such scraps of gossip are committed to paper, the words bear a heavier weight than when the same information is imparted huskily between draughts of champagne in the noise of a crowded room.' That was what he said, through Jenkins of course, in *A Buyer's Market*. So to soften the impact of the comedy he has recourse to that cushion of qualification, circumlocution, tentativeness and obliquity which is the hallmark of both his and his character's style. As a result of this his readers' interest tends to be deflected from the scene and caught up in that unruffled, sceptical well-bred tone. Often, when they assume they are being amused, they are actually being uplifted, and what they are being uplifted into, linguistically, is a class above themselves.

Though this is the effect so often produced by the way Jenkins addresses the reader, we have seen also how Powell manufactures distinctive comic effects by drawing our attention, ever so gently, almost as if he were not noticing, to the particular timbres and undertones of the prose. This was what he achieved in his description of the chamber-pot incident in *A Question of Upbringing*. But there I also suggested that a false note was struck by the insertion of mock-heroic phrases. I should not wish to leave the impression that Powell's comedy, in this descriptive mode, invariably depends on maintaining an air of colourless equanimity, even when the subject he has invented is a more spectacular one than Jimmy Stripling's perambulations with the potty. On the contrary, on other occasions (as we have seen in the opening and closing paragraphs of the sequence) Powell shows considerable skill in applying the strokes of a highly coloured language to produce what might be called baroque pictorial and linguistic effects – though always in association with that sceptical, disenchanted tone of voice that sounds throughout *A Dance to the Music of Time*.

The opening chapter of *The Soldier's Art* provides an excellent example of Powell's baroque prose. Nicholas happens upon the dissolute Lieutenant Bithel at night during an air raid. After a brief, muttered conversation, description of the raid is held up by a passage of reminiscence about the history of the cricket pavilion towards which Nicholas and Bithel are strolling. It is a petty history, of disagreements among the officers about when the door should be locked and when not. But this is the background against which Powell sets his bravura description of the raid:

The noise of the cannonade round about was deepening. An odour like smouldering rubber imposed a rank unsavoury surface smell on lesser exhalations of soot and smoke. Towards the far side of the town – the direction of the harbour – thin greenish rays of searchlight beams rapidly described wide intersecting arcs backwards and forwards against the eastern horizon, their range ever reducing, ever extending, as they sliced purposefully across each other's tracks. Then, all at once, these several zig-zagging angles of light would form an apex on the same patch of sky, creating a small elliptical compartment through which, once in a way, rapidly darted a tiny object, moving like an angry insect confined in a bottle. As if reacting in deliberately regulated unison to the searchlights' methodical fluctuations, shifting masses of cloudbank alternately glowed and faded, constantly redesigning by that means half-a-dozen intricately pastelled compositions of black and lilac, grey and saffron, pink and gold. Out of this resplendent firmament – which, transcendentally speaking, seemed to threaten imminent revelation from on high – slowly descended, like Japanese lanterns at a fête, a score or more of flares released by the raiding planes. Clustered together in twos and threes, they drifted at first aimlessly in the breeze, after a time scarcely losing height, only swaying a little this way and that, metamorphosed into all but stationary lamps, apparently suspended by immensely elongated wires attached to an invisible ceiling. Suddenly, as if at a prearranged signal for the climax of the spectacle – a set-piece at midnight – high swirling clouds of inky smoke rose from below to meet these flickering airborne torches. At ground level, too, irregular knots of flame began to blaze away like a nest of nocturnal forges in the Black Country. All the world was dipped in a livid, unearthly refulgence, theatrical yet sinister, a light neither of night nor day, the penumbra of Pluto's frontiers. The reek of scorched rubber grew more than ever sickly. Bithel fidgeted with the belt of his mackintosh.

The word 'theatrical' is used only once in this passage, but it is impossible not to notice how the raid has been transformed into an elaborate theatrical spectacle. The distance customarily present between Jenkins and what he is describing is created here mainly by the absence of sense impressions that, we are bound to feel, would immediately have struck anyone recording what he experienced at the time the raid was actually taking place. There are no appeals to the senses of smell, taste or touch after the first reference to an 'odour like smouldering rubber', until the reminder at the end of the paragraph of the 'reeking of scorched rubber'. Everything in between is conveyed to us in visual terms. The only suggestion of a sense of sound, even, is in the images of an insect trapped in a bottle (no sound, no buzzing, actually mentioned) and of nocturnal forges in the Black Country (again the verb – 'blazed' – is not an auditory one). And the visual images used are almost always artificial ones, insisting on cosmetic aspects of the raid, transforming it into a picture or a stage set. The feeling that movement has been arrested to create a gorgeously coloured painting, that a terrifying reality has been transformed into a baroque artifice, is reinforced by the way the syntax depresses the energy of the verbs by crowding them back into repeated participal phrases. The sentence beginning 'Clustered together in twos and threes' is a striking example of this device. There is plenty of movement in this passage: after 'Suddenly', the 'swirling clouds' and the 'flickering torches'. But it is movement as one imagines it in a painting; especially, perhaps, a painting by Gaulli or Pozzo, or Powell's admired Tiepolo – a ceiling painting stretched under the dome of the night sky.

Jenkins warns of an 'imminent revelation from on high'; but it is clear from his tone that to speak 'transcendentally' is to speak fancifully too. There is no serious attempt to adduce a meaning from the spectacle. In fact there is no doubt that, in spite of the two references to the smell of scorched rubber, Jenkins has transformed a terrible reality into a feast of words and colours. A raid has been converted into an opera, or a *fête galante* with Japanese lanterns, shifting scenery, and *dei ex machini* drifting down from cloudbanks. Then, at the 'penumbra of Pluto's frontiers', we are returned to Bithel, fidgeting with his belt, and worrying about 'a spot of bother with a cheque' that bounced. What Powell has done, in short, is to overlay the real horrors of war with descriptions of sub-farcical trivialities on the one hand, and vivid but fanciful pictorial artifice on the other. Between these two discrepant stylistic triumphs, the raid has been squeezed out of existence. It is beautifully done, but it makes the war seem curiously remote. One does begin to wonder whether Jenkins, and Powell, ought not to show a little more respect for reality, betray a little less willingness to indulge in elaborately stylised versions of it.

As with events, so with people. Describing them, Jenkins frequently has recourse to comparisons with the visual arts. The psychological inferences he draws from his study of the physique of a character is often helped along by speculations about a figure in a painting whom he resembles. Charles Stringham, for example, resembles a figure in an Elizabethan miniature; or a younger version of Alexander receiving the children of Darius after the battle of Issus in Veronese's painting. Norman Chandler, playing the part of Bosola in a production of *The Duchess of Malfi*, reminds Moreland of a figure from Picasso, 'one of those attenuated, androgynous mountebanks of the Blue Period, who haven't had a meal for weeks'. But the finest and most detailed comparison from painting is the comparison between Moreland himself and the personification of Folly in Bronzino's 'Venus Disarming Cupid'. At first Moreland's head is compared with Beethoven's, in an approximately musical parallel (Moreland is a composer). Afterwards we are told that

> On the other hand, his short, dark, curly hair recalled a dissipated cherub, a less aggressive, more intellectual version of Folly in Bronzino's picture, rubicund, mischievous, as he threatens with a fusillade of rose petals the embrace of Venus and Cupid; while Time in the background, whiskered like the Emperor Franz-Josef, looms behind a blue curtain as if evasively vacating the bathroom.

But there is a difference: 'Moreland's face in repose, in spite of this cherubic, humorous character, was not without melancholy too; his flesh suggesting none of that riotously healthy physique enjoyed by Bronzino's – and, I suppose, everyone else's – Folly.'

The question we shall want to ask about this comparison is, On what has the author's eye most clearly focused? At the beginning of *The Soldier's Art* we found that his description of an air raid played second fiddle to the stage set that had been erected over its demise. What is at the centre here: Moreland's face or Bronzino's painting? Is the comparison performing the same function of some of those long epic similes in Milton, in which the classical and biblical references multiply as the event in the narrative that gave rise to them slips unnoticed from the mind; or is it at all points contributing to a detailed picture of Moreland's physiognomy? At first glance it seems as if the reference to Bronzino has accomplished all it set out to do by the time we get to 'rubicund, mischievous'. The fusillade of rose petals and the elaborate description of Time looming behind the blue curtain seem unnecessary. They are accurately observed: Time *does* look like the Emperor; and the phrase 'as if evasively vacating the bathroom' amusingly describes what he *could* have been doing, if we were to be so tactless as to ignore his allegorical pretensions. But it is nothing to the point. The non-comparison that follows, in which Jenkins says that, after all, Moreland's rubicund and mischievous appearance has more of melancholy and illness in it than the riotous good health of Folly, seems to take back the little that has already been given. Even so, I think Jenkins is being scrupulous in his comparison here, because we have to keep in mind the reference to Moreland's 'Beethoven-shaped head', and read the comments about melancholy and illness into that as well as into the figure in the painting. If we do so we get a surprising and vivid conflation of two portraits – one heavy, massive, and glaring; the other mischievous, cherubic, and intellectual – which come together to create a distinct visual impression. And, as the faces fit over each other so perfectly, so do the temperamental qualities they express. Therefore, in spite of Franz-Josef and the bathroom, this painterly comparison works rather well. It is a pity that, when he appears elsewhere in the novels, the character suggested by it does not entirely live up to the promise of this description.

How does the way Powell manipulates language affect his representation of Widmerpool, the best known and most controversial character in *A Dance to the Music of Time*? I have suggested that there is some uncertainty about the extent to which Jenkins uses his medium as an invitation to the reader to rise linguistically into a class above himself; or as a Trojan horse inside the walls of linguistic gentility, available there to break down from the inside what might otherwise have been impregnable social barriers. The way he handles Widmerpool should do more than anything else to resolve the uncertainty. For Widmerpool is the most persistent and probably the most distasteful *arriviste* in the novels. His function is to rise, and go on rising, in the world he has entered, if not through the tradesmen's entrance, then not through the front door either. I think Widmerpool's career demonstrates that there are in fact two worlds in which one might rise, or fall. They look the same. The political, professional and financial world *seems* to be the same as the social world. The same people, more or less, inhabit them both. Advancement in the one, therefore, would appear to entail advancement in the other. Yet Widmerpool's career shows us (I am not sure whether it shows him) that this is not so. The very ambition, energy and pushing qualities that, for a long time, carry him upwards and onwards in his public life are the same qualities that make it impossible for him ever to enter the world of society on terms that will allow it to remain social, and sociable, when he is inside it.

A good place to start thinking about Widmerpool's character is towards the end of *Hearing Secret Harmonies*, at Fiona Cutts's wedding, where he abases himself before Sir Bertram Akworth. Widmerpool's behaviour here is histrionic and absurd. Having thrown in his lot with Scorpio Murtlock's squatters and failed to browbeat Murtlock into submission to his authority, he has become a pathetic wretch, his will totally dissolved in an orgy of penance and self-humiliation. Sir Bertram's reaction to his self-exposure is cool, though disgusted, and Powell's prose mirrors it faithfully. The composed discrimination of the balanced clauses ('Sir Bertram either did not . . . or, more probably . . .', etc.) and the pressure of expressions such as 'more than a trifle' or 'socially to discompose him', all conspire to produce an impression of well-bred disdain, ever so slightly lifted eyebrows, precisely an immunity from social indisposition. This is what I take to have been Michael Ratcliffe's point in his *Times* review of the series when he referred to Powell's 'resources of metropolitan detachment'. Whilst it may have played its part in the composition of passages I have confessed to admiring in *The Kindly Ones* and *The Valley of Bones*, it seems to me to be most in evidence in descriptive comic scenes such as this one between Widmerpool and Akworth. Most of the celebrated comic scenes in the series take this form: Barbara Goring pouring sugar over Widmerpool's head at the Huntercombe ball; Pamela Widmerpool being sick in a Chinese vase after Erridge's funeral. The sugar-pouring episode is the first of these public humiliations we see Widmerpool endure. We have *heard* about his problems at school, through anecdotes spoken by another person, usually Stringham or Templer. But this is the first time we have come face to face with the kind of incident out of which such anecdotes are made. Looking at it, I think we shall find interesting parallels to the scene with Sir Bertram.

Barbara Goring pours a castor full of sugar over Widmerpool's head near the end of *A Buyer's Market*, 1, as a reaction to his annoyance at her intention to leave the table at which they have been sitting together. Widmerpool has been displaying what we are already beginning to realise (see the Örn and Lundquist incident in *A Question of Upbringing*) is a basic element, perhaps *the* basic element, of his nature: a need to use his will power in order to exert influence over other people. The trouble is that on this occasion – as on another, much later one (in *Temporary Kings*), when he takes his wife by the throat – the only way Widmerpool can do this by direct physical assault. He snatches at Barbara's wrist and tells her that she cannot leave him. Barbara will have none of this, and, saying that Widmerpool is sour and needs sweetening, takes the sugar castor from the sideboard with the intention of sprinkling a few grains over his head. Unfortunately the bottom of the castor is loose, and an avalanche of sugar descends on him.

For the most part the episode is narrated in a mock heroic style: not, on this occasion, by periphrastic descriptions of commonplace objects in the seventeenth and eighteenth-century manner (which we saw Powell using *à propos* the chamber pot); but by slowing down the pace of the narrative to a point where something that took a couple of seconds to happen ('an instant of time', Jenkins says), takes three pages of prose to describe. The moment of the downpour takes almost as long to pass as the moment when Belinda's lock is severed in Pope's *Rape of the Lock*, the *locus classicus* for this kind of writing. What follows is only the very last phase of the description:

Barbara now tipped the castor so that it was poised vertically over Widmerpool's head, holding it there like the sword of Damocles above the tyrant. However, unlike the merely minatory quiescence of that normally inactive weapon, a state of dispensation was not in this case maintained, and suddenly, without the slightest warning, the massive silver apex of the castor dropped from its base, as if severed by the slash of some invisible machinery, and crashed heavily to the floor: the sugar pouring out on to Widmerpool's head in a dense and over-whelming cascade.

Again the event has been transformed into a theatrical spectacle. The 'invisible machinery' looks as if it has been assembled somewhere above a stage curtain. Widmerpool's embarrassment is described as a 'display', to be inspected by 'the eye of an attentive observer'. The spectacle itself, whilst being accounted for in the most circumspect and precise terms (Widmerpool's brilliantine making the grains of sugar stick firmly to his hair), suggests that Widmerpool's fate is to be viewed as something containing an equal measure of riotous farce and Vergilian epic beauty: 'The sugar sparkled on him like hoar-frost, and, when he moved, there was a faint rustle from leaves of a tree in some wintry forest.' The prose suggests that Widmerpool buried beneath these 'glittering incrustations' is a more acceptable spectacle than Widmerpool as he normally appears. His 'rather sparse hair', 'liberally greased with a dressing' which gives off 'a sweetish smell' and which Jenkins recalls as being a 'disagreeable . . . lubricant' (in tones that suggest 'lubricity' in the sense of 'lewdness' also), is inspected from a fastidious distance. The words Jenkins uses seem to fend off Widmerpool, indeed fence him off – as a creature of another species. And in a sense that is precisely what he is. None of the people Nicholas likes and gets on well with ever smells. Widmerpool, one infers, with his greasy complexion, his brilliantined hair, his boils, and what Stringham calls his 'contortions of the bottom' (a particularly displeasing, because incomprehensible, innuendo), sounds as if he does smell. He certainly possesses offensive bodily attributes – owns a body, in fact, which performs routine functions of a kind most of the other characters seem to have no need of. At any rate Jenkins never mentions them. Having a father in liquid manure cannot be much help, especially as, in the past, he has taken delivery of it to Barbara's father, Lord Goring; thus for ever, as it were, interposing a bad smell between himself and his social 'peers'.

Widmerpool's first response to his humiliation over the sugar castor is to betray a certain enjoyment. As on the occasion when Budd threw a ripe banana at him, 'an absolutely slavish look came into Widmerpool's face'. But it does not last for long. He pushes his way out of the room in a towering rage, never to visit the house again. Jenkins, though, alone among the guests, has noticed that moment of servility. I think Powell intends his readers to connect Widmerpool's behaviour at the Cutts wedding with his behaviour here at the Huntercombe ball. His relationship with Scorpio Murtlock, in which competitiveness and the willingness to undergo humiliation fuse into a simple emotional state, reflects the same facet of his personality. We notice it, too, in his relationship with women: not only Barbara, but also Gipsy Jones, Mildred Haycock and, above all, Pamela Flitton. Perhaps it is the master key to his angular and uncomfortable personality. If so, it is a key that will turn only from the outside, providing an explanation of his behaviour without any deeper access to sympathy or understanding from within. Well, Widmerpool is a comic character. It might be argued that we should not expect that kind of understanding of a comic character. On the other hand it might be argued that, with the exception of Nicholas, he is the only person of any major importance who plays a significant part in all twelve novels. This odd blend of arrogance and servility is demonstrated at too great length for it to be appreciated merely as the hallmark of a comic, even of a supremely comic, fictional character.

Sexual diffidence, sexual clumsiness and aggression, rumours of emotional problems attendant on his marriage with Pamela Flitton, all have the effect of arousing in us a curiosity about Widmerpool's inner life which is never satisfied at the appropriate level. The rôle he plays in *A Dance to the Music of Time* is not unlike that played by the Baron de Charlus in Proust's *A la Recherche du Temps Perdu*; and Marcel, in spite of his self-preoccupation (which Nicholas, of course, in no way shares) tells us a great deal about the Baron's feelings, at the same time as he creates the external impression of him as a supremely vital comic character. Something is missing from Widmerpool, and I suspect it is missing because Jenkins, and Powell, are not prepared to be sufficiently serious about him. Unlike Stringham, or Moreland, or Barnby, he is an outsider, socially unacceptable in spite of the status Jenkins confers on him as a sort of landmark in his life. This allows Jenkins to paint him with rather broader strokes than he does these other characters – giving him a vitality and comic verve none of them shares. But it also has the effect of closing off his inner life even more effectively, and more disappointingly, than is the case with the other inhabitants of Jenkins's world.

So in the representation of Widmerpool what Ratcliffe calls Powell's 'metropolitan detachment' often strikes me as being only in a special sense a 'resource' – presumably, he implies, of literary excellence. Though it is responsible for many of those muted comic effects which delight us as much by their variety as by their lightness of touch, it seems to be responsible also for a ringing down of the curtain on descriptions of feelings and obsessive emotional states which are not of their nature inimical to comic treatment on any but a superficial, uncomprehending level. Powell's inclination remains to stick to the surface and trust to the transparency of social behaviour as an accurate register of what exists beneath it. Thinking of General Conyers practising the cello (*At Lady Molly's*, 2), Jenkins calls to mind 'one of those Dutch genre pictures . . . impressive . . . from the deep social conviction of the painter'. Powell's social conviction is also very deep. In *A Buyer's Market* he has Jenkins say that 'human life is lived largely at surface level', which means for the most part in social terms. Or at the very most in terms that make it susceptible, without much distortion or censorship, to treatment by means of social comedy.

Where it is not lived on the surface, Jenkins finds it virtually impossible to articulate: 'close examination of what happened at any given period in itself provokes an unnatural element, like looking at a large oil painting under a magnifying glass, the over-all effect lost' (*Temporary Kings*, 1). There is something commendable, and tactful, about such an insistence on the limits of art, or of communication generally. But it can run to undue caution, undue reticence. It can also encourage too great an insistence on tone at the expense of matter, an air of literary gossip about fictional people. In Powell's case I believe something like this has happened and that it has become more damaging since the war volumes because of the growing area of social life he insists on noticing, but refrains from investigating at all thoroughly. It was present back in the old Walpole–Wilson–Warminster–Tolland days but the fact of social homogeneity made it less startling; and Widmerpool's carefully documented origins in the lowest stratum of Jenkins's and Powell's own social class provided a firm backbone to a plot which elsewhere betrayed some purposelessness and irresolution – inseparable from the restrictions Powell imposed on his hero's contacts with other people. In recent volumes the other side of Powell's reticence, the shallowness of his insight into what are potentially his most interesting characters – Trapnel, Gwinnett, Pamela Widmerpool – has become more pronounced. But the tone remains genial, tactful, civilised to many people's way of thinking.

English critics have emulated Powell's metropolitan detachment and conferred on his novels an almost unanimous accolade. It was left to an American, Edmund Wilson, to sound a cautionary note. He did not see why the English made so much fuss about Powell: 'He's just entertaining enough to read in bed late at night in summer.' That was a frivolous remark, but a useful corrective none the less. As an American, Wilson felt no need to be uplifted into an English class from which the style and tone of the prose extend such a seductive invitation. He did not see the need to dignify accounts of life as it is lived socially, however amusingly and at whatever great lengths, with metaphors of art, mythology, and transcendental intuitions. That is what I suggested Powell was doing when I drew attention to the unusually large gap that exists between the artistic metaphors he deploys – the sustained analogy with Poussin's painting 'A Dance to the Music of Time' – and the social connections, and severances, they 'stand for'. English men of letters have fewer defences than Wilson, partly, no doubt, because their temperaments are more attuned to the distinctions of class and language on which Powell rings so many and such various changes. Powell, I am sure, is not a snob in the modern sense of the word. But I have more than a little suspicion that, in the subtlest and least deliberate of ways, he has exposed a vein of snobbery in the old, eighteenth-century sense, masquerading as comic appreciation, in some of his readers.

The snobbery travels far beyond its basis in idiom and tone, because the content of Powell's social observation grows progressively less important as the cultivated sensibility which is responsible for it ('half way between dissipation and diffidence') attracts more and more attention. From the first we find out extraordinarily little about even the most superficial of the

characters. Yet this is what Jenkins calls 'an unsentimental grasp
on human conduct', available, we remember, only to those, such
as Powell and himself, 'whose minds have been attuned by early
association to the constant give and take of an ancient and
tenacious social organism'. It seems to me that, whilst such
attunement may be very real, and in an earlier age had a great
deal to do with, for example, Jane Austen's success as a novelist,
this attempt to separate it from critical thought by 'apparently
more perceptive persons' is disingenuous; and incidentally inap-
plicable to Powell's own best work. My point is that Powell has
been taken at more than his word by critics who have noticed the
felicities of his detached comic method whilst remaining blind to
the exclusive tone through which so much of it is irradiated. And
this is because it is the charm of this tone that it provides the
illusion of a shared attitude and a shared status. It makes
exclusiveness inclusive. Readers in general may be flattered into a
sort of class collusion, which they interpret as emotional poise,
comic detachment, a restrained delicacy of appreciation. In the
end tone is almost all that is left. It flutters elegantly in a void at
the back of which Trapnel, Gwinnett, Murtlock, even Widmerpool, have been done away with. Metropolitan critics of matching
resource have not been slow to fill it with their own professions of
significance.

5 Angus Wilson

In one of Angus Wilson's short stories, 'Fresh Air Fiend', a young graduate student, staying with her professor and his wife in their country home outside Oxford, tries to get her hosts to face up to the reality of their sterile marriage. The girl, Elspeth Eccles, is an example of a type of person who is to appear often in Wilson's stories and his novels. Almost invariably young, and female, she is the fresh air fiend of the title, eager to dispel the deceit and hypocrisy of those around her. Elspeth knows that Professor Searle has been prevented from continuing with his research by his neurotic and dipsomaniac wife, and she suspects that Miranda Searle's neurosis has been caused by the death of her only son some years ago. She decides that the best way to alert Mrs Searle to the damage she is doing is to confront her with the memory of her son and force her to understand how she is sacrificing the living to the dead. There is much thought of 'putting the issue fairly and squarely before Mrs Searle'. When Elspeth puts her plan into practice Miranda creates a terrible scene. Later Professor Searle has a nervous breakdown and has to leave the university.

A depressing story, in more ways than one. Reading it, we feel depressed by the emptiness of the lives the characters live in it, and the apparent impossibility of anybody doing anything effective about it. And the characters themselves, with the exception of the girl, are depressives – the Professor turned in on himself, failing to share his sense of failure and frustration with those around him; the wife incapable of facing the world on any but aggressive and bitterly sarcastic terms. Elspeth's supposition that she can tear down the barriers by going straight to the essentials of the matter, by 'preferring to have things straight instead of crooked', is callow to say the least. Professor Searle warns her against such a course: 'I'm more and more disinclined to expose skeletons that have been so carefully buried', he says. 'I suppose it's reticence that comes with old age.'

We never discover what are the most carefully concealed skeletons in the Searle family's cupboard. Whatever the reason for the breakdown of the marriage, however, both partners seem to have adapted to it. As Professor Searle tells Elspeth before she witnesses the terrible scene between himself and his wife,

> What takes place between my wife and me has occurred so often now, the pattern is so stereotyped, that, awful though it may be, my mind, yes, and my feelings have become hardened to the routine. To you, even though it is only guessed at, or perhaps for that very reason, it will seem far more awful than it can ever again seem to me.

But he is proved wrong when Elspeth shakes up the 'pattern', and the stereotype is forced to give way to a more raw assault on his nervous system. In his condition, fresh air can only cause a chill. By opening the window, Elspeth has destroyed the man she had so naively intended to 'save'.

The Elspeth sort of person appears in one form or another throughout Wilson's work. Usually the basis of her willingness to undeceive others in an equally pronounced tendency for self-deception on her own part is given greater emphasis than it is here. The origins of this sort of person go back to the plays of Ibsen, in which we know Wilson has taken a great interest. In one of the later stories, 'After the Show', interference in the broken life of another person follows immediately on two of the principal characters' attendance at a performance of *The Wild Duck*. But Gregers Werle usually takes a female form in Wilson's fiction, and in both of his first two novels the character who is most like Elspeth, or Gregers, is a woman: Elizabeth Sands in *Hemlock and After* and Elvira Portway in *Anglo-Saxon Attitudes*. Oddly enough, in both of these cases the character is more sympathetically treated than she tends to be in the short stories. In *Anglo-Saxon Attitudes*, however, there is a much less sympathetic attitude of the type in John Middleton, the hero's younger son. As a television reporter, he specialises in making a public exhibition of other people's private lives through his largely unwarranted and undesired interference in them.

Miranda Searle is the first of many dissatisfied and embittered wives whose dissatisfaction expresses itself in a shrill mockery of the pretensions of other people and a habit of organising life at arm's length. In her case this is demonstrated in the way she goes about her gardening: 'It was at once one of the shames and one of the privileges of gardening, she thought, that one was put in this godlike position of judgement and analogies.' Such observations look forward to a passage of dialogue between Ella and Bernard Sands in *Hemlock and After*. Here also a neurotic wife finds in gardening an outlet for the straightforward exercise of authority. Ella has no difficulty in separating the weeds from the flowers. Her certainty here contrasts with her indecisiveness about human relationships, prompting her husband to say to her, 'Yours may not be the conventional approach, but it is, after all, the proper exercise of authority.' This compensation for inner neurosis by an outer display of firmness and authority is frequently displayed by Wilson's characters.

Unlike the two women, Professor Searle belongs to a type of person who appears very rarely in Wilson's short stories. But a part of what he represents exists somewhere in the background of many of them – in the way Wilson himself looks at the world he has created. A sensitive man, with a squeamish respect for his own and others' privacy, Searle reacts to personal difficulties by erecting makeshift barriers of evasion and self-deception. By the time the story opens he has insulated himself for years from a resurgence of hope or despair. Of course Wilson recognises this. He is himself a writer of the utmost moral scruple and psychological refinement. Even so, my suggestion that he shares some of the weaknesses as well as the strengths of his hero is a serious one. There really is a sense in which Wilson, with all his subtlety in examining and exposing the consciences of others, is not entirely free from self-deception. I suspect he is at least half-aware that this is so.

Taking 'Fresh Air Fiend' as a model of Wilson's fiction, we can predict what we are likely to find in much of the rest of it. People who pride themselves on their honesty in facing up to the reality of a situation, especially when that situation is someone else's, will be likely to do more harm than good. On the other hand, people who disguise their own weaknesses or obscure the weaknesses of others, often with the best intentions, are also likely to come to grief. But the Miranda Searles of this world will manage to survive on their own depressive and sometimes hysterical terms. None of the characters in this story is admirable. Each of them is in possession of a false idea about himself or about one or both of the other characters. The world of deception Professor and Mrs Searle have built around themselves is stifling and unattractive. But the world outside, as represented by Elspeth Eccles, is only superficially more likable. Her insistence on facing up to things is only in the most naive sense honest and realistic. Invariably it results in damage and distress. No human activity seems to be free from evasion and self-deception. Depression seems to be the only alternative to more energetic response to lives grounded in ignorance and heading towards despair.

'Fresh Air Fiend' is a story about a family – not the less so on account of the absence of one of its members. This also is a conspicuous feature of Wilson's short stories and his novels. Perhaps this sounds like a superfluous and rather silly comment to make about a novelist. Of course most novelists write about families: think of Jane Austen, Thackeray, or E. M. Forster. But there is a special sense in which it can be said that Wilson writes about families, in a more intensely inward way than the great English novelists of the past. I shall explain what I mean by this at greater length when I come to look at the novels, especially *No Laughing Matter*. Even in a common or garden sense, however, it is remarkable how deeply absorbed in family problems Wilson is in these early stories. Sometimes the family is a large, sprawling affair, with in-laws and aunts and uncles to spare, as in 'Union Reunion' or 'Crazy Crowd'. At others it is reduced to a close relationship between two or three members, drawn together as a result of some crisis in their lives or those around them. 'Mother's Sense of Fun' and 'A Story of Historical Interest' are good early examples of this genre, as is the title story of *Such Darling Dodos*.

A great deal has been written about the way these stories of the late forties and early fifties caught the mood of the time; how they painted brilliant satirical portraits of people who seemed typical of those years of austerity, black-market, faded gentility – then a somewhat brash and uncertain recovery. Wilson did do this, and it would be wrong to overlook his contribution to the new image of themselves English people acquired during the immediate post-war period. Wilson shows little interest in what goes on behind the public face of the period he is writing about. He is interested in what it looks like, as well as in what individuals in the privacy of their families feel like, but his gestures in the direction of how it works, as a social organism, are perfunctory.

I want to make clear this fact about Wilson's novels, because, in the past, attention to the social and historical aspects of his work has tended to obscure aspects of it that I consider to be more important. Only when we notice the extent to which Wilson is preoccupied with family relationships, from a position very close to that of the members of the families he is writing about, are we able to acquire some sort of insight into his moral evaluation of certain recurrent psychological attitudes. The same applies to the characteristic tone – which contrives to be evasive and corrective at the same time – by recourse to which he is able to give expression to these things.

In an excellent essay on the early fiction, Ian Scott-Kilvert* describes Wilson as a 'human killer'. He draws attention to the distinctively unpleasant effect of the satire on those whom it selects as its victims. Wilson's thrusts, says Scott-Kilvert, are anything but painless. 'They hurt, as they are intended to do, and not only hurt but degrade, and yet he is a writer who is emotionally involved with his victims.' Now this really is a most unusual way for satirical writing to operate, because, in spite of what we may unreflectively suppose, satire does not usually degrade. To degrade is to place the victim below the level at which justice can be administered; and justice, or at any rate the appearance of justice, is what satirists usually want us to suppose they are administering. To degrade, on the contrary, is to expose the victim to either pity or contempt – or both. That is what Scott-Kilvert says happens to Wilson's victims. 'It is difficult to rouse ourselves wholeheartedly against them. They yield to temptation so easily, betray themselves so inadvertently, in short are so obviously vulnerable, that the readers' feelings are divided between pity, amusement and contempt.' This is as true of Minnie and Flo, in 'Union Reunion', getting a spurious personal satisfaction out of the roles they played in young David's death, as it is of Margaret and Malcolm Tarrant in 'A Visit in Bad Taste', ruthlessly and self-righteously disencumbering themselves of responsibility for their disgraced brother Arthur.

What accounts for this satirical bias of Wilson's, in which the characters are caught in demeaning postures of vulgarity, pretentiousness and hypocrisy? Why is it that these people open their wounds so readily for Wilson's pen to slide into them? And what sort of surgeon or torturer deliberately probes an open wound?

---

* In 'Angus Wilson', *Review of English Literature*, I (1960) 42–53.

Where the victim exposes himself, exposes what we should expect to be his most secret and most private inadequacies, it seems sadistic to probe deeper. Mere observation is tactless enough. Hence the coincidence of pity and contempt at the spectacle of a degraded humanity. Amusement, too, of a sour, embarrassed sort.

I think the quality of the satire has a great deal to do with the fact that the people who are its victims are members of families. Unhappy families. We have it on the best authority that unhappy families are all different. But one way in which they are alike is in the awkwardness its separate members feel when they are forced into the sustained intimacies of family life. Wilson's characters usually feel this. The title alone of 'A Visit in Bad Taste' indicates the awful and awkward embarrassment felt by the Tarrants in the presence of their pathetic, child-molesting brother. Donald Carrington cannot bear the sounds of bustle and activity which wake him at six in the morning and remind him of his sickeningly possessive mother 'scurrying . . . like mice in the wainscotting' below. And, in 'Crazy Crowd', though the Cockshott family might like to see themselves as eccentric, amusing and, yes, crazy, the point is surely that, when an outsider is introduced into the household, even an outsider who is predisposed to be admiringly sympathetic, they are exposed as a collection of irresponsible, childish egotists without charm, grace, or even elementary hygiene.

'Crazy Crowd' is an unusual story for Wilson to have written, because the egotism of the individual Cockshotts immunises them from the embarrassment that usually flows from the proximity other Wilson households enforce on their members. More to the point, Wilson himself seems to react to his characters as if he were a member of the family to which they belong. And so he experiences a distaste for their manners, their habits of speech, their overworked idiosyncrasies and underrehearsed powers of discrimination, that a novelist who is less closely involved with his characters, in this 'family sense', would not feel. He is particularly sensitive to unwholesome aspects of their appearance. Spots, acne, blemishes of the skin, blackheads, are everywhere in Wilson's work. Wherever you look, you are likely to find a soiled pair of dentures gazing up from a dirty bowl, the spent flakes of a half-eaten sausage roll sneezed onto a greasy carpet. Observed in the behaviour of other people this is simply nasty. But within the bosom of your own family it is a source of acute embarrassment. The distaste evinced in the prose arises out of the author's complicity in all that he describes as degrading. The delinquencies of a family touch on every member of it. By imposing his own membership on each and every family he describes, Wilson feels that touch. His response is one of shame, distancing and contempt – in that order.

The most well known, and one of the best, of Wilson's short stories is the first he wrote, 'Raspberry Jam'. I should like to look at this story in detail, because there are brought together in it most of the themes, inclinations, oddities of mood and point of view, that I have been discussing more generally so far. Also Wilson has written very interestingly, and strangely, I think, about it in his literary autobiography, *The Wild Garden*. The strangeness of the story and the even greater strangeness of Wilson's commentary on it, tell us a great deal about the kind of writer Wilson is.

'Raspberry Jam' tells the story of a small boy, Johnnie, who takes refuge from his unloving and hypocritical middle-class parents in the house of two eccentric old sisters, the Miss Swindales. These old ladies are the daughters of gentlefolk. Although they have fallen on hard times they manage to maintain an air of gaiety and playfulness that is totally foreign to Johnnie's own parents. One of them, Miss Marian, is besotted by the memory of her admired father and will not hear a word spoken against him. The other, Miss Dolly, has been a great beauty and still fancies herself as such. From time to time they have behaved ridiculously. Both of them have spent some time in a mental institution. Nevertheless they possess a certain *joie de vivre*. In spite of their addiction to the bottle they provide entertaining and lively company for young Johnnie.

The story opens with a typical family get-together. Johnnie's aunt and uncle are paying a visit to the house and are being served malicious gossip about the Swindales by his mother. The selfishness and unimaginative conceit of the three adults is communicated entirely through the dialogue, and through our appreciation of the fact that what is being said is being said in Johnnie's presence. The rest of the family appears to have forgotten he is there. And it transpires that they are right to have forgotten, since, unbeknown to them or to us, Johnnie has taken himself off upstairs at some unspecified interval in their appalling conversation. So far the story reveals most of the features of Wilson's short fiction: a vivid picture of the hypocrisy and selfishness of adult human beings, self-exposed and self-condemned; an embarrassing sense of family intimacy and nastiness, registered from somewhere inside the family, and then pushed to a bearable distance by Wilson's fastidious but disgusted prose; and our sense of a healthy deflection from the norm in the person of the little boy, Johnnie, who keeps himself at a distance from the grown-ups, playing games alone in his room upstairs – and trying to keep out of his mind the horror of his last visit to the old ladies.

The horror arises out of Johnnie's witnessing of a terrible and cruel act inflicted by the Miss Swindales on a bullfinch they have caught stripping their raspberry canes. Driven to madness by the bird's depredations and angered by the fact that they will not be able to offer Johnnie home-made raspberry jam, they torture the bullfinch and, finally, put out its eyes with a pin. All of this occurs in Johnnie's presence, and he is not unnaturally appalled by it. Everything he admired and loved in the old ladies pales before this evidence of their lunatic cruelty and sadism. Yet, in spite of Johnnie's horror at what they have done, the old ladies are the nicest adults in the story. They have been driven to cruelty by the attitude of the rest of the villagers towards them, and by the fading of their hopes and ambitions in the course of time.

In *The Wild Garden* Wilson explains the torture of the bullfinch in terms that emphasise the fundamental goodness of the Swindale sisters. 'This act,' he says, 'though to the boy it is just an incredible horror, is in fact a culmination of rising paranoia produced in two simple, imaginative, generous old women by the narrow-minded malice, jealousy and frightened detestation that their originality has aroused in the village.' Throughout his commentary, Wilson plays down the horror of the treatment of the bird ('just an incredible horror'), which is gone into in harrowing detail in the actual story. Instead, he concentrates on the states of mind of the women who are responsible for it. When he wrote the story, he says, he saw the two old women 'as the embodiments of that saintliness which the mediocrity of the world seeks to destroy'. The killing of the bird (actually Wilson does not mention this; he says 'their craziness and their destruction of their young friend's peace of mind') is not their fault 'but that of the world which has failed to cherish them'. Since that time, however, Wilson has placed a different interpretation on what he wrote. Now he supposes that the story draws a comparison between the old ladies and the young boy, because all three of them (after all, the boy is thirteen) are trying to retain a childish innocence and ignorance in the face of realities which make this not merely undesirable, but a culpable act of self-deception. The result must be that they will 'inevitably destroy themselves and in all probability those that they love'.

Wilson is trying to explain that what he thought he wrote and what he actually wrote are two very different things. When he wrote, he thought he was describing 'true simplicity'. Now that he looks at what he wrote, he finds that he was exposing 'the falsity of preserved innocence or ignorance'. But it seems to me that, although discriminations of this kind are useful, and although we can agree with Wilson, even while unable to speculate about his motives at the time of writing, that what he wrote is what he now supposes he wrote, nevertheless there are features common to both accounts which remain deeply disturbing. Whatever the reasons were for what the old ladies did, there must have been a foundation of motive for the actual and prolonged act of torture which went deeper than any feelings they entertained about the hostile world around them. this would be the case whether they were saints or simpletons. In other words, the attribute of the saint or the simpleton must have been a less basic quality in them than a deep impulse to cruelty, an ability to continue to be cruel over a period of minutes, not seconds or split seconds, which they evinced in their torture of the bullfinch. In the story Wilson makes us feel this very strongly. We sense not merely its horror, but its disconnection from everything else about the two women that could account for their drunkenness or their rudeness or their unpleasantness to Johnnie. Elsewhere in Wilson's work we encounter gratuitous acts of violence and cruelty, and he has written interestingly on the problem of evil in the world and in the novel. In 'Raspberry Jam', however, Wilson simply presents the evidence and leaves us to try and make sense of it. When he himself tries to make sense of it in *The Wild Garden*, he makes any number of thoughtful and relevant observations, but none of them touch on the fundamental issue, which is not the innocence or ignorance, or saintliness, of the two sisters, but the inexplicable evil of their behaviour. In the face of this Wilson remains not

merely baffled but apparently uninterested. The word 'evil' is not
used at any point in Wilson's description of this incident.

Bernard Sands, the hero of Wilson's first novel, *Hemlock and After*
(1953), has little in common with most of the characters of the
short stories. The people amongst whom he moves, though, are
familiar. Celia Craddock's possessive attitude towards her son
Eric, for example, is similar to Mrs Carrington's attitude to
Donald in 'Mother's Sense of Fun'. Bill Pendlebury's parasitic
attachment to Bernard derives from several variations on the
same theme: Mr Nicholson's living off his son-in-law in 'Rex
Imperator', for example, or Maurice Legge's dependence on
Greta's money in 'What do Hippos Eat?' The subsidiary characters and relationships of *Hemlock and After* repeat those exposures
of greed, hypocrisy, irresponsibility and hysteria that were at the
centre of the short stories. Indeed, the first chapter, 'The Prophet
and the Locals', could well have started off as a short story. It is
cast in the typical mould Wilson had created for his first two
books, in which the distasteful characteristics of a group of people
are illuminated by the intrusion of someone who does not share
their particular kind of vulgarity and selfishness.

Looking back to 'Fresh Air Fiend', however, we might recognise something of Bernard Sands in the figure of Professor Searle.
He is different from almost all the other characters in the short
stories on account of his moral scruples and what follows from
them: his hesitancy in judging and acting, particularly where his
relationship with his wife is concerned. Discussing Professor
Searle at the beginning of this chapter I said that, though he
differs from other people in the rest of the stories, he does seem to
share something of the sensibility of their author, in so far as his
involvement with his family is concerned, and his detachment
from any tendency to positive moral evaluation of what goes on
inside it. Bernard shares Professor Searle's tentativeness and
detachment where judgement of human motive is concerned. His
most positive commitments to other human beings are not what
they seem to be. There is a vacuum at their centre of which
Bernard becomes more and more aware. But nature abhors a
vacuum, and so do the ethical predilections of a humanist
novelist, or a humanist in a novel. When such a vacuum is
discovered, however, we are given to understand that what rushes

in to fill it is not necessarily, or even probably, anything that is itself ethical, anything that is likely to satisfy the conscience of such a man as Bernard or such a novelist as Angus Wilson.

At the beginning of the novel Bernard appears to be a much more positive, practical and self-satisfied person than I have been suggesting. His plans for the opening of a writers' hostel at Vardon Hall have just come to fruition, and the first thing we see of him is his delight at receiving confirmation of this fact in a letter from the Treasury. This informs him that all of his suggestions about how the hostel should be run have been accepted by the Government and the Civil Service departments concerned. Bernard is exultant at having met authority 'at its most impersonal level' and succeeded in having impressed his will on it in the service of an outlook on life which is basically opposed to all it stands for.

Critics of Wilson have compared Vardon Hall with James's Great Good Place or (a more immediate and perhaps more dangerous influence) E. M. Forster's Howards End. It is a place artificially cut off from the rest of society, an experimental station of the human spirit. In it, notions of freedom, conscience and moral sensitivity can be put into practice without interference from external authority. Wilson is fond of these artificial societies within society. He likes to speculate about their internal viability; also about how they are likely to respond to the inevitable infection they will receive from outside pressures. This is what happens to Dr Leacock's wildlife reserve in *The Old Men at the Zoo*. Lord Godmanchester brings it into being and then destroys it in order to further his own political ambitions. Andredaswood, David Parker's nursery garden in *The Middle Age of Mrs Eliot*, is another experiment in withdrawal from a wider society. Finally Hamo Langmuir's plans to improve the 'hopeless lands' of India out of money from the Rapson Trust in *As If By Magic* carry with them some of the ambiguous idealism and humanist contradictions that infect the projects for Vardon Hall and its successors. But in *Hemlock and After* a succession of blows to Bernard Sands's self-respect and to his trust in the soundness of humanist instincts that have given it its character is what it takes to destroy his belief in the place, and, eventually, to convert it into something quite different from anything he had intended it should be.

The first blow to Bernard's belief in himself comes some little time after his appearance at James's cocktail party. It is

administered by his daughter Elizabeth, when she confronts him
with her knowledge of his homosexuality. But, before his dis-
closure, contradictions in Bernard's humanism have already been
suggested by James himself. James is an unreliable, and unsympathetic witness. Even so he possesses several insights into his
father's character which go deeper than he himself is aware. He
accuses his father of self-deception in defending Mrs Curry, an
unpleasant and unpopular neighbour, from the gossipy accusations of his guests at the party:

> He and Sonia were perfectly well aware of the vulgar stupidity
> of the greater part of these local people, quite as well aware as
> his father, but they were capable of a little civilized tolerance. It
> was typical of his father's endless self-deception. All this
> universal understanding, this Dostoyevskian emotional
> brotherhood, and, at bottom, he had nothing but utter
> contempt for nine-tenths of humanity; as for the other tenth he
> probably hated their guts for not being susceptible to his
> patronage.

This is the first of several occasions on which it is suggested that
Bernard feels nothing but contempt for other people. Perhaps
Bernard's humanism is more a device for evading the truth about
his own life than a means of understanding the truth about the lives
of others. Deep inside him there is a damaging ignorance –
ignorance about the real nature of his relationships with other
people, and ignorance at the deepest level about his own motives
and his own nature. We have seen that in 'Raspberry Jam' one of
Wilson's main preoccupations was with the dangerous innocence,
and ignorance, of both Johnnie and the old ladies. We saw to what
horrors such ignorance could lead – though, as I have argued, we
did not see how the connection between ignorance and cruelty,
the central themes of that story, was forged. In *The Wild Garden*
Wilson advances the view that the quality Bernard Sands shares
with the other two central figures of his first three novels – Gerald
Middleton and Meg Eliot – is this ignorance of their real natures.
He goes on to say that they all, in their different ways, seek to
conceal from themselves the fact that they are so ignorant. And
they do so successfully for as long as they are able to circumvent 'a
habit of rigorous self-inquiry and a trained observation of . . .
other people' which is second nature to them. What also accounts

for their failure is a suspicious tendency to relax when called upon to contemplate aspects of their own personalities which they sense would go better undisclosed. In so deceiving themselves, Wilson says, 'They are practising the final hypocrisies of the educated and the worldly.'

Bernard's suspicion that a flaw exists at the centre of his humanist approach to life is intensified through a succession of discoveries about his relationships with other people, shortly before the opening of Vardon Hall. But the incident that brings it into clear and appalling focus occurs quite by accident one evening, when he is waiting to meet his ex-boyfriend Terence in Leicester Square. Here he is approached by a young man in a mackintosh who makes rather crude homosexual advances to him. Bernard turns away in disgust, despising himself for being the object of such an approach, which he considers vulgar and 'second rate'. He has just left his club in the company of Charles Murley, a high-ranking civil servant, whose acceptance of power and habitual exercise of authority Bernard has been weighing in the balance of his humanist beliefs and finding wanting. Now he envies Charles his exclusion from the world to which his own curiosity and claims to imaginative freedom have allowed him access. In the earlier parts of the novel this world have been represented by Mrs Curry, Sherman Winter, Celia Craddock and Louie Randall – all very different people, but all 'second rate failures' in Bernard's opinion. It is a fact that the people to whom Bernard refers here are as contemptible as he believes they are. However, now that they have been joined by this new apparition of nastiness and vulgarity, Bernard allows his contempt for them to assume a more sinister character: they are 'stagnant little pools' beneath Charles's notice, from which 'mists and vapours arise which circle round his head like . . . bogies in the night . . . like Hitler, like . . .'. It is at this point that his reflections are broken into by a police officer, who asks him to give evidence of the young man's importuning. Of course he refuses, but his response to the policeman's request and the young man's terror in the face of it, is violent and, perhaps, unexpected. Certainly, in spite of all his earlier self-doubts and self-accusations, he does not expect this of himself:

> it was neither compassion nor fear that had frozen Bernard. He could only remember the intense, the violent excitement that he

had felt when he saw the hopeless terror in the young man's face, the tension with which he had watched for the disintegration of a once confident human being. He had been ready to join the hounds in the kill then. It was only when he had turned to the detective that his sadistic excitement had faded, leaving him with normal disgust. But what had brought him to his senses, he asked himself, and, to his horror, the only answer he could find was that in the detective's attitude of somewhat officious but routine duty there was no response to his own hunter's thrill. Truly, he thought, he was not at one with those who exercised proper authority. A humanist, it would seem was more at home with the wielders of the knout and the rubber truncheon.

Several critics of *Hemlock and After* have found this incident contrived. My own reaction to it is more positive and admiring. The description of the event itself, as well as the representation of Bernard's later broodings and anxieties about it, is powerfully written. There is a precision, an excitement in the prose that seems to well up from sources deep in Wilson's psyche. The horror and bewilderment Bernard feels when he is made to face the fact of his enjoyment of the young man's terror are rendered with a hallucinatory accuracy. The transition from 'normal disgust' to 'sadistic excitement' is described without tender qualifications or evasive excuses. There is no similar occasion in either of Wilson's later novels, before the fantasy of *The Old Men at the Zoo*. Where incidents involving cruelty or sadism do occur – such as the one in which Yves Houdet forces his mother and her companion to re-enact their concentration-camp exercises in *Anglo-Saxon Attitudes* – they do not involve the complicity of the main character in the same way as Bernard's complicity is involved here.

But why is he an accomplice? What has caused his sadistic enjoyment of the suffering of others? Wilson insists – the whole novel is based on his insistence – that what Bernard feels here is what all of us feel or are capable of feeling, under the polite disguise of whatever beliefs we have consciously espoused. When Bernard looks back over the events of the preceding weeks he sees the behaviour of all the 'second rate' people he has become involved with as not merely unpleasant and vulgar, but evil: 'Bernard . . . saw all the fragments, the threads of evil which had been weaving in and out of his thoughts . . . worked together before his eyes, in the hard bright colours of the afternoon sunlight, into a huge tapestry of obscene horror.' Then, more damagingly, he discovers that the 'little patterns of hostility, or violence, and of cruelty' that he had thought belonged only to the people he disliked and found contemptible, actually applied to himself:

> it was not an external picture of concerted enemies that he saw, but the reflection of his own guilt, of his newly discovered hypocrisy, his long-suppressed lusts. Whatever happened here, whatever collapsed of his humanistic ideals, whatever disaster to those he loved, seemed to him now the price of all that had been revealed in his thrill at the arrest of man's horror.

What Bernard is forced to accept, as a result of his experience in Leicester Square, is the 'dual nature of all human action'. *All* human action. And in *all* human beings – humanist like himself, or infantile and anarchic like Hubert Rose. Basically there is no difference. That is what Bernard is convinced of as a result of this incident. And that appears to be Wilson's conviction too. But need such a conviction follow from what Bernard has discovered about himself in the earlier part of the novel, from what Elizabeth, Bill Pendlebury, Terence, and Celia Craddock have told him and reveal to him there? In other words, do the feelings Bernard experiences as a result of his encounters with the homosexual and the policeman follow naturally and necessarily from what he has already learned from (at the time) less radically damaging though severely mortifying discoveries about himself in the course of his normal life at Vardon?

What has Bernard learnt in these last few weeks when he has been fighting to secure Vardon Hall? Several things, and none of them complimentary. From Elizabeth he has learnt the extent to which his homosexual relationships have alienated him from his family. Also that his suppressed homosexuality before this period probably goes some way towards explaining his wife's withdrawal and neurosis. Other people force him to recognise other ways in which his behaviour is capable of being represented in a less flattering light than he has been accustomed to view it. All this is honestly exhibited by Wilson. His representation of the workings of Bernard's conscience, its complicated mixture of revelation and evasion, is subtle and penetrating. But does it lead us to the conclusion that Bernard not merely is, but must be, capable of the evil he experiences in himself at that moment in Leicester Square? Once again there is a passage in *The Wild Garden* which helps to clarify what in the novel remains problematic. Discussing his work at an inter-services organisation deep in the countryside during the war, Wilson describes how he fell in love for the first time – at the age of thirty-three. In the course of his love affair Wilson 'painfully learned that I had far too little capacity for anything except demanding in such a relationship'. In a slightly later passage, writing about the same relationship, he goes further than to confess merely that his love was exclusively 'demanding'. He accuses himself of a capacity for hatred and cruelty that reminds us very forcefully of what Bernard Sands discovered about himself in Leicester Square:

> Bathed in the glow of the cosiness of my earlier life, I had always thought of myself as a person of unusual gentleness and a natural liking for other human beings. I now learnt that I could hate intensely, if not for long periods, and that I was capable of cruelty, indeed addicted to it, particularly towards those who attracted me most strongly. Finally I was forced to think that my sophistication, easy sociability and worldly tolerance had been a form of carefully protected ignorance of life that had fooled myself as well as many around me.

All the terms of reference are familiar. There are references to Wilson's own 'ignorance of life' concealing itself beneath a disguise of 'worldly tolerance' and 'easy sociability' – the things James detests in his father at the cocktail party with which *Hemlock and After* begins. And the emphasis on 'cosiness' in his description of his earlier life is striking because 'cosiness' is always synonymous with evil in Wilson's work. It is used to describe Mrs Curry, one of the two most hideous exemplars of evil in *Hemlock and After*, and it is a word, like 'sweetness', which she herself often uses to camouflage the real cruelty and perversion that lie at the centre of her vision of life. To return to the passage from *The Wild Garden*, Wilson goes on to confess how he was not only capable of acts of hatred and cruelty, but actually became 'addicted' to cruelty, 'particularly to those who attracted me most strongly'. Here is an astonishingly honest testimony to the 'dual nature of all human action' that Bernard had been forced to face up to and that

Wilson is seeking to convince us is, in this particular form, a fact of life which Bernard and all the rest of us ignore at our peril.

The same movement from acknowledgement of human error to confession of personal evil and corruption is repeated in his address to the public at the inauguration of the Vardon Hall project. Wilson does not repeat this speech verbatim, except for one or two sentences. But its general character is suggested by his summary of what followed Bernard's appeal for a new humanism. 'And yet', he goes on,

> Motives were so difficult, so double, so much hypocrisy might spring from guilt, so much benevolence from fear to use power, so much kindness overlay cruelty, so much that was done didn't matter. If the scheme failed, if the young writer ceased to write, it was of small account in time; better failure than deception, better defeat than victory where motive was wrong. He seemed quite unable to leave the subject of motive, so that the more attentive of his audience got the impression that they were involved in a discussion of some mysterious crime.

Leaving aside the Leicester Square incident for the moment, we can understand the reasons for Bernard's suspicion of motives. His treatment of Ella, of Terence and of Eric affords plenty of evidence of his own ambiguous motives. Apparently eager to promote their happiness through a genial interference in their lives, he has actually made use of them to satisfy his own selfish demands. It requires the exercise of a sophisticated and tenacious conscience to bring this to Bernard's attention but, Wilson is claiming, and I think his claim carries conviction here, the kind of manipulation of other people under the guise of doing them good is consistent with the possession of such a conscience. Where the drift of Bernard's confession seems to exceed anything in his past that might help to account for it, however, is in the equation of duplicities of motive with the commission of a 'crime'. For Bernard, evil is a necessary part of the world, a necessary part of his own and everyone else's psychological make-up. Humanism is a subtle distraction from the truth of this, an evasion of the reality of human evil. Any honest appraisal of human motive must take into account the fact of evil and the necessity of violence:

> 'No culture that reposes on resistence and strength alone can survive', Bernard urged. 'No culture that doesn't accept its own

decadence is real. I trust I shall not be convicted of false *mystique* if I dwell on the sweetness of the forces that oppose us, on the renewed life that may come from capitulation to their primitive power.'

What follows from Bernard's expression of these views, as regards his own behaviour, is logical and comprehensible. The only course of action for a humanist to follow is one of quiescence. Or, since quiescence may come very close to acquiescence, it might be possible to act positively, though with intense self-distrust and circumspection, in an attempt to restrict where possible the largely inevitable and damaging effects of an infected will.

Bernard is able to put this view of life into practice in only one particular case before he dies. That is when he takes steps to prevent Hubert Rose from interfering with the young girl Mrs Curry has procured for him. In taking the decision to do this Bernard finds himself doing what he had never been able to do before. He deliberately wounds another human being at his most vulnerable point, takes brutal advantage of the weakness of another person. For Hubert is weak, in spite of his cynical profession of inhumanity and decadence. The first thing Bernard notices when he comes to see Hubert is the 'pathos' of his setting, the bareness, the functional barrenness of his inner sanctum: 'Only the desolate moonlit horror of a single Samuel Palmer summed up in coherent statement the world of its owner – the empty hopelessness of a desert universe, which had almost wound down to its end.' Hubert's despair of the world, his consciousness that he lives 'on the level below good and evil', leads him to presuppose Bernard's complicity in what he is doing. He cannot see the difference between his enjoyment of Elsie Black and Bernard's enjoyment of Eric Craddock. They are both illegal acts, both examples of an older man's taking advantage of the innocence of youth.

Some critics, notably A. O. J. Cockshutt,* share Hubert's incomprehension. Bernard, however, tries to convince Hubert that there is a fundamental difference; that, though both of them are 'disciples of negation', he, Bernard, cannot separate his despair from his compassion. 'If your despair does not lead you to compassion,' he says, 'then I can only limit its field of devasta-

---

* 'Favoured Sons: The Moral World of Angus Wilson', *Essays in Criticism*, IX, no. 1 (1959).

tion.' He insists that there are 'two despairs', and that the fact that
they recognise each other's failures gives Hubert 'no brotherly
claim on my acquiescence'. I think there is some point in the
distinction Bernard makes between himself and Hubert Rose, and
that Bernard's recognition of his capacity for evil does limit the
extent to which he is shown to exercise it in damaging and harmful
ways. The motive might remain corrupt, but to act as though it
were not is likely to prove effective in the world outside the self,
so long as the corrupt man can live with the knowledge of his
corruption and not despair. Bernard comes very close to despair
but he is still able to open the Hall, and he is still able to recognise
that, for example, 'Eric and Terence needed guidance no less
because he now distrusted his motives for giving it.' Above all he is
able to prevent Hubert Rose from molesting Elsie Black. To go
further, however, and expose Mrs Curry and her evil establishment to the full rigours of the law, Bernard is not prepared to do.
And not merely because her knowledge of the weakness of his own
position deters him. The reasons are more inward, more conson-
ant with his new distrust of his motives: 'I had to save that
innocent, but I do not want to take vengeance. How do I know
where the action may lead or who it may hurt far beyond my
control?'

Shortly after making this confession to Ella, Bernard has a
heart attack and dies. The actions he was loathe to perform are
performed by Ella, who has undergone a somewhat miraculous
transformation of a result of her knowledge of Bernard's distress.
Her interference can be judged in a variety of ways, not all of them
flattering. But the main point is that it is unlikely Bernard himself
would have interfered at all. This is not because of his self-
distrust, or even self-disgust – of the kind he had already
experienced before his encounter with the young homosexual. It is
because of his knowledge that the springs of his action are
poisoned with sadistic violence, and that this means that his
motives cannot be trusted and that the effects of whatever actions
he performs, except in such very obvious cases as Hubert Rose's,
are unlikely to be desirable. This makes his end very much more
pessimistic than the ends of his humanist successors, who do not
experience this kind of shock to their most private visions of
themselves. Both Gerald Middleton and Meg Eliot learn things
about themselves which they never expected to learn or sought to
discover. But what they learn releases them into useful activity.

Their liberal pretensions appear to belong to less fundamentally vicious personalities than Bernard's ever did.

I have referred to A. O. J. Cockshutt's essay on *Hemlock and After*. Examining this novel, the critic is much preoccupied with what he takes to be Wilson's indulgent attitude towards Bernard Sands. Looking at some of the parallel cases to Bernard's (Celia Craddock's possessiveness over Eric, Mrs Curry's and Sherman Winter's various perversions of innocence, Bill Pendlebury's inferiority as a writer) Cockshutt notices how 'the fire of the reader's moral criticism is naturally drawn by each of these more palpable targets in turn. It is very natural for the reader to slide from "Look how much better Bernard is than X" to "Look how very good Bernard is"; and it is this slide which we are apparently asked to make.' This approach to the novel has some truth in it, but I think it does less than justice to the insight Wilson has achieved into Bernard's moral duplicities. Particularly into his almost paralysing experience of sadistic impulses that are so closely related to his championship of the weak and the inadequate. This was the point I made about Bernard's confrontation of Hubert Rose. Nevertheless there is, I think, an ambiguous note in Wilson's final comment on Bernard, and I am not sure how far this weakens the general impact made by his character or how far it confirms my view that, overall, his character is presented with unwavering honesty, but questionable consistency (I am referring to the connection Wilson discovers between Bernard's ignorance and his sadism). How we understand Wilson's final comment on Bernard makes a great deal of difference to our assessment of the whole of *Hemlock and After*. It might also make a difference to the way we approach his next two novels, *Anglo-Saxon Attitudes* and *The Middle Age of Mrs Eliot*, because a similar ambiguity attends the representation of the central characters there also.

The last word on Bernard is spoken by Ella, to their daughter on a journey by aeroplane from England to the South of France. Aeroplanes are important in Wilson's novels. Both *Anglo-Saxon Attitudes* and *The Middle Age of Mrs Eliot* also end with a journey by aeroplane. In Gerald's and Meg's cases perhaps, in Ella's certainly, the journey represents a movement away from responsibilities which may or may not have been fulfilled (Ella certainly assumes hers would have been fulfilled). What Ella says to

Elizabeth about her father is puzzling. Elizabeth has advanced
the view that it seems strange Bernard's books will have such a
great influence 'when in life he got so little done'; ' "My dear,"
Ella replied, "doing doesn't last, even if one knows what one's
doing, which one usually doesn't. But Bernard *was* something to
people – lots of people – me, for example – and that has its effect in
the end, I think." '

What effect has Bernard's 'being' had on Ella's 'doing'? It has
galvanised her into activity over the Vardon Hall arrangements,
by getting her to persuade Charles Murley to take Bernard's place
on the Committee. It has made her persuade Bill Pendlebury to go
to the police about Mrs Curry, which has the effect of putting Mrs
Curry behind bars and providing Bill with the money he needs to
live off whilst he writes his books. It has also resulted in the arrest
of Hubert Rose and Ron Wrigley; the opening-up of a relationship
between Terence and Elizabeth; and the promotion of Bernard's
plans for Eric Craddock. Few of these achievements, however, are
as desirable as they seem. Charles's administrative flair gets the
better of his humanism and Vardon Hall becomes a bureaucratic
plaything. Bill Pendlebury's books are no good. Mrs Curry is
released after two years and makes the most of the contacts she
has made inside to expand her services to lonely gentlemen when
she gets out. Ron Wrigley seems to get on well in prison too.
Meanwhile Hubert Rose commits suicide and Terence breaks up
his relationship with Elizabeth. This might be good for both of
them. The only unambiguously satisfactory result of Ella's
activities is the new life Eric Craddock is able to live. All the same,
this is much less than Ella had hoped for, and to suppose
otherwise is yet another form of self-deception. Perhaps she
realises this. Wilson surely does. That is why, after she has spoken
to Elizabeth, he makes her turn to the window of the plane and, we
are told, 'it was really easier to concentrate on the clouds moving
above and below like great golden snowdrifts'.

So Ella's achievements on her husband's behalf, the expression
of his being in her doing, have come to very much less than Ella
suggests to Elizabeth. The weaknesses of Bernard's humanism
continue to show through even where that humanism is enacted
by someone who is less inhibited by the flaws in her character than
Bernard was. And, if we trace back the deficiencies of Ella's doing
to the kind of being she attributed to Bernard, then we are unlikely
to go as far as Cockshutt in emphasising Wilson's special and

incomprehensible affection for his hero. The tone in which Ella speaks of him is very much at variance with aspects of his character which have given rise to it. At the end of this novel, almost all the successes of the characters are tinged with failure, or are on their way to being transformed into failures. Bernard has achieved little, either by himself or through Ella. The deficiencies of his character and the limitations of his humanism have both been emphasised at the expense of anything more indulgent, or more morally consoling.

It would be tedious to offer the same amount of detail about the lives of Gerald Middleton and Meg Eliot as I have given about Bernard Sands. Both of them suffer from some variant of the ignorance Bernard discovers in himself, as Wilson makes clear in *The Wild Garden*. Gerald's inability to meet the world honestly and directly on its own terms has been caused by two blunders he made when he was a young man and which have coloured his attitude to life ever since. One of these blunders has ruined his professional life as a historian. Though in many respects he has been outwardly successful, his belief in the integrity of his scholarship has been undermined by what was almost certainly a fraud in which he had played a small part many years ago. The other blunder has to do with his private life. Years ago Gerald broke off his relationship with the only person he ever loved in a mature and adult way, and married instead a sentimental Danish beauty called Ingeborg. His marriage to Inge has proved a disaster. But since she has borne his three children, for whom he feels responsible, he cannot leave her. Even when he resumes his relationship with Dollie Stokesay (Gilbert's widow), and even when Inge's apparently altruistic but actually selfish interference in that relationship results in its termination, he cannot summon up the will to break with his wife. Or at any rate he has not been able to do so by the time the novel begins. Then, in the course of a dismally unsuccessful Christmas party at Inge's house, Gerald has a change of heart. Memories of the past stirred up by what he hears there push him back into life, and provide him with the opportunity of making much more effective contributions to the two worlds (of family and scholarship) that he values than Bernard and Ella Sands were ever allowed to make.

Meg Eliot, at the opening of Wilson's next novel, is a very much more exuberant and active character than Gerald. She is a vigorous chairman of the Committee for Aid to the Elderly, a ceaseless adviser on the problems of her own and her husband's friends, and also (a superficial link with Gerald Middleton, this) a collector of antique china. But her busyness and outward show of self-confidence conceal a profound ignorance of her own nature. The danger note is sounded most clearly when Meg draws attention to the '*cosy* self satisfaction' (emphasis added) with which she prides herself on the range of her interests and the sensible combination of public good and private pleasure that they exhibit. When her husband is killed she is forced to re-examine her past, and come to terms with what it actually was rather than what she had assumed it to be. Armed with a new self-confidence, she goes out to play an active part in the world. Like Gerald Middleton she has overcome self-delusion and depression and won through to a life of limited but effective usefulness, both to herself and to society at large.

I have said that I do not want to go into a great deal of detail about these heroes of Wilson's mid-term fiction. There are two aspects of them, however, that connect in interesting ways with what I have already written about Bernard Sands, and I should like to draw the reader's attention to these. The first is that neither Gerald Middleton nor Meg Eliot ever experiences anything remotely similar to what Bernard experiences in Leicester Square. True, Gerald's evasion of his responsibility to his family includes his refusal to believe (what he really knows) that on one occasion far in the past Inge deliberately burnt the hand of her favourite child, Kay. What Gerald chooses to ignore here is a covert sadism in his wife's character which helps to explain other kinds of interference in the lives of her husband and children which at first sight seem merely stupid and uncharitable. But there is all the difference in the world between Gerald's averting his eyes from this kind of knowledge about someone else, and Bernard's ignorance of his own corrupt nature. Both are guilty of evasion, but what it is in themselves about which they are evasive is quite different. Similarly with Meg Eliot. The shooting-down of her husband is an evil and random act. It reveals an arbitrariness, a lack of justice in the workings of the world, which humanists like Meg find it difficult to understand. In fact she has been in a sense prepared for what happens at the airport by her experience in the 'plane as it crossed the desert before landing. There she had felt herself 'lost' in a totally meaningless landscape. She was 'completely and absolutely bereft of all that made sense of her life, forsaken, and ready for annihilation'. But for Meg the vacuum remains a vacuum, until what happens at the airport produces unforeseen consequences. Meg is not at any time tempted to behave with deliberate cruelty, as Bernard was in Leicester Square. The cruelty and viciousness remain outside. What is inside might have the effect of creating unhappiness and pain, but, as Wilson would argue, intention and motive are everything here. And, though Meg Eliot's motives may be selfish and trivial and uncharitable, they are never vicious.

This leads naturally to the other aspect of these two novels which differentiates them sharply from *Hemlock and After*. For some reason, which may have to do with their failure to share Bernard's sadistic impulse, Gerald and Meg do succeed in making something of their lives. They do manage to pierce through the miasma of self-satisfaction or self-distrust, or self-satisfaction leading to self-distrust, which would otherwise have stifled their ambitions and led them into failure and despair. Gerald leaves Inge, he forms a new and unpossessive relationship with Dollie, he recommences work on his life of Edward the Confessor, and he accepts the chairmanship of the historical association. Meg uses her qualifications as a typist and a secretary to make a life for herself in politics and business.

The trouble with these two successful adaptations to reality is that the route by which they are reached is unconvincingly described. Wilson is clearly determined to give substance to the (ambiguously) up-beat ending of *Hemlock and After*. He wanted to show how people who had suffered from the same general debility as Bernard Sands could, in a real and responsible way, overcome that debility. He wanted to show how they could win through to an honest self-appraisal and thence to involvement in some kind of activity which will give scope to their new found belief in themselves, their resurgent humanism. But the devices he chose to convince about this process of recovery are either transparently artificial or suspiciously over-subtle. In *Anglo-Saxon Attitudes*, Gerald's determination to act decisively over the Melpham fraud and the failure of his marriage arises extraordinarily suddenly from mere reminiscences. It is true that the reminiscences occupy almost half of the novel. But they are reminiscences about facts of his past life which Gerald always knew about, and which nothing that has happened at Inge's party can be said to have radically changed. In *The Middle Age of Mrs Eliot*, Meg's awakening to a new life follows her long stay with her brother David at Andredas-wood. I want to look at her experience there in more detail below. But for the purposes of my present argument I want to insist that the environment within which Meg undergoes her change of character, and the experiences there which cause that change of character to take the form it does, are highly artificial. Of course neither of these things means that the change must be unconvincing. Nevertheless the combination of them does have the effect of making Meg into a very special case, much more so than anything in her life before her return to David would have led us to expect. So there are very great obstacles in the way of Wilson's success in convincing us of Gerald's and Meg's change of heart. It seems that escape from depression and sterile self-disgust is difficult to achieve even where the peculiar circumstances that accounted for Bernard's admitted failure in this direction do not apply.

This approach to *The Middle Age of Mrs Eliot* has omitted any detailed account of Meg's life with David at Andredaswood. It is important that this omission should be made good, because the scenes in which David and Meg work out their personal salvations bring together many of the preoccupations Wilson is habitually drawn to, and they expose certain oddities in those preoccupations which require some looking at. I have already suggested how the garden at Andredaswood fits into a pattern of societies within societies that we see taking up a great deal of space in several of Wilson's other novels. Wilson's interest in families is narrowed here to an exhaustive analysis of a brother–sister relationship. The sister, though widowed, is childless, and the brother is a practising homosexual whose partner is either dying or dead during the period in which the events of the novel take place. David Parker represents an alternative style of humanism from that of previous Wilson heroes. It is a humanism founded much more deliberately on disengagement from the world than we have seen up to now. Indeed what David stands for, though it goes by the name of humanism, is the diametrical opposite of everything Bernard Sands, Gerald Middleton and Meg Eliot have been struggling to achieve.

David's most complete exposition of his views is offered to Mrs Paget after her son's funeral:

I think that passivity [he says] – I don't say quietism because
that has religious connotations – is an entire way of living. . . .
I'm not saying that the passive way of living is an absolute good
right at all times of history. . . . Only in ages like the present
one, where violence and self-expression and complication of
motive have become so great that we need a *détente*. It's the
commonplace of the newspapers when they talk of the cold war.
But I believe this disengagement should take place inside all of
us. We need a simmering down of human personality, of human
achievement too if you like, in order that we can start up again.
Otherwise all will be lost in the boiling over.

Later he talks of keeping alive 'on the simmering level'. He
recommends a life of 'Martha daily duties' in which people will
lower their aspirations deliberately in order to maintain an
undynamic equilibrium. What Bernard and Gerald most feared –
the ambiguously motivated interference in other people's lives – is
to be prevented not by purging the motives or (if that's possible, as
Bernard believes) evaluating with utmost moral scruple the likely
consequences of any proposed course of action, but by almost
total withdrawal. In view of the mess Bernard got into as a result
of his own spectacular *and* tentative interferences, and the mess
Gerald got out of only at the expense of the happiness of a lot of
other people, we are inclined to ask ourselves whether this is not
an attitude to life Wilson comes close to endorsing. It is a fact that
those by-and-large admirable characters who use their authority
carefully, but without undue exercise of conscience – characters
such as Charles Murley in *Hemlock and After* or Sir Edgar Iffley in
Anglo-Saxon Attitudes – are conspicuously absent here. The novel
changes, with David's appearance in it, from being a novel of
social comedy and humanist anguish to one where the postures of
ambition, competition and egotism are played out against a
background of extreme moral alternatives. This imposes a heavy
duty on Meg Eliot to demonstrate, in her own untheoretical way,
how the values of such earlier more ambitious humanists as
Bernard Sands and Gerald Middleton might compete with this
new quietism.

In my view Meg has an uphill struggle. There is something
about the way David's life at Andredaswood is described that
makes it very difficult to adopt a critical attitude towards it. At
first the timidity, the lack of vitality seems undesirable. The

details of David's and Gordon's life together sometimes appear absurd. For example, we learn that one of the ways they have put into practice their beliefs has been to produce books which are deliberately innocuous – 'their very insipidity was their value; they pretended to nothing'. It is hard to take this kind of thing seriously. Still, the cogency and fervour of David's argument makes us do so. Even this sort of apparently silly contrivance is hedged about with so many reservations and qualifications that we have difficulty getting through to a position where we are able to make a simple judgement. The trouble is that David is so preternaturally aware of all the subtle evasions involved in this behaviour that any criticism we might choose to make about his conduct is almost certain to have been anticipated by him. What Wilson said about the earlier heroes and about Meg in *The Wild Garden*, that their concealment from themselves about their ignorance about life 'has to be subtle because it must deceive a habit of rigorous self-inquiry' (etc.), is doubly true of David. So true that neither he, nor (I submit) we, are able to get round that sublety to acquire a clear and unambiguous understanding of the nature of his ignorance. The ignorance either does not exist at all, or it is so profound that it has sunk beneath a level where anybody, including David, can detect it.

The passages describing Gordon's death provide many examples of David's subtlety about these matters. This is a very interesting part of the novel, because it tries to deal with an area of human experience – our attitude to the dying – which writers are notoriously bad at describing. Perhaps because, for understandable reasons, we are most of us bad at facing up to this kind of experience with much competence in real life. In Wilson's novel, David's relationship with Gordon makes his ability to deal with it more difficult in some ways, easier in others. The total honesty with which they have treated each other throughout their life together makes it impossible for David to disguise the real facts of Gordon's suffering, and the certainty of his death. Also his attachment to a life 'encompassed by simple immediate duties and reactions – an ordered present' does not allow him to dramatise or artificially to heighten in any way the circumstances of his friend's dying. For 'an ordered present demanded at least the fiction of an immediate future with simple duties and recreations to be planned. Only such a life, he had come to believe, could allow one to cross the shapeless tracks of human existence with grace and with gentleness'. David cannot pretend to himself that he does not have an immediate future, and it has to be attended to. On the other hand David reaps the benefits of Gordon's complementary honesty, which happens in his case to coincide with a belief in Christian redemption. This affords Gordon some real comfort – a comfort which David cannot share. Nevertheless the fact that it ameliorates his friend's suffering ameliorates his own, up to a point. It is an accidental bonus that has nothing intrinsically to do with both men's humanistic beliefs.

As usual, David is aware of this fact. As usual, he has anticipated our criticism and met with an acknowledgement of the unsolicited advantage the situation affords him. He is also sharply aware of the way his rather distanced compassion for Gordon might be in danger of sliding to self-congratulation, a smug satisfaction at his ability to rise above his friend's tragic circumstances. He blocks any tendency in this direction by continuing to exercise his powers of judgement, by refusing to sentimentalise Gordon's character merely because he is being forced to submit to a condition which tempts to sympathy – often at the expense of a real understanding of the person on whose behalf that sympathy has been evoked. David is unassailably scrupulous, incontrovertibly subtle, in his rejection of this temptation:

> He had wished then, more than at any time he could remember, that he were able to say, I observe, I don't judge. But this sentimentalism, that passed as a wide and deep love of humanity, as the gentle wisdom taught by the years, was surely the negation of real respect for men. It would never do, least of all where respect and love were involved. Where you respected and loved, you esteemed, you judged. If these self-styled adult 'observers' simply meant that judgement should not impair one's love, they spoke in platitudes; if the love was deep enough, no judgement would impair it.

'In any case,' he says, 'he had long felt that the patronage, the godlikeness implied in this sort of compassion from above was far more displeasing than the action of judging.' In the face of this kind of self-analysis, our own judgement is in danger of being suspended. How can we object to the behaviour of a man who has counted whatever objection we might like to make, long before it ever occurred to us to make it? David's assessment of his own character, and his adaptation of his conduct to make good any defects he has discovered, is always at least two steps ahead of our own. There is something positively Jamesian in David's exposure, and correction, of his motives.

It was with relief as well as surprise that I opened the pages of *The Wild Garden* again and saw that Wilson agreed that something was wrong. Wilson's discussion of David's character, and his beliefs, is startling and dismissive. His suspicion of David and all he stands for is emphatic, even intemperate. So much so that I am inclined to ask myself whether the case against David is as clearly made out in the novel as Wilson assumes it is in his commentary. As usual, however, there are ambiguities in the commentary, ambiguities of which Wilson is well aware, which leave one uncertain about the depth of his disenchantment with the experiment at Andredaswood.

Wilson begins by pointing out the pun on the word 'nursery'. When he reflected on Meg's regression, after her breakdown, to a '*cosy* and comforting childhood relationship' (emphasis added) with her brother, the phrase 'back to the nursery' came to mind. And this feeling that the garden nursery was also as David used it, a children's nursery, stayed with him during the writing of the Andredaswood chapters of the novel. It is important we realise that the fictional garden was created by Wilson some time before he developed an interest in real gardens. When he wrote *The Middle Age of Mrs Eliot* he 'knew only a little of the working and economics of nursery gardening, and . . . I was uneasy in describing or imagining where I did not have some solid background of fact'. Therefore, Wilson believes, he used Andredaswood as an emblem of infantile regression: 'my sympathies . . . appeared to be very directly marked against gardens, country living, and the values that symbols implied'. However, he finds that he has to agree that this is not what most readers felt about David's garden. They felt, as I still feel, that in the novel Andredaswood appears to be a place of genuine healing. It expresses a sensitive new approach to human relationships. I think Wilson likes it, in spite of what he says in his retrospective commentary.

The reason for this is given by Wilson in a later paragraph in *The Wild Garden*. Although at the time of writing *The Middle Age of Mrs Eliot* Wilson had not developed a taste for gardening, and did not possess a garden, he was spending much of his time at a friend's house on the edge of Ashdown Forest. This house had a garden which was 'the centre of the household existence'. Incidentally, there was also, Wilson tells us, a wild garden attached to his brother's prep school on the Sussex Downs. What appears to have happened in the novel is that Wilson's early suspicion of gardeners (as with Miranda Searle in 'Fresh Air Fiend' and Ella Sands in *Hemlock and After*) has begun to give way to his new-found enjoyment of gardens when they are tended by close friends and relations. So the superficial aspects of Andredaswood remain undesirable – the name itself is pretentious, the nursery pun hovers in the background. And it is true that the scheme of the novel is intended to show that David Parker's gardening is 'a mechanical exercise devised to provide material means on which to live out a deliberately flattened ascetic existence'. Again, 'Since he had once loved gardening, there was a purposeful destruction of that pleasure instinct in himself.' But we have seen that the 'deliberate flattening' David espouses is hedged about with ironies and qualifications which have the effect of protecting it from the charges Wilson claims he was making, and which the image of the garden, even in its overcultivated form, tends to support rather than expose.

None of this is a chance or merely random importation of autobiographical details into the novel. I am not just talking about whether Wilson did or did not like gardens when he wrote *The Middle Age of Mrs Eliot*. What I am talking about is the way Wilson is apparently using Meg to demonstrate the inadequacy of David's view of life whilst he is actually doing something different. There can be no argument that Meg's escape into purposeful existence occurs as a result of what she discovers to be unsatisfactory in her relationship with David. I think we are left in two minds about the plausibility of the argument she uses to justify her leaving Andredaswood. But we are also left in two minds about the satisfactoriness of the Andredaswood experiment itself in so far as it is presented as a viable alternative to Meg's attitude to life. An alternative, that is to say, for such people as her brother and, perhaps, Angus Wilson too, at some deep level of their personality.

In spite of the intelligence Wilson displays in *The Wild Garden*, I am not sure that he has grasped the fundamental contradictions between what comes over most powerfully in his work and what he thought he was doing at the time he wrote it. The same uncertainty, the same blur at the centre of his appreciation, is present in his comments on Meg's and David's experience at Andredaswood as I have argued was present in his comments on the genesis of 'Raspberry Jam'. Wilson shows the same introspective subtlety and refinement of moral analysis in his description of his own states of mind as he has shown in the workings of the consciences of heroes such as Bernard, Gerald, Meg and, especially, David. But he shows, in *The Wild Garden*, that he is deeply suspicious of the way these subtleties and refinements are manipulated by the characters, in order to evade rather than to confront the deepest reality of their being. In David's case we are to suppose that this reality has been suppressed by a spurious philosophy of quietism and withdrawal from the world. But in fact Wilson's ambiguous attitude to this philosophy, his uncertainty as to whether to deplore its basis in regression and infantilism or to approve its tough as well as tender-minded attention to the minutiae of personal relationships, makes us unsure of just how we are supposed to feel about what David has achieved. And this ambiguity is expressed in Wilson's coincidentally ambiguous attitude to the wild garden which he has selected as his metaphor for David's view of life.

But Andredaswood is *not* a wild garden. It is a carefully cultivated garden, and that is one of the reasons Wilson says he deplores it. The ideal garden is one which will encourage the greater psychological freedom, the instinctual pleasure, which has been thwarted by David's experiment. What is required, in other words, is 'limited liberty', a phrase that might be used to define the objectives of all Wilson's heroes, but that is actually used by Dr Leacock, one of the old men in Wilson's fourth novel, *The Old Men at the Zoo*. 'Limited liberty' is a somewhat vacuous phrase. It can mean very different things to different people, depending on the view they take about what constitute the proper limits of personal satisfaction, and where the line is to be drawn between freedom and anarchy. These are some of the issues Wilson sets out to explore in what I think is a very brilliant and original novel.

Leacock's intention in setting up his wildlife reserve is explained most fully in a television broadcast he makes when the project is still only a pious hope. In it he says that those who profit by the naturalists' way of life will be 'the pioneers in our society carrying the developed instinctual way of life to balance the top-heavy intellectual growth of today':

> After all because we do not want to live in chaos . . . there is no reason why in our fear we should die in captivity. . . . Liberty we can find if we accept some limitation on its definition, liberty thus limited we may feed on. . . . Only so I believe can we restore the psychic balance, the soul's health of a very sick civilisation.

These are respectable liberal sentiments. But, though Leacock theoretically approves of a relaxation of the human will and an enlargement of the scope of animal instinct, he fails to see how the putting into practice of this theory about life might have the most harmful consequences. The animals which escape from the reserve do not, as a matter of fact, do much damage. But, on a more personal level, Harriet Leacock's nymphomaniac proc- livities – a sad perversion of the nurturing of animal instincts championed by her father – drive her to acts of bestiality with her pet Alsatian, acts of bestiality which eventually cause her death. The irony of the situation is that these acts have sprung from sheer desperation on Harriet's part, and that her desperation has sprung from her father's inability to recognise what is going on inside her – at an animal instinctual level – so preoccupied is he with his intellectual schemes for the reserve.

The reason why *The Old Men at the Zoo* is such an interesting novel is that in it Wilson deals more directly with the connection between liberty and violence than he had done at any time since *Hemlock and After*. The character in whom this is most vividly dramatised, however, is not Dr Leacock but the narrator, Simon Carter. Simon is secretary to the London Zoo and a man with considerable administrative gifts. But he also has a powerful desire to relinquish this largely intellectual flair in favour of a more instinctual attitude to life. In the first two chapters of the novel, before the broadcast and the move to Stretton, Carter's main preoccupation is with an accident that has occurred at the zoo. A giraffe has kicked its keeper in the balls and killed him. Absurd though this incident is – the title of the chapter in which it happens is called 'A Tall Story' – there is real suffering involved. Carter does not forget this. Indeed he makes his awareness of it a high-minded excuse for conducting an enquiry into the circumstances of young Filson's death. This gives reign to what might be described as the Elspeth Eccles aspect of Carter's personality. On the other hand, his attempt to see that justice is done by investigating the circumstances in which something unpleasant, or merely negligent, took place is not strictly comparable to those other attempts by Bernard Sands and Gerald Middleton to establish the truth of a tangled and painful situation. The inquiry is dropped less than half-way through the novel, when more important matters absorb Simon's attention.

After a conversation with the curator of mammals Simon discovers that he is 'bored with the whole affair' of Filson's death. His involvement with all the petty moral problems that surround the event make him feel suffocated. The air of the room in which he and the curator have been talking becomes stale and fetid, 'like the breath of the great cats in the Lion House'. Simon takes his cue from the simile that has been brought to mind, reflecting that 'I felt myself not a guardian but a prisoner of the caged beasts. My delight had been in their free movements, their untamed terrors and cruelty, the slow discovery of a pattern of life as I watched it unfold for hours at a time had freed me from all consciousness of self.' He goes on to delight in his memories of watching animal life in the wild – something set apart from the caged animals in the zoo and the old men who superintend them, men who appear to Carter to be equally caged and confined by their petty rivalry and competing egotisms.

There are two interesting features of Carter's attitude to the wild animals. The first is that his interest in them, with all that implies about his endorsement of Leacock's views on the 'naturalist's way of life', takes the form of a compensation for what he recognises as the sterile character of his administrative gift. His delight in squirrels in the Suffolk beechwoods takes place at the expense of his responsibilities for the administration of the zoo, which include such things as making up his mind what course of action he should take over young Filson's death. It may be that he should leave well alone; or it may be that he should continue his investigation. But to worry away at the issue so as to leave almost everyone concerned in it unhappy and uncomfortable and then just drop it because squirrels and badgers are so much more interesting does not seem to me to be very different from doing what David did at Andredaswood – except that David's theoretical justification for it is lacking. The point here, though, is that Wilson recognises Simon's self-deception. He makes this clear when he sends him to Stretton as both administrative secretary to the whole reserve and warden of the British reserve which is a part of it. In other words Simon is being allowed to suppose that he can get the best of both worlds: he can be the conscientious administrator, exercising his ability to make patterns out of muddled details; and he can be the intent, inactive naturalist who observes the patterns made by other creatures, in which he can play no active part. But this cosy arrangement fails when the artificial division between human beings and animals breaks down – after Harriet is savaged to death by her Alsatian; and after the destruction of the zoo, with its horrible carnage among the beasts who escape and the men who shoot them down.

The second peculiarity of Carter's delight in the free movements of the animals on the reserve (or what, at this stage, he imagines they will be) is its easy contemplation of their savagery as well as their freedom. He emphasises their 'untamed terrors and cruelties' and seems to enjoy calling them 'beasts' instead of 'animals' or 'mammals'. Later, when the zoo is being bombed during the Third World War, his usual concern for the animals is momentarily averted by the music Bobby Falcon has had switched on through the amplifiers all over the Gardens. He hears a 'sweet' soprano voice singing 'Home Sweet Home' and, we are told, 'Everything that was absurd about Victorian England seemed to come from that genteel, sugary, drawing-room-parlour voice and yet it filled me with a deep nostalgia, a willingness to surrender myself to the prettiness and to die.' The suffering of the animals goes for a moment unnoticed whilst Simon surrenders himself to an infantile pleasure in the music. Another hint of Simon's regression to a state of mind and a form of conduct that are not so much healing as violent and sadistic occurs when he protects himself from Bobby and accidentally knocks the older man to the floor. The incident is absurd, but 'I felt a strange and unfriendly sense of power. I think I could have shot him, if someone had told me that the circumstances called for it.' The questions one is disposed to ask about Simon here are: is he acting as a responsible human being like Charles Murley or the policeman in Leicester Square in *Hemlock and After*; or is he displaying something more like the uncontrollable excitement, the sadistic pleasure in the misfortunes of other people that

Bernard Sands discovered in himself when he looked into the arrested homosexual's face? Taken by itself the incident with Bobby could be understood in either sense; 'unfriendly' can be read in two ways. But coincidence of his reflections on the wild beasts and his behaviour at the zoo during the air raid (momentary aberrations both) suggest that Simon is not free from an anarchic delight in cruelty and that this might infect his administrative competence as well as his naturalist's detachment. Later in the novel he is able to continue working with the new fascist authorities at Regent's Park, and the final effect of his favourite pastime – watching badgers – is disquieting to say the least.

Simon does not go so far as to throw in his lot entirely with Blanchard-White's uni-Europeans, though the reason for his disaffection – his wife's contempt for him – hardly represents the committed opposition that we should expect from a liberal and a humanist. In fact Simon has something fundamentally in common with the 'sad-faced men and women' who provide Blanchard-White with a following. Wilson says they have come from 'the ranks of those who were too obstinately individual to fit in, yet too weakly individual to make their mark'. On one level that might be description, as Wilson says it is, of 'the handicapped or handicap prone in all their many kinds, the ranks of those who had been our proles ever since the end of the Hitler war'. On another it might be a description of Simon. For he is also handicapped by weaknesses in his character which have made possible those moments of sadistic excitement and infantilism that we have noticed play a significant part in his response to the reserve, the war, and the rise of the anti uni-Europeans.

But, by the time he has come to examine Carter's predicament, Wilson has placed the impulses he could not cope with in Bernard Sands into a more adult and less obsessed perspective. The real test of Simon's character comes when he is struggling for his life in the wilds of Essex after his escape from the zoo. Here he is tended by a mother and her son who, like everyone else, are swiftly running out of food. Simon realises that one way of obtaining food is to kill the badgers. He and the young man go out into the wood and wait by the sett. The appearance of the badger family is described in some detail. They spend most of their time simply playing: 'this was the happy family play whose healing innocence I had been cheated of again and again in the days of watching at

Stretton'. The horrifying fact is driven home to us that Simon can stay alive only by destroying these animals which have given him hope that there might be an alternative to his desiccated humanism and administrative efficiency. Now, it seems, he is to keep these worthless characteristics alive by eating the flesh of the very creatures who taught him how, temporarily, to set them aside; creatures in whom are incorporated a life of instinct, a playfulness, with which Simon's best self has tried to keep in touch during all those weeks spent in quiet observation. It seems that, by eating the badgers, Simon is eating his own spiritual salvation.

Or is this to convert the badgers too eagerly into appropriate symbolic properties? It is not as if Wilson is not in the habit of developing parts of his narrative symbolically. One thinks of the phallic figure found in Bishop Eorpwald's tomb in *Anglo-Saxon Attitudes*, and the way this conjunction of pagan sexuality and christian idealism suggests a pattern that underlies the whole novel; or of the dungong that Hamo Langmuir finds being clubbed to death in the Tamil country of Ceylon, and the subtly symbolic connections that are established between the creature and the commercial and psychedelic uses to which it is put by some of the characters in *As If By Magic*. I believe, therefore, that Wilson does intend us to think of the badgers as symbols of a non-human, instinctual innocence. More to the point, I think he is drawing our attention to the fact that that is what Simon feels about them too. Symbols in Wilson's novels are always recognised as such by the characters. They are not mysterious receptacles of wisdom. Instead they are a convenient way of bringing together in decisive areas of the plot some of the principal issues with which Wilson is trying to engage. The badgers exist symbolically on this level. Simon knows what they represent for him, and he comes to realise that, if he is to survive, this representative function must be set aside in favour of the living body in which it has been lodged. In the same way Gerald Middleton must expose the historical fraud of the Melpham idol, even though he has to recognise, through his reacquaintance with Dollie Stokesay, the extra-truth represented by its presence in Eorpwald's coffin. And though Hamo Langmuir makes use of Mr Jayasekeri's 'Dugong' press as an *entrée* to the favours of his dishy young servant (and later tries to expose the fraud of a religious cult that uses the dugong as a symbol of its nonsensical beliefs), when he sees the real dugong being stoned to death he is instrumental in freeing it and returning it to its natural environment. It is interesting how the symbolic props of these novels progressively take on the form of animals, rather than of objects such as the phallic idol. In an animal it is difficult to disengage the concept being represented – vitality, instinctual life, the values of playfulness and conscienceless enjoyment of existence – from the body in which that concept is lodged. This is what Simon Carter has to do when he kills the badgers. But he does not experience any perverse thrill. And, coincidentally, the prose in which the killing is described is not excited and hallucinatory, like the description of the Leicester Square incident in *Hemlock and After*. Instead it has the objective clarity and force of a passage from Defoe:

> I nudged the boy's arm. He fired and the boar fell, screeching, on his side. Instantly the mate was down the sett, followed by her cubs. But before they had reached the entrance, the boy had fired again and one of the cubs lay dead. The boy walked over to where the old boar lay, only grunting now; he knocked it on the head with the butt end of his rifle, half crushing its skull. Even together we had not the strength to carry the body back. The boar must have weighed around forty pounds. So, for the next hour, in the clear light of the now risen moon, I hacked away at the carcass; and the boy and his mother made journeys to and from the cottage, carrying badger joints. The cub required only the one journey.

A great deal of feeling is being controlled by the easy movements of this prose. The limpid elegance of that last simple sentence admirably sums up the pathos of the situation, without drawing attention to any of Simon's feelings that might be interpreted in an ambiguous or suspect way. Next morning, when he eats the badger, his responses are extreme but not excessive. He is hungry and at first he enjoys the meat: 'to my surprise, it tasted rich and delicious'. But by the end of the meal he is physically sick. This, I should have thought, is psychologically credible and morally defensible. The most important aspect of Simon's experience here is that it does not develop the incipient enjoyment of cruelty and violence that we saw in some of the earlier scenes. Sadism is not an essential part of the equipment of a naturally humane and intelligent man.

In his commentary on *The Old Men at the Zoo* in *The Wild Garden* Wilson again gives us penetrating insights into problems that were raised by its choice of subject and the ways in which he tried to resolve them in the process of writing. Also, once again, I think, he fails fully to understand the significance of what he has done. But this time his misunderstanding works to the advantage of his fiction, in a way that, I have tried to show, it did not with *The Middle Age of Mrs Eliot*.

Wilson begins by noticing the way cruelty to animals has played a significant part in his early novels and short stories. Maurice Legge's callous recollections of Indian tigers in 'What do Hippos Eat' are not allowed to set before us any particular example of sadistic violence towards them. But we have already noticed the horror of the Misses Swindales' treatment of the captive bullfinch in 'Raspberry Jam', and we might also recall the scene in which Larry Rourke kills a baby owl in *Anglo-Saxon Attitudes*. Most interesting of all is Gordon Paget's decision to put all his pet animals to sleep before he dies; because he cannot trust anyone else to care for them properly. The extent to which Wilson is drawn to describe human beings' behaviour towards animals, and the animals' response to being treated in the way they are, reveals an interest in the relation of animal life to human life which goes to the heart of Wilson's morality. Because in his novels human beings so often behave cruelly towards animals (and in a ruthlessly authoritarian way towards plants, also) the suggestion is made that there is in us some ineradicable stain, a kind of original sin, that expresses itself in violence towards the unprotected, and comes into being through an unholy alliance between animal instinct (which is good) and moral conscience (which is also good). In other words the two essential aspects of human beings, when operating separately, are capable of great good. But their combination in a single being, working upon each other in mysterious and unfathomable ways, often creates the opposite effect. The link between conscience and instinct that could, theoretically, produce such desirable results actually produces thoroughly undesirable ones – of sadism, violence, the deliberate excitable infliction of suffering. 'All these aspects of the animal world', Wilson writes, 'come to a climax in *The Old Men at the Zoo*.' The dilemmas that confront Simon Carter in this novel are 'dilemmas which I find insoluble on any but an empirical basis, although they persist in troubling me as being at the root of the contemporary dilemma, the junction point of social ethics and metaphysics'.

Simon's job at the zoo places him at the cutting-edge of Wilson's dilemma. His competence as an administrator at the wildlife reserve should be enhanced by his knowledge of British wildlife that the other part of his job, as warden of the British reserve, is expected to afford him. But it does not work out like that. True, 'our moment in history demands both forms of activity, and yet they seem so contradictory that inevitably Simon the administrator swallows up Simon the naturalist'. And Wilson goes on to generalise from this to what he takes to be the fundamentally humanist dilemma of our time. For 'this need at one and the same time for contemplation and social activity, for a secularised form of grace and good works, confronts the humanist as a paradox that can only be imperfectly solved at every level of life'. Wilson is surely right to claim that this is the fundamental humanist dilemma. For human activity, according to Wilson, is automatically drawn in the direction of authority, power and the will to possess.

But I believe Wilson has done himself less than justice when he comments on the most striking incident in the novel, where the relation between men and animals assumes an apparently predatory character. Wilson dwells for a long time on the events that occur at the cottage in Essex after Simon's escape from London. He stresses the fact that the journey was undertaken at the insistence of a colleague whose wish to preserve specimen animals for anatomical research is far removed from Simon's 'considered reverence for animal life'. In other words, the motive that lies at the back of everything Simon does during this episode is a false motive. Then Wilson traces the journey from London to the cottage, and discovers that in a half-conscious way Simon has been following a roundabout country route not in fact to Essex but to his own (Wilson's own) wild garden in Suffolk, and that the events in the cottage and garden in Essex in the fiction must actually have been occurring, in Wilson's own mind, in his own house and in his own wild garden. This makes the eating of the badgers a much more private image than we had thought. And Wilson makes this point in no uncertain – indeed, rather self-despairing – terms. The badgers, he says, symbolise 'peace and gentleness'. 'Unconsciously I had placed the defeat of Simon in my own cherished garden in the wild, my own symbol of resolution. The ambiguous symbol when it finally emerged directly into my work proved to be central to my own life.'

But why 'defeat'? It is true that, partly as a result of his experience in the Essex cottage, Simon throws in the sponge, almost until the last minute, when the uni-Europeans, with their shameless abuse of both animals and men, take over the zoo. But I have stressed the way we have to disengage the symbolic content from the body of the creature in which it has been lodged before we can properly come to terms with Simon's failure or success at this crucial moment. And, if we do this, I think the writing tells us that Simon has not been defeated. His weaknesses and self-doubts and evasions of the truth are as powerful as they ever were. But he has, at the most rudimentary level of his being, behaved properly, with a correct if inarticulate understanding of the relationship between men and animals, in the decision he took about the badgers, and his willingness to feed off them. Here is no sadism, no enjoyment in what he is doing – only the acceptance that to live he must eat, and there is nothing else to eat. His later rejection of what he has done here is a perfectly natural response. It was horrible. But it was not enjoyably horrible. That is the difference between Bernard and Simon. That is why I think *The Old Men at the Zoo*, whilst confronting directly the difficult issues raised in most of Wilson's previous work, arrives at a more honest and less despairing resolution of them then he had managed in any of the earlier novels.

Near the beginning of *Hemlock and After* Isabel Sands reflects on Bernard's novels and finds them wanting. 'She did not care for her brother's works, the earlier satirical ones seeming hard and frivolous – she felt they did not do justice to the depth and courage of his humanity. . . .' We have seen that Bernard's character had much in common with Wilson's at the time of writing. Here I should like to dwell on Isabel's dismissal of his early writing, the writing, in Wilson's case, that we should identify with the first two volumes of short stories.

One of the ways Wilson brings out the frivolous behaviour of his characters in these stories is through mimicry. I have implied above that the peculiar quality of Wilson's satire has to do with the simultaneously detached and involved position he occupies among the families who are exposed to it. And I have emphasised the characteristic effect such exposure has on those of us who have read the stories and responded to it: a sort of sour amusement built on a foundation of pity and contempt. Now, mimicry is an appropriate vehicle for satire of this sort. And, however Wilson might have changed as a writer, he has kept this gift of mimicry intact. He has continued to use it to remarkable effect in all of the novels from *Hemlock and After* onwards.

He has also populated his novels with a large number of equally brilliant mimics. Simon Carter is one of them. Jane Falcon testifies to this when she persuades him to exercise his talents on the members of the zoo staff, including her husband. It sounds like an amusing game – but, in spite of its having been played at her own request, Jane is not amused. She draws attention to the limitations of mimicry, to the superficiality of the mimic's understanding of the person he is mimicking: ' "You are extraordinary Simon. You will persist in thinking that people can 'know' about each other. Especially that *you* know about everybody else. Martha [Simon's wife] was quite right, my dear, you 'get' people awfully well but you get them all wrong." Later, Martha points out that 'everybody you described is ridiculous and a bit sad. Oh I don't mean that nastily. You do see very funny things in people and you have got a feeling but you paint the whole world that way." '

Wilson seems to have taken these accusations by Isabel Sands and Jane Falcon very much to heart. However, this has not meant that he has suppressed his natural talent for mimicry. Indeed his next long novel (written after *The Old Men at the Zoo* and *Late Call*), *No Laughing Matter*, depends more on mimicry and parody than any of his earlier ones had done. The book ia a collage of styles, building up a history of the Matthews family through interior monologue, parody, little playlets of a Shavian, Chekhovian or, later, Pinteresque character. This subordination of the writer's identity to the exigencies of whatever style he has judged appropriate to his purpose at any given moment has been discussed in a recent essay by Malcolm Bradbury.* In *No Laughing Matter*, Bradbury says, society is presented 'not as a solid substance but as a seeming'. 'The point of the writing is to release energy and invention, to generate fable, to draw deeply on

* In *Possibilities: Essays on the State of the Novel* (London and New York, 1973).

autobiographical feeling and awareness, afterwards shaping and designing what comes forth.' The result is a kind of novel which is less concerned with 'moral poise' than with 'vigorous invention', the novelist 'putting himself at risk by indulging the power of his own imaginings and obsessions'. My own view is that if this were so it would be a pity. Wilson has already shown himself capable of inventing fictions that explore the most obscure and ambiguous of private obsessions. But at the same time he has managed to stay in touch with a great deal of the world of 'solid social substance', which is by no means lacking even in such a fantasy as *The Old Men at the Zoo*. *No Laughing Matter*, though it is the largest and most ambitious of Wilson's fictions, does not possess the vitality and inner complexity present in so many of the other novels. The reason for this takes us back to Wilson's mimicry, and his reproduction of this activity in the behaviour of one of the Matthews children, Margaret, who is also a novelist. Indeed she is a novelist who has much in common with Angus Wilson himself.

Margaret Matthews's reputation as a writer depends on the stories she has written about the Carmichael family, a family in all important respects like her own. But she writes about it in such a way as to direct attention away from what the real experience of living amongst them must have been like, towards a detached, unsympathetic scrutiny of their absurdities, their petty malices and jealousies. This cannot help but remind us of Wilson's own short stories, many of which we now know to have grown out of his personal experiences of life with his mother and father and three brothers. Under the title of one of Margaret's stories, reproduced in full in *No Laughing Matter*, Wilson has inserted a brief sentence from what we are to suppose is a typical review of her work: 'The ironies of Miss Matthews's stories expose our most cherished evasions.' Just like 'Mother's Sense of Fun' or 'Flat Country Christmas' in fact. But like Wilson, and like Bernard Sands (if Isobel is to be believed), Margaret has grown dissatisfied with this cleverly satirical style, with its easy mimicry, itself not free from evasions more subtle, but no less personally damaging, than those of its intended victims. Under the influence of a passionate love affair with an unworthy but not altogether imperceptive young man, she develops ambitions to write something very different from the stories she has written until now:

She has begun something fuller, something that, instead of putting a sharp line under life's episodes, would capture the fusion of all the moments, happy, unhappy. A Carmichael novel in which the surface absurdities and conflicts and bitterness were only one theme in a much larger symphony, where the faithfulness, the enduring affection of the seemingly comic and vulgar Sophie and George were the real still centre of all the little storms. 'The Countess and B. P.,' she wrote, 'seeing each other still as they did thirty years ago on their Madeira honeymoon. They pretend to see each other in more hateful or ridiculous images for public consumption, so that they shall not seem to have failed to notice the stress and storm of the years. But this is only the surface, the public picture they offer to us, their children . . . your Mother's aged pathetically, your Father's lost all sense of pride . . . but behind that, when they're alone, or even in company, the old wedding photo remains as fresh as ever, ready to pop up at the most unexpected moments. Not realizing this basic continuity, we are dissatisfied with the disjunctive joys and sorrows, and seek to impose other patterns – the C. resents B. P.'s failure, we say, or B. P. cannot forgive the C. for seeking warmth with other men – but these imposed patterns falsify, blotting out both the lifelong vision and the immediate joy . . . .'

This is what we are to take *No Laughing Matter* itself as being. The caustic satire and eye for people's absurdities are still present. Indeed Wilson has made use of Margaret's stories, as well as Rupert's acting and Quentin's speechifying, to enlarge his armoury of satirical weapons. But these weapons, as I argued above, are used to expose the most vulnerable hypocrisies and embarrassments of family life – from a point of vantage very close to the members of the families concerned. With the result that, as with Margaret, there is always a tendency to push the victims of the satire to a fastidious distance, for the writer to protect himself from the embarrassment that follows from too close an emotional connection with those who are being attacked.

The difference between *No Laughing Matter* and either Wilson's or Margaret's short stories is that here Wilson tries to place these comic-deflating devices in the service of his characters. He does not use them directly himself. By doing this, he hopes he will be able to have his cake and eat it. Have his cake – because his pictures of the Matthews family will be touched in by that demeaning satire he had practised so astutely in the short stories. Eat it – because, not being responsible for the satire himself, he can call on the sympathetic involvement of the reader with the family he has placed at the centre of his novel. He can do so all the more effectively because now he seems to take the view that mimicry is an essential expression of our personalities, not just a rather special habit of 'taking off' other people.

Margaret seems to be trying to do the same thing in her novel, for she hopes that its surface absurdities will be only 'one theme in a much larger symphony'. The characters in it will be represented as both 'comic and vulgar' *and* dignified and sympathetic. But Wilson invites us to be sceptical about Margaret's success in achieving this. There is something in her tone, rather sentimental and coy ('the old wedding photo remains as fresh as ever . . .'), which alerts us to the likelihood that she is not actually going to be able to do what she can see needs to be done. In any case the failure of her relationship with Clifford Arbuckle makes her assume a detachment from life and an indifference to her art that are unlikely to provide the creative energy she will need to sustain her new literary ambition.

Margaret's later career shows her learning how to take more account of the way people adopt contradictory styles to bring together the separate and often conflicting parts of themselves. In real life these conflicting parts mysteriously cohere to form a whole personality which, when reproduced on the printed page with all the power of Margaret's mimicry, tends to fall apart again into apparently unrelated fragments. Wilson aims to succeed where Margaret has failed. He has tried to assemble the different ways of looking at each member of the Matthews family so as to produce a picture that is at the same time credible and vigorously animated.

To my mind the complications inherent in his ambition prevent his doing so. His ambivalent attitude to the family is more expansively and, I should guess, more intimately represented here than anywhere else in his fiction. But the long and not very excitingly plotted narrative lacks dynamism. It seems to be unconnected to anything outside family life that has hitherto provided a stimulus to Wilson's imagination.

In *No Laughing Matter* a longstanding ambition to make something genuinely creative out of the ambiguous feelings he had always entertained about his family caused Wilson to misdirect what by this time had become his most formidable talents. These still have to do with the issues raised by his handling of the characters of Bernard Sands and Simon Carter. What should be the proper connection between concern for other people, on the one hand, and an inevitable urge to satisfy one's self, on the other? This issue is raised again in *As If By Magic*. In Hamo Langmuir we are brought into close contact with someone who experiences the contradictions of modern humanism directly and painfully. The result is Wilson's funniest novel to date. The fact that Hamo undertakes his enquiry into motives during a year-long peregrination through the countries of South East Asia gives the novel an air of displacement, strangeness, often near-hysteria. These mirror very accurately the feelings of a man suddenly uprooted from all of his known landmarks and forced to make something coherent out of a multitude of alien experiences. Since Hamo's temperament and homosexual – infantile proclivities are as they are, this is to anticipate disaster. And disaster, farcically and picaresquely exhibited, is precisely what we get.

The most exhilarating thing about this novel is that Wilson makes no bones about Hamo's thoroughly reprehensible perversions. For his sensuality is not complicated by a simple homosexual twist to his affections, but by a love of boys (boys, it seems, between the ages of fourteen and twenty-four), which is very difficult to distinguish from mere lust. Before Hamo leaves England we learn that he has broken off relations with his latest boyfriend because he has become too muscular, heavy and generally adult. Throughout the journey he is to be found chasing the houseboys, drivers, beggars and hangers-on of all kinds – anyone who measures up to his simple physical requirements. Yet at the same time Hamo is a world-famous agronomist, inventor of the wonderful strain of rice called 'Magic', which has made a dramatic contribution to the Green Revolution throughout Asia. He is also a humanist, a man of conscience, whose paedophiliac absurdities walk hand in hand, so to speak, with the operations of a most delicate sensitivity.

Hamo's scientific eminence and his paederasty come together in both hilarious and tragic circumstances. The hilarious aspects are beyond my brief. Even so, I should like to draw the reader's attention to Hamo's efforts to seduce a beautiful houseboy in the establishment of Mr and Mrs Jayasekere. These are a couple of pro-Western 'liberals' Hamo meets in Colombo, whose overriding ambition is to force a Western-style education on the students of Ceylonese universities, with the object of creating a market for textbooks printed on Mr Jayasekere's private press. Issues that are raised by this episode, of the uneasy conjunction of Western technology and Eastern life styles, are central to the novel's concerns, and yet they are handled in such a surrealistically comic manner that the point is driven home in places where we might have least expected to find it. More serious, though, is the upshot of another of Hamo's quests for young boys. His irresponsible lust has already caused the disappearance of one youth and the drowning of another. Now he tries to make up for the disasters he has caused by giving a brand new pair of binoculars to a wretched young man who has been following him about, tipping him the wink, but failing to rouse his sexual interests (he is pock-marked and ugly). But Hamo's gesture – an expression of his 'new-found weakness for the weak' – has the effect of producing yet another tragedy. The boy uses the binoculars to spy on naked European hippies sun-bathing on the beach. Angry townspeople discover him there and kill him. Riots develop in which another near-acquaintance of Hamo's is brutally raped. And Hamo's gesture contributes to the inflammation of feeling during the procession on St Xavier's Day which almost destroys his goddaughter and actually results in his own destruction – he is stoned to death and drowned by a crowd of Goanese peasants.

The circumstances in which all these things happen are complicated and fast-moving. But the central issue is the irrational combination in the principal character of the most vicious sensual proclivities, and a tolerant, liberal, circumspect intelligence. Like many other characters in the novel, Hamo has in his possession and in his gift a form of 'magic'. In his case it is the rice strain, called 'Magic', on which the pun of the novel's title depends. But magic, as one of the other characters points out, draws to it two kinds of people: the power-hungry and the neurotic. In most respects there is all the difference in the world between Hamo's 'Magic' and the magic, for example, of the Austrian swami, who plays a very important part in the climax of the novel. But the fundamental thing they have in common is their inappropriateness to the requirements of those who think they need them most. The unproductive paddy fields of Asia look as if they need Hamo Langmuir's scientific 'Magic'. But on closer inspection it transpires that the use to which 'Magic' has been put (by power-hungry politicians and landowners) has made many Thais, Indians and Ceylonese worse off rather than better. Looking at it from the other point of view, it seems as if disturbed and neurotic people such as Alexandra Grant and Elinore Tarbett need the swami's magic, his system of Atlantean wisdom and Lemurian powers to give direction to their naive religious aspirations. But, if we look at what happens when they get involved in a kind of magic which, however synthetic and tawdrily eclectic, has considerable destructive power, we are likely to come away with a different opinion.

Alexandra's contribution to the debate arises out of her discovery that she is pregnant. This has happened as a result of what she calls 'tripling', i.e. having sex more or less simultaneously with two men. The fact that she has relinquished one scientific form of Western magic (i.e the contraceptive pill), whilst continuing to practise another, 'superstitious' variety of it, has thrust her into a situation where she is in two minds as to what course of action to follow: to give up 'magic' altogether, or to accept it as a way of life she can no longer afford to do without. At first she opts for 'magic':

The two young men looked away from her. In all their triplings, she has used the basic words only tenderly; and *they* had used them in this brutal way, on occasion, in a little side game they had of speaking of her body coarsely to one another as she lay naked between them. The game was spoiled. Rodrigo voiced it.

'Then the Fellowship of the ring is at an end', he said, trying with mockery to lighten the atmosphere.

'Oh, no,' Alexandra told them, 'just because you've been weak and silly and let yourself be used, doesn't mean that you cease to want your users. At least I don't think so. I don't feel any different to either of you. Why should I? I mean you aren't different because Ned urged me not to take the pill and Rodrigo fucked me when I hadn't. It's just that we aren't protected by magic. And, of course, I knew we weren't, but our game seemed so important that it made me feel we were different. And I think I want to go on playing it. What else is there to do?

'What else is there to do?' The rest of the novel, in so far as
Alexandra's participation in it is concerned, is an attempt to
answer that question. Magic represents 'togetherness', hippy
communion, a sinking of the West's sterile intellectual contri-
vances in games, fantasy ('the Fellowship of the Ring') and
Oriental mysticism. 'What else' eventually identifies itself as
Hamo's sceptical humanist intelligence, functioning in terms of
diminished expectations and, in Alexandra's case, without the
fatal admixture of Hamo's amoral sensual anarchy. She has a
great deal to learn about fantasy before she is able to put Hamo's
ideas into practice. In spite of a superficial eccentricity and
absurdity, Alexandra's behaviour is very little self-deceived. That
is why she is able to accomplish what she does accomplish, limited
though that might be.

Oriental magic, then, is inappropriate to the real problems of a
developed Western society and an overdeveloped Western intelligence and conscience. Conversely, Occidental magic, or science,
is inappropriate to the real problems of Eastern poverty and the
population explosion. Or is it? Certainly it seems so to Hamo. As
his itinerary lengthens, and his contact with the Asian experience
grows closer, the hopelessness of that experience strikes him with
increasing force. His wonderful 'Magic', the product not only of
scientific intelligence but also of humanist concern for the
problems of underdeveloped countries, has done nothing to
alleviate suffering. This is vividly and comically brought out
during one of Homo's tours of the state of Madras. He is shocked
by the way the substitution of his 'Magic' for the inferior grain
that used to be sown in the paddy fields has encouraged a method
of farming that excludes the poor smallholders, whose land has
been rendered worthless and who have been forced to work for
subsistence wages on the big new estates that produce Hamo's
mutation. His host, Mr Gupta, breezily dismisses his argument.
How can a famous scientist such as Hamo prefer an inferior,
unproductive system of agriculture to a modern, efficient system
that provides better quality rice in greater quantities? Besides,
what right has Homo, a stranger to the East, to pronounce
judgement upon Oriental attitudes to these things? The peasants
do not share his views about the importance of individual human
beings and their god-given right to life, health and happiness.
This is proved a few seconds later when the car in which they are
travelling swerves to avoid a couple of cows lying in the road near

heaps of inferior white rice grains the peasants have laboured to assemble in the heat of the afternoon. As the car barely avoids running into one of the cows, by driving over two or three of the little hoards of rice, the peasants shout and shake their fists. But they do this not because of the destruction of the rice that provides them with their livelihood, but because of the damage that has almost been done to the sacred cows. In this situation Hamo comes close to despair. Both his science and his humanism seem to be irrelevant.

In the end, though, Hamo avoids despair. Like Bernard Sands, he cannot be sure whether the 'high, distant overtone of perpetual, desperate woe' he can hear is really out there, in the world at large, or exists only in himself. Eventually they both come to realise that the evil exists in both places. But, unlike Bernard, Hamo does not allow this knowledge to paralyse his ability to accept the one, and still be able to make an effort to do something about the other. Bernard's feeble defeat of Hubert Rose is replaced, in Hamo's case, by an ambitious, though realistic, report to his foundation about what can be done to help those who have suffered so appallingly as a result of its own good intentions. Equally important, he understands that the only way to do this is to press on with the developments of his own particular kind of 'Magic' and use it to counter the ill effects of its hitherto misdirected application: 'Our work on Magic', he says in his report, 'will never be complete until the human . . . . , the moral concerns involved are made clear to the beneficiaries, above all, until that acceptance of "hopelessness" so endemic in the past has been clearly and manifestly rejected'.

That is an altogether more strenuous and less defeatist attitude than was represented by Bernard at the end of *Hemlock and After*. Though Hamo also dies before he can do much to put his new beliefs into practice, he has been able to demonstrate how an awareness of personal and social evil need not lead to despair, nor even to the sort of quietism that is represented by David Parker in *The Middle Age of Mrs Eliot*. The translation of a humanism of despair into a humanism of renewed hope, which Wilson was unable to demonstrate convincingly in Gerald Middleton or Meg Eliot, and which he only touched on in a very private way, somewhere between the text and the life, in *The Old Men at the Zoo*, is made here with total conviction and exceptional honesty. The fact that Hamo's report is written, and that Alexandra inherits it, shows that Wilson has not lost his belief in humanism. What he has lost is what he calls, in *The Wild Garden*, 'panic', creating in the person who experiences it paralysis and despair. And the image which expressed this confident reassertion of humanist belief is not altogether surprising. It is a grain of rice, a magic mutation, which, one day, might create a new wild garden in the Green Revolution all over Asia.

At the end of the novel the time is not ripe, the conditions are imperfect, and the man who has identified the nature of the problem is dead. But Hamo has understood the 'make-believe', the 'divine idiocy' of his ambition. He has accepted the 'muddle' (an interestingly Forsterian conception) through which things might be made to come right. In the end Alexandra, his beneficiary, cannot put into practice his ideas about the power of 'Magic'. She does not possess the professional skills and she is unable to persuade those who do possess them to follow Hamo's lead. But she possesses another sort of magic that she does learn how to use. Money. Money that has come to her from Hamo himself and from his great-uncle James. The way Alexandra uses the money has no effect at all on the starving hordes of Asia. But it does have an effect – a more limited, but largely beneficial one – on a relatively small number of less spectacularly deserving people.

Evidently there is a large area of practical usefulness to be staked out between a panicked, paralysing sense of evil on the one hand, and mere quietism, a serene spiritual withdrawal from the world, on the other. More than any other of Wilson's heroes or heroines, Hamo and Alexandra manage to occupy that territory. It is a triumph of their humanism that they do so, and a triumph of Angus Wilson's humanism that he is able to believe that they do so. I do not think we should minimise the extent of his achievement here, nor the fascination of the route by which he came to realise it.

6 Kingsley Amis

Near the middle of Kingsley Amis's second novel, *That Uncertain Feeling*, there is a very funny scene in which John Lewis and Elizabeth Gruffyd-Williams are almost discovered making love in the lounge of Vernon Gruffyd-Williams's house. Lewis, escaping into the hall, avoids bumping into Gruffyd-Williams and his guests by concealing himself in a cloakroom under the stairs. The whole of the next chapter (10) is given over to a farcical account of Lewis's travels around the house, part of the time disguised as a plumber, part of the time as a Welshwoman; and his escape in the Welshwoman's clothes out of the house, onto a bus, and, finally, through the streets of the town to his own front door. Though it is a not untypical Amis situation, its general aspect, and some particular incidents, recall scenes from Whitehall farces of the forties and fifties, or from Ealing films of about the same period. Indeed, it provided one of the high spots of the film *Only Two Can Play*, a free adaptation of this novel which, though released in 1962, employed the services of several of the old Ealing hands of the 1950s.

Other features of the episode, however, are typical Amis. None more so than the display of motive, or rather lack of it, for Lewis's extraordinary behaviour. For Amis deliberately removes Lewis's most obvious reason for behaving as he does (i.e. to conceal from Gruffyd-Williams the fact of his presence in the house) by having Elizabeth get up and dress quickly enough to go and tell her husband that Lewis is visiting them – in entirely uncompromising circumstances. So Lewis has no good reason to leave the house at all, certainly not to go to great lengths to escape from it unseen. Having decided that that is what he *will* do, he has no reason to prolong the plumbing charade for as long as he does, and none at all, so far as I can see, for disguising himself in the Welshwoman's dress. Later this dressing up is interpreted as an act of therapy to enable Lewis to face the outside world again. But, by the time he leaves, the disguise has become a mere encumbrance. Just beforehand he had promised himself that he would 'soon have these farcical garments off', and would have had them off in a couple of Gruffyd-Williams's guests had not entered the room and been about to draw back the curtain of the window-seat in which he was hiding. Lewis's behaviour in the Gruffyd-Williams house is psychologically quite implausible. Amis has made it so deliberately. He has gone out of his way to divert our attention from Lewis as a comprehensible, motive-driven human being, to the sequence of events into which he has been precipitated by the controlling whim of his creator.

What does this incident tell us about the kind of novelist Amis is – beyond the fact that he is an accomplished writer of comedy which usually has broad farcical overtones? I think, first of all, there are a number of things it tells us about the kind of novelist he is *not*, but that many critics have assumed he resembles much more closely than in fact he does. I am referring to two, related traditions of English writing with which Amis has been associated: the tradition of the Edwardian novel of social comedy, as represented by Wells in such novels as *Kipps* and *Mr Polly*; and the 'tradition' (hardly established by 1954, when Amis published his first novel) of the post-war novel of revolt against middle-class *mores* and middle-class literary, as well as social, assumptions. This latter tradition is represented by 'working-class' novelists of the fifties such as Alan Sillitoe, David Storey and Keith Waterhouse; and it has had lumped with it, by association of a rather facile kind, the picaresque early fiction of John Wain and Iris Murdoch.

The Wellsian aspects of Amis's work have been discovered in his 'realistic' presentation of lower-middle-class heroes in situations that dramatise movements among different social groups within the same waveband of the English class system. But, whatever the reality of Amis's interest in a similar area of the English social structure half a century after Wells, his method of dealing with it is totally different. In any case, movements across the classes during those fifty years have been so rapid, so perplexing, that it cannot ever be said that Amis is describing the same social groups that Wells described. Other novelists, such as Thomas Hinde and V. S. Pritchett, have come much closer than Amis has to emulating Wells – as even a cursory reading of *Mr Nicholas* or, especially, *Mr Beluncle* will make abundantly clear.

Pritchett's description of how Beluncle's house is furnished, for example, with its emphasis on the impermanence of chairs, tables, even carpets that are 'on loan' from the directors of the business ('Be careful with it. It may have to go back'), is both funny and informative about Beluncle's character. He is a queer mixture of obstinacy and diffidence, of overbearing pomposity in no way mitigated by a disturbing undercurrent of financial worry. All of this is vividly suggested by Pritchett's description of the rooms he occupies. Amis's writing has something of the ebullience of Pritchett's, but little of its capacity to bring to life that area of a character's personality which lies half-way between the sort of person he really is and the effect he makes on other people. The description of Patrick Standish's room (*Take a Girl Like You*, ch. 4), for example, in the 'row of Auntie Minnie houses' where he rents a flat, is serviceable, in so far as it establishes the physical location of Patrick's attempts to seduce Jenny Bunn and Sheila Torkington. Its *décor* of books and gramophone records also tells us something of Patrick's tastes and outlook. But it goes no farther than that. The success of Amis's descriptions of what happens in the room has more to do with the play of Standish's mind over and beyond the objects in it than with any imaginative interaction between the room and its owner. When Amis does make an imaginative observation about some aspect of his hero's environment, it is likely to be of a less personal and more generally characteristic kind. His description of the bar at the Queen's Head (in *That Uncertain Feeling*), for example, establishes the pretentiousness of the place, and of all such places, with its list of warming-pans, soup ladles, candle-snuffers hung around the walls, 'and a thing that would have come in handy for getting fried ostrich eggs off a frying pan'. The uselessness, silliness and typicality of this last object, which we have all seen at some local Queen's Head, are brilliantly caught in the reference to ostrich eggs. But beyond adding to the impression we have already received, that pretentious people patronise pretentious pubs, the description tells us nothing.

Externals have a way of remaining external in Amis, while even in an extravert novelist such as Wells or Pritchett they tend to enliven our appreciation of the characters' minds at, it is only fair to say, a relatively unintrospective level of activity. Pritchett handles those elements of a situation that lie both on its surface and just a little below it in brief, almost aphoristic passages that would not have discredited Dickens. In *Mr Beluncle* 'Miss More did not know how to leave; she knew only how to be replaced'; 'Mr Chilly watched his restless hands, surprised they had remembered to come with him'; and Mr Beluncle's meetings with Mrs Robinson at Lippard's tea-rooms 'were a kind of suicide pact in which their voices and their autobiographies died together over the counter twice a week'. There is none of this affectionate curiosity about people in Amis. His characters' negotiations with the world around them is consequently embattled and irritable, lacking authorial intervention by recourse to which the one might have been explained by reference to the other.

Though Amis's heroes share something of the awkwardness and social inexperience of their Edwardian predecessors, as mediated through the work of Pritchett and Hinde, their place in the world is more exposed than Kipps's, or Beluncle's, or Mr Nicholas's. This is because their author's prose has the effect of detaching them from the things that are in the world – things that in Wells and Pritchett are also devices for 'colouring' their characters, and giving them a purchase on life in linguistic terms even when their purchase on the life of society remains precarious.

Amis's lack of common ground with the 'angry' novelists of the fifties is much easier to show than his separation from the Edwardian tradition, mainly because it is much more complete. Beyond a rather cavalier treatment of plot, there is nothing much in Amis to compare with Sillitoe or Waterhouse. Not only is the class background of his heroes completely different from theirs (if his characters are a class above Wells's and Pritchett's, they are as much as two classes above Sillitoe's); the form their rebellion against society takes is also strikingly at variance with that represented by Arthur Seaton in *Saturday Night and Sunday Morning*, or the anonymous Borstal boy of 'The Loneliness of the Long Distance Runner'. Seaton and the boy are possessed by a nihilistic destructive energy. But their urge to destroy is revealed mainly in their detestation of people who occupy superior positions to their own in the social hierarchy, people who are placed in positions of authority over them, such as the works manager or the governor of the Borstal. Although it may seem unfocused and hysterical much of the time, Sillitoe's anger is directed at what he seems to agree with his characters is a large-scale social abuse, a fundamental defect in the system. In spite of his early leftward leanings, nothing could be more different from Amis's own very real anger, and its relation to the view of society that emerges from a reading of his novels.

For Amis's anger is anger at the human condition. That sounds a portentous way of describing the achievement of a popular comic novelist, but I believe it is true all the same. Anger – apparently aroused by the pretensions and hypocrisies of society, actually by something having little to do with real social abuses – is the characteristic response of the Amis hero to his situation. Before we go on to look at how that anger is expressed, and how it is related to other emotional traits – lust, boredom, irritability and panic – we need to trace its origins to a deeper stratum of the English literary tradition, the eighteenth-century picaresque novel. Here is a form and an expression of attitudes more closely resembling what Amis is trying to achieve than was present in either of the two more recent fictional analogues I have been looking at. Reference to the eighteenth century might also help to explain the peculiar nature of farce in Amis, to which I referred *à propos* of the passage from *That Uncertain Feeling* with which this chapter began.

Amis's admiration of the eighteenth-century novelists is no secret. The most categorical statement of it is made by Garnet Bowen, the publisher hero of *I Like It Here*, whose views on Fielding closely parallel Amis's own:

> Bowen thought about Fielding. Perhaps it was worth dying in your forties if two hundred years later you were the only non-contemporary novelist who could be read with unaffected and whole-hearted interest, the only one who never had to be apologised for or excused on the grounds of changing taste. And how sensible to live in the world of fear. Did that make it a simplified world? Perhaps, but that hardly mattered beside the existence of a moral seriousness that could be made apparent without the aid of evangelical puffing and blowing.

Before we look at this more closely it might be a good idea to throw into the melting-pot two other, less well-known passages on the same subject. The first of them is spoken by Roger Micheldene, the hero of *One Fat Englishman*, and suggests an evaluation of Samuel Richardson almost as high as the one Bowen offered of Fielding. Micheldene claims that 'Even before *Clarissa* there had only been a few touches in Aphra Behn and Defoe (*Colonel Jack*, of course, not *Crusoe* or *Moll Flanders*), and what was there since?' Precious little, according to Maurice Allington, landlord of the 'Green Man', who, though unamiable, like Micheldene, nevertheless, also like Micheldene, shows good taste in his choice of reading. Allington has no novels in his library. He finds the art of the novelist 'puny and piffling',

> one that, even at its best, can render truthfully no more than a few minor parts of the total world it pretends to take as its field of reference. A man has only to feel some emotion, anything differentiated at all, and spend a minute speculating how this would be rendered in a novel . . . to grasp the pitiful inadequacy of all prose fiction to the task it sets itself.

Of course, we shall be reminded, Micheldene, Allington *et alia* are characters in a novel, not Amis speaking *in propria persona*. I hope I shall be able to expose the fallacy of looking at Amis's principal characters in this way (a fallacy so far as anything critically useful can be extruded from it) at a subsequent stage of my argument. However, it is true that, some one hundred pages after Allington has expressed the views quoted above, he does make at least one literary judgement with which we might expect Amis to disagree. Stopping by a supermarket in Cambridge, Allington (who is speaking) 'went in and bought something I had never heard of by a writer whose first book, a satire on provincial life, I remembered had been commended at the time . . . I got through about forty minutes' worth of this . . . before going out and dropping it into a rubbish basket.' It looks as if *Lucky Jim* is to be included in the list of post-Smollett novels Bowen, Micheldene and Allington can't bring themselves to read.

Two features of Bowen's confession, and one of Allington's, strike me as being of more than passing significance. Bowen acknowledges that Fielding's is a 'simplified world'. Nevertheless it is one in which moral seriousness, divorced from a too explicit advertisement of didactic aims, is plainly at work. The more recent novelists to whom Allington refers – Stendhal and Proust – are dismissed because they are unable to render in their chosen form any kind of emotion, or indeed 'anything differentiated at all'. Taken together these comments suggest something about Amis's ambitions as a novelist, and about his achievement too. He has created a flattened-out world in which, or on the surface of which (it is *all* surface), the complexities and subtleties of human feeling have been deliberately excluded. Poetry, even Lord de Tabley's poetry according to Maurice Allington, can do that kind of thing much better. The novelist's job, in Amis's view, is different. His seriousness will show itself in the way he handles characters and situations that have been simplified in the interests of moral clarity. As in Fielding, this leads in the direction of the picaresque. Even more than in Fielding, it leads in the direction of farce.

It also leads to parody – not just within the novels (though there is plenty of that too, of which more later) but also in their overall structure. After all, Fielding began his career as a novelist with a parody of Richardson's *Pamela*. So why shouldn't Amis make his fourth novel (*Take a Girl Like You*) into a parody of *Clarissa*? That is what we get when Patrick Standish, the Lovelace of the story, spends his time in the novel trying to seduce pretty little Jenny Bunn (also pursued by the odious Dick Thompson – i.e. Soames in a fifties semi), and rapes her whilst she is unconscious at the end. *That Uncertain Feeling* is probably a parody of Fielding, John Lewis being pursued by aristocratic Elizabeth Gruffyd-Williams just as Tom Jones was pursued by Lady Bellaston – although nice ordinary Jean, like Sophia Western, is the girl he really loves. Late novels such as *The Anti-Death League* and *The Green Man* make their moral point to a large extent by parodying more contemporary fictional genres – the Le Carré–Deighton spy thriller, and the later nineteenth- and early twentieth-century ghost story respectively. There are pronounced hints of parody too (coming closer to home) in such novels as *I Want It Now* and *Girl, 20*. I hasten to add that these are affectionate parodies, not vicious lampoons. Amis delights in mimicking the novels he admires, and clearly feels that the plots and situations deployed in them contain much that can still be made morally persuasive.

It is possible to agree, I think, that Amis has succeeded in his ambition to simplify his material, at the same time as denying that he has got away from the expression of emotion. But the emotion belongs to him, the author. It is a prominent feature of his moral awareness, and through him it infiltrates a sizeable percentage of his characters. These characters are not free inhabitants of a world Amis has created for them to live in. They are expressions of his own temperament, usually in a very direct way. That is to say,

in a quite simple sense they tend to 'stand for' him; they have been
constructed so as to enable him to speak from them in his own tone
of voice, often, but not always, expressing his own opinions. Other
characters are set up as targets against which this tone of voice
and set of attitudes is encouraged to expend itself. Ieuan Johns,
Professor Welch and Bertrand in *Lucky Jim*, Gareth Probert and
Bill Evans in *That Uncertain Feeling*, Dick Thompson, F. B.
Charlton and Charlie Crosland in *Take a Girl Like You* are
examples of such characters. Almost everybody except Micheldene in *One Fat Englishman* is one of them.

Women usually don't qualify, Amis being on the whole too
idealistic or too chivalrous (more eighteenth-century virtues?) to
insult them in the downright way he goes about insulting the
men. This is usually bad for the women, because, not having been
allowed to exist as free characters, they are not being allowed to
exist as comic stooges either ('stooge' is in any case a word that
they use about men, never about other women – see Jenny Bunn
in *Take a Girl Like You*). That leaves them in a sort of limbo from
which only one or two of the minor characters (such as Lewis's
landlady and his colleague Jenkins's wife) and perhaps one of the
major ones (Margaret Peel in *Lucky Jim*) escape into some
semblance of life. The others, even girls such as Jenny on whose
behalf Amis has put in a great deal of work, are inert. Their
behaviour is either discontinuous and therefore baffling (thus
Jean Lewis: who could believe that she would in any circumstances enter into a clandestine affair with Gareth Probert?) or
utterly hazy in a mannishly idealising sort of way (see Catherine
Casement in *The Anti-Death League*). I think the trouble is that,
since none of these women can be allowed to be exposed to the full
brunt of Amis's comedy, and they can't become like some of the
men and act as substitutes for Amis's own presence in the novel,
they have no alternative open to them but to become characters –
separate and discrete – and Amis can't manage characters of this
sort, as Bowen's comments on Fielding make clear. Therefore
they end up as nothing much at all, except fixed points in the plot
towards which the men can advance or from which they can
retreat, as the situation requires.

I made the point that many of Amis's male characters speak in
his tone of voice though they might not invariably express his own
opinions. Ever since Jim Dixon resented Professor Welch's
singing 'filthy Mozart' in his bath on the night of the burnt sheets

(*Lucky Jim*, ch. 6) most if not all of Amis's most sympathetic, or at any rate centrally positioned, characters have given expression to opinions that we know, from other, non-fictional sources, Amis doesn't hold, indeed positively detests. Jim's hatred of Mozart is just one early example of this. Standish's dismissal of the Latin authors (he teaches Classics at a public school – and incidentally also hates Beethoven) is another. But the most atrocious un-Amisian opinions are ventilated by two characters – Micheldene in *One Fat Englishman* and Sir Roger Vandervane in *Girl, 20* – who at other times speak a lot of sense where we would usually expect to hear humbug. And they do this in a rude and forthright vein characteristic of their author. With his usual strokes of broad comedy Amis has established Micheldene as an appalling snob, snuff-taker and Americaphobe, and Vandervane as an aging Humbert Humbert who goes into youth culture and the pop scene in a big way. We have to pay attention to the nonsense they speak about all these things at the same time as we have to admire their welcome dismissal of other forms of cant – such as the rubbish that is represented by Irving Macher's novel, *Blinkie Heaven*, in *One Fat Englishman*; or the politics of envy and meanness Vandervane keeps brushing up against in *Girl, 20*.

The most reliable guide to Amis's approval or otherwise of his male characters is their attitude towards women. If they show due appreciation of women as sex objects, then they can invariably be counted on to be 'above the line'. This is the one consistent area of comparison between Jim Dixon, John Lewis, Roger Micheldene, Maurice Allington, James Churchill, and so on. This, of course, is bad news for the women, not only because they might prefer to be thought of as something more elevating than sex toys, but also because they can't very well go about making passes at each other, because then they'd be lesbians, and nowhere in his novels before *The Anti-Death League* (with the sympathetic portrait of Max Hunter; Joyce Allington and Diana Maybury in *The Green Man* show a great deal of physical interest in each other too) does Amis display any enthusiasm for homosexual practices. However, this lowest common denominator does help us to separate one goat from another, even if it leaves us nowhere so far as the sheep are concerned. So long as the sex thing is all right no amount of twaddle about drink, snuff, books, music or Americans will finally bring the hero down – even if he is fat, filthy or, like Graham McClintoch in *Take a Girl Like You*, a 'stooge'.

The description of Amis's novels I am skirting is one that sees them as comic, satirical and irresponsible. Comic I have already discussed, and I shall go into the detail of the comedy in due course. But satirical *and* irresponsible? Here again I am bearing in mind Amis's tastes in eighteenth-century fiction, and the most recent exemplars of what it was that he found to admire in that fiction. I am thinking of Swift and Evelyn Waugh in particular. We know that Amis admires Waugh's novels (see his essay 'My kind of Comedy', *Twentieth Century*, July 1961), and an article he wrote for the *New York Review of Books* (7 July 1957) strongly suggests that, when he thinks about satire, Swift is the satirist who is most likely to spring to mind. 'A society such as ours,' he writes, 'in which the forms of power are changing and multiplying, needs above all the restraining influences of savage laughter. Even if that influence at times seems negligible, the satirist's laughter is valid as a gesture – a gesture on the side of reason.' 'Savage laughter'; *'saeva indignatio'*. This is the laughter of Swift at the end of *Gulliver's Travels*, where Gulliver, returned from the land of the Houyhnhnms and the Yahoos, is the ridiculous mouthpiece of his author's despair at the fact that he would have men behave reasonably, if it were a reasonable thing to expect men so to do.

Amis would have men behave reasonably. But he would have them behave lecherously too. The illogical compatibility between reason and lust, both of them distractions from what otherwise would be the unbearable boredom and futility of life, is what Amis wants to show us. Even though it makes you look ridiculous, the portraits of Standish, Micheldene *et alia* are telling us, it is possible to be intelligently civilised and downright randy at the same time. Just as the author of *Gulliver* can approve and detest his character's behaviour at the end of the *Travels*; and just as, two hundred years later, Evelyn Waugh can admire and despair of Sebastian Flyte's views on contemporary life and manners, so Amis can invite us to judge Micheldene's behaviour commendable and ridiculous. That is what I meant when I used the phrase 'satirical and irresponsible'. Something in the nature of life makes our best judgements about it perversely inappropriate. To be most aware of how far existence falls short of what we are inclined to suppose are legitimate claims on it, to realise how deficient and unsatisfactory it is, is to be most dangerously and comically exposed to the consequences of that deficiency, that unsatisfactory quality of being. Such a perception about life underlines whatever else Amis's most 'sympathetic' characters say and do. It is what makes them so ridiculous and so right, so misanthropic at one moment and so exuberantly involved with life at another, so alternately admirable and offputting. It is, in fact, what makes them so much like Kingsley Amis himself.

The difference between the kind of novelist many people think Amis is and the kind of novelist I am arguing he is can be highlighted if we put side by side with his work the work of another gifted and very funny writer several years his junior, Malcolm Bradbury. It so happens that they both began their adult lives as university teachers of English (Bradbury still is one) and both of their first novels were set in provincial universities rather like the ones in which they taught. But 'rather like' in a different sense, depending on which author is being discussed. Because, although Amis and Bradbury are both comic novelists, and being a comic novelist involves some degree of stylisation of reality, nevertheless there are discriminations to be made. Bradbury's university in *Eating People Is Wrong* is much more realistically presented than Amis's is in *Lucky Jim*. No professor in Bradbury is quite so monstrously caricatured as Amis's Neddy Welch. Indeed his sympathetic central character, Stuart Treece, *is* a professor – not a junior lecturer like Jim Dixon. Also there is no occasion, like Dixon's lecture on 'Merrie England', that so patently belongs to a never-never land in which the most humble functionary in a university department is chosen to deliver a set-piece lecture on the occasion of the university's open day. In any case nobody in a university history department in 1954, the date of the novel's first appearance, could have imagined for one moment that he could get away with a lecture on this subject, which was as clearly understood then as it is now to be a fiction of one of the more trivial aspects of the Victorian Gothic revival. All of Bradbury's situations in *Eating People Is Wrong* are plausible. Something like them could have happened – even Mr Eborebel-osa getting stuck in the lavatory. Many of the incidents in *Lucky Jim* couldn't have happened at all. They are conventional exaggerations of what university life is supposed to be like, further exaggerated in the service of Amis's farcical requirements.

More important, Amis's novel is not in any serious way interested in the role the university should play in contemporary society. How can it be, when the people who inhabit it are so grotesquely unrepresentative of the people who teach and learn in such places? Dixon hates the very thought of books, libraries, history, the Middle Ages, anything that could conceivably be expected to interest a university lecturer in Medieval History – which, of course, Dixon knows nothing at all about. Treece, on the other hand, knows a fair bit about English poetry. He is interested in Proust, enjoys conversation with members of the Sociology department, and spends a lot of his time, when he is not failing his driving-test, brooding on the place of the academic intelligence in modern life. He is outraged when he finds that someone in the university has been pulling pages out of the current edition of *Essays in Criticism* and argues, passionately as well as amusingly, about the changing function of the intelligentsia and the effect this change is likely to produce on liberal values in society at large. What follows is a transcription of Treece's thoughts as he reflects on the violation of *Essays in Criticism*:

> The ordinary laws of sound human conduct were slipping; and the people who were selling out were those within the citadel – one's own friends, people one invited to one's home, people who did not destroy aimlessly but with a philosophy of life that comprehended destruction. To Treece, the existence of people, of liberal intellectuals, like himself was infinitely precious. . . . But those who live by the liberalism shall perish by the liberalism. Their own lack of intransigence, their inevitable effeteness, betrayed them. Already liberal intellects like his own found themselves on the periphery. The end was coming, as people like him had less and less of a social function, and were driven out into an effete and separate world of their own, to the far edge of alienation. It was on communication that they depended, and the channels were being closed from the other side; and in the tearing up of *Essays in Criticism* Treece saw the end of the liberal tradition.

This is what *Eating People Is Wrong* is about: a serious issue, not, as in *Lucky Jim*, a farcical transformation of reality into fantasy. Earlier, Treece had described himself as a liberal humanist who believes in original sin. Here he examines the consequences of being that sort of person. Of course there is a comic discrepancy between the nature of the offence Treece is contemplating, and the tone of outrage it has elicited from him. That is funny. But what he is saying, funny in the circumstances, may also be true. The trivial event might be a sign of something altogether more important, something that might assume very much more serious forms in the future. In *Eating People Is Wrong*, for the most part it doesn't. The emphasis falls instead on the discrepancy, to which Treece testifies here, between his sense of the importance of his liberal beliefs and the peripheral position he occupies in society. There is a further discrepancy between Treece's theoretical convictions about liberalism (and the value they attribute to personal relationships), and the difficulties he experiences in forming satisfactory personal relationships with almost everyone in the novel, from Mr Eborebelosa, the African visiting student, to Emma Fielding and Louis Bates. The comedy arises out of Treece's failure to make very much, or anything at all, of these relationships. It arises out of the mismatching of his genuinely humble appreciation of other people and his pompous supposition that, even when the way he treats them is causing irritation or dismay, his view of life makes him responsible for them. The humour arises directly out of the moral concern Bradbury shares with Treece. It is not the anarchic farce of Amis. It stands in an altogether different relation to reality.

In his 'Afterword' to *Eating People Is Wrong*, accompanying the 1979 reprint, Bradbury claims that 'the liberalism that makes Treece virtuous also makes him inert'. Treece represents 'both the absurdity and the virtue of liberalism . . . engaging with its own inconsistency and anticipating its own destruction'. This is fair comment, though, as Bradbury would admit, in the novel itself the date at which liberalism is doomed to destruction seems very far away. That is why its tone is so effervescent, its treatment of the humanist dilemma so untouched by anxiety. Until the end, that is to say, when Treece's fortunes take a sudden turn for the worse. We leave him in a hospital ward also occupied by Bates, who has tried to commit suicide after being told by Emma that she has been having an affair with Treece. This is a gratuitously dark note to close on, and one that doesn't indicate very clearly the way in which Bradbury's comic talent was to develop over the next twenty years. More to the point are references in the 'Afterword' to a change in cultural circumstances that has taken place since *Eating People Is Wrong* was first published. It seems we no longer share 'a sense of possessing a common . . . reality, as I think the fifties did'. The destruction of liberalism is well under way, at the hands of the 'stern historicism' and the 'collectivist passions' of the sixties. This, and the 'contradiction between our humanist expectations and our sense of ourselves as exposed historical performers', also referred to in the 'Afterword', are what darken the foreground of the very different comedy of Bradbury's most recent novel.

The events described in *The History Man* take place in 1967–8. People like Stuart Treece have little or no place in the University of Watermouth, where Howard Kirk, senior lecturer in Sociology, dominates the scene. He and his wife Barbara have manufactured out of an 'interpretation' of their own lives a critique of the liberal cultural values which are collapsing all around them. The ineffectuality of liberal attitudes is demonstrated by the conduct of Annie Callender, a young lecturer in the English department, and Henry Beamish, a renegade from the collectivist passions that Howard exploits with totalitarian rigour and Marxist–Freudian illogic. For Howard, human beings are not the unpredictable, free and opaque individuals who puzzled Stuart Treece in *Eating People Is Wrong*. They are predictable, determined and transparent. Especially transparent. They can be explained completely, explained away one might almost say, in a 'socio-psychological context'. As a result, human nature has become 'a particular type of relation to the temporal and historical process, culturally conditioned and afforded'. It is 'a particular performance within the available rôle sets'. The only way anyone can develop is by 'innovating' through 'manipulating options among the rôle sets'. At first Barbara shared Howard's views about human nature. She even conspired with him to publicise his views about the determination and innovation of social roles. But, when Howard makes a career out of the publicity and leaves Barbara holding the (inevitable) baby, she begins to change her mind. She wonders 'what it's got to do with real people'. She accuses him of being 'a kind of self-made fictional character who's got the whole story on his side, just because he happens to be writing it'. That is exactly what Howard does. He confuses history, or at any rate his little bit of history, with a programme of self-advancement, and identifies necessity with the quest for self-satisfaction. This produces one kind of comedy, expressed through the plot of the novel. Something rather like it, but not quite the same, produces another kind of comedy, which has very little to do with the plot, much more to do with Bradbury's manipulation of sociological jargon. I find the second kind of comedy more subtle and more satirically exposing than the first.

I think this is because the plot of the novel cheats Howard of the little that is his due. He is an arrogant but confused person, much more at the mercy of his own self-justifying ideas about history and social determinism than he would need to have been to have perpetrated the moral outrage upon which the plot of the novel turns. For at the very end of the novel Howard more or less agrees with Miss Callender that he organised the scandal of George Carmody's grades so that he could make use of him and Felicity Phee to worm his way into Annie's bed. ' "But what was it for?" asks Annie. "I wanted you," says Howard, "I just had to find a way to you." ' This seems to me to show a calculating selfishness on Howard's part, a willingness to damage two other people's lives in the service of entirely trivial schemes of self-advancement, which is inconsistent with his identification with the historical process that lies at the root of the comedy. Isn't the point Bradbury is making in *The History Man* that Howard Kirk is a stupid, not a vicious man? His relationships with his wife, his children, his colleagues, lack seriousness. He simply doesn't understand them. His materialist beliefs about progress and privacy and history fail to provide him with a moral vocabulary, or even more beliefs, which might enable him to make sense of himself and the world he lives in.

To claim that Howard lacks seriousness, or anything more than a rudimentary moral sense, is not to imply that he lacks idealism. It is to suggest that his ideals are completely identified with history, and that the only way he can develop consistently is to 'innovate' by 'manipulating options among the rôle sets'. But the impression has not been given that the 'rôle sets' include unscrupulously plotting his own self-gratification by devising a play and forcing everybody else to accept rôles in it – rôles of which they themselves are quite unaware. Or has it? Is Kirk in fact endowed with a sort of Leninist intelligence, making use of events whilst pretending to be controlled by them? That is what the plot tells us. The breathless present-tense narrative, showing Howard as totally wrapped up in the present, oblivious to the realities of past and future, seems to be implying the opposite. So does the way he tends to disappear under the levelling barrage of sociological jargon he is made to speak every time he opens his mouth, or his book. The plot seems to be pulling in the opposite direction to the dialogue, and to other ways in which the prose underlines Bradbury's attitudes. But either way the comedy is making a serious moral point about contemporary life and thought. It is a technique for dramatising and making comprehensible those 'collectivist passions' of the sixties to which Bradbury referred in his 'Afterword' to *Eating People Is Wrong*.

Compare this with what happens in *Lucky Jim*. Dixon has nothing of the morally representative existence Treece shares with Howard Kirk. His presence on the teaching-staff of a university is in any but a superficial sense an irrelevance. That is where his author was at the time, and to put him there too was a matter of convenience rather than strategy. Intelligent conversation is non-existent; students, even, are non-existent (with the exception of Michie, who makes no contribution to the plot, but appears occasionally to remind us that students do crop up from time to time in universities). Dixon has colleagues, such as Goldsmith and Johns; but Goldsmith says nothing about history, and Johns's position on the administrative staff is made use of only in so far as it allows Dixon to flush a sample of his insurance policies down the lavatory. I have already discussed the fantasy figure that is Professor Welch, and the fantasy occasion that is Dixon's lecture. Clearly the university is nothing but a geographical location, a building with people rushing about inside it for Dixon to bump into or avoid as the progress of the plot dictates.

Dixon's revolt isn't a revolt against anything that can be described as academic values, liberal or otherwise. Such values do not exist in *Lucky Jim*. Several instances of pretentiousness, hypocrisy, pomposity and humbug exist, but these qualities are merely personal. They don't establish a moral or cultural context to be investigated and ridiculed. That is why F. R. Karl, in his otherwise intelligent account of what he thinks is an Amis–Wain–Sillitoe axis in contemporary English fiction, is mistaken when he takes Amis to task for 'nowhere making it clear that Jim's level of revolt is not also his'.* But Jim's level of revolt *is* Amis's. Jim is one of those characters I discussed above, who are mouthpieces for the expression of Amis's own dissatisfaction and annoyance with the world. To have subjected him to the ironic

---

* Frederick R. Karl, *A Reader's Guide to the Contemporary English Novel* (New York, 1959; London, 1965).

treatment Karl thinks is appropriate would have been to convert him into a free character of a kind I have suggested Amis takes no interest in. Of course Amis wants to outrage the reader by emphasising the philistinism and sheer rudeness that accompany Dixon's hatred of cant. He also makes Jim physically unprepossessing in order to put some superficial distance between his character and himself. But, in all the important senses, Jim acts on Amis's behalf – pulling his faces, enacting his fantasies, perpetrating his jokes. In this respect Amis is not a bit like Fielding. The irony has to be missing where the Fielding-*like* comic incidents are being used to display a temperament rather than to create a world.

In so far as anything morally interesting is going on at all in *Lucky Jim*, it has to do with Dixon's decision to sever his relationship with Margaret Peel and run away with Christine Callaghan. Although Jim's scenes with Margaret allow her to let off a little psychological steam (Margaret's success as a character anticipates Amis's other successes with temperamentally 'difficult' wives and girlfriends – Martha Thompson, for example, in *Take a Girl Like You*, or Adela Bastable in *Ending Up*), they are on the whole rather tedious; as are Jim's reflections on his guilt, or unwillingness to accept his guilt, over the way he has treated her. 'Whatever passably decent treatment Margaret had had from him', he supposes, 'was the result of a temporary victory of fear over irritation and/or pity over boredom'. The irritation and boredom come over very well. It is the fear and the pity which remain mere words, and rather too many of them. In any case, Dixon is let off the hook with Margaret when Catchpole, her previous 'lover', tells him the truth about the overdose of sleeping-pills she took the night Dixon was expected to call at her flat. This has always struck me as a reason for Dixon to stay with Margaret rather than to leave her. Her phoney suicide attempt was clearly an act of desperation. Although Dixon might well take the view that he owes her rather less in the emotional sense than she has led him to believe he does, he surely can't think that her behaviour in this matter provides him with a *carte blanche* to forget about her altogether and run off with Christine. In spite of the moral fuss Dixon makes about Margaret, his preference for Christine is really no more than a consequence of his frequently articulated conviction that 'nice things are nicer than nasty things', and that Christine's character is 'workable', while

Margaret's is not. That doesn't seem like a very profound solution to Dixon's dilemma. He has simply substituted pragmatic for moral reasons for behaving as he does. The inconsequentiality of this form of moralising by a character is demonstrated even more graphically in *Take a Girl Like You* when Standish subjects Sheila Torkington to an earnest, carefully considered, ever-so-closely-reasoned lecture on why it would be wrong for him to enter into an affair with the seventeen-year-old daughter of his headmaster, and then goes on to say 'However, since you've taken the trouble to turn up . . .' and seduces her. Standish is one of Amis's most admired male leads. I suppose we must interpret his behaviour here as just another of those occasions when nice things are nicer than nasty ones, even when the nice thing in this instance has a long chin and turns out to be two months pregnant.

At the end of *Lucky Jim* Dixon doesn't only get the girl, he gets the money too. More precisely, he gets the job in London, as Julius Gore-Urquart's secretary, that Bertrand Welch was fishing for at the university dance. Bertrand obviously doesn't deserve the job. He is a talentless nincompoop with genteel *fin de siècle* views about art, which Dixon quite properly ridicules. Besides, he is Neddy Welch's son. But does Dixon deserve it? Gore-Urquart's opinion is that, although he hasn't got the qualifications for the work, 'or any other work', he hasn't got the disqualifications either. What are the disqualifications Dixon hasn't got? No doubt being a conceited bore and pretentious twit like Bertrand is one of them. But aren't knowing nothing about art, and not having a clue about how to make oneself socially acceptable to people rather massive disqualifications too, for the private secretary to a 'rich devotee of the arts' who intends to use him for 'meeting people or telling people I can't meet them'? This is not the real world of art and patronage, any more than the university was a real place where people taught things and learned things. It is a world in which farcical vitality and advanced powers of ridicule are rewarded by material success, as a gesture in the direction of comic justice. Just as the funnier the things are that John Lewis does in his effort to escape from Gruffyd-Williams's house, the better time he deserves to have with Elizabeth on the beach, and the greater success he deserves to have at his interview with the library committee (later cancelled in favour of renewed marital harmony and a decent job with the coal board); so Dixon's reward is a reward he earns through his contribution to the farce rather than any sterling moral qualities he has displayed. Although there is more than enough moral fussing in *Lucky Jim*, there is hardly any moral content, in the sense of a correspondence between the moral complexion of what any of the characters *do* and the way the reader is invited to pass judgements on the kinds of people any of them *are*.

One other 'moral' aspect *Lucky Jim* shares with many of Amis's later novels is the reappearance of the eighteenth- (and nineteenth-)century novel's dependence on rich benefactors, who are there to impress the hero with their admirable styles of life, and often to provide him with a route to salvation through a lavish display of financial patronage. Gore-Urquart is the first of such figures in Amis's work – as free with his whisky bottle as he is with his sinecures. Gruffyd-Williams plays the part in *That Uncertain Feeling*. Although at first he seems a dull stick, later it transpires that he is a sensitive soul and a handy *deus ex machina* to have about when Lewis and Elizabeth are involved in a car accident. He turns up again in a different guise in *Take a Girl Like You* as Julian Ormerod – treading a delicate balance between the predatory sexuality, and the decent respect for other people (note his attitude over the rape of Jenny Bunn), that Amis admires. Evidently the stream of seemingly inexhaustible financial benevolence shamelessly admired in characters ranging from Fielding's Squire Allworthy to Dickens's John Jarndyce, has not been dammed up by the welfare state. John Wain's Joe Lumley also benefits from such liberal patronage, in his employment as Mr Bracewright's chauffeur in *Hurry on Down*. None of these notably angry novelists is in the slightest degree angry about Mr Bracewright and his ilk. But I don't think this is immoral. It is just another piece of evidence that their characters don't live in anything resembling the real world. They are all creatures of fantasy, metaphors of the author's imagination kept busy by being projected onto the accidental twists and turns of an eighteenth-century picaresque narrative.

'Lumley is characteristic . . . of most of the Angry protagonists. They rebel and then find some niche for themselves that fails to accommodate their former intention. The honesty of the intention becomes transformed into the expedience of reality' (Karl). Well, Lumley is characteristic in this way. So are Dixon, Standish, Douglas Yandell (the narrator of *Girl, 20*) and others. But what Karl calls 'the expedience of reality' has more in common with

those merely literary rewards and punishments that eighteenth-
century and Dickensian heroes have handed out to them in the
final chapters of the novels they belong to. Amis isn't saying,
'Look, Jim, everything you've done proves that you're a fundamentally good and decent fellow, just the right chap for the job
Gore-Urquart wants to offer you, and the right chap for that nice
girl Christine too.' He is saying something much more like, 'Well
done, Jim, very funny performance. Off you go now and collect
your money and give Christine Callaghan an extra one for me.'
The one interpretation is consistent with reading the book as if it
were a basically serious, though comic, commentary on aspects of
modern life and society. The other implies that the book is nothing
of the kind, but a device for allowing Amis to let off steam about
some of his favourite likes and dislikes by matching a persistent
mood of exasperation with the kind of story that usually serves the
purpose Karl believes this one does. I can understand why he
thinks so: there is a fair amount of 'evangelical puffing and
blowing' in some of the 'dead' scenes from the book. But these are
superorogatory. On the other hand Amis does claim that he
admires 'moral seriousness' in novels, and we shall have to
inquire as to how he gets this over in his own fiction. First,
however, more needs to be said about the comic devices by means
of which he conveys his exasperation, irritability and general
dissatisfaction with the world, the foundation on which his novels
are built.

Abasing himself before Margaret Peel after she has discovered his
preference for Christine Callaghan over herself, Jim Dixon finds
himself saying things about how he should stick by her, do the
decent thing, not throw her over just because he finds another
woman more attractive than he finds her. A minute or more
passes by, and then Dixon realises that it wasn't really himself
speaking. He wasn't really there at all, except as a sort of
ventriloquist's dummy manipulated by someone else from outside:

> Dixon felt that his role in this conversation, as indeed in the
> whole of his relations with Margaret, had been directed by
> something outside himself and yet not directly present in her.
> He felt more than ever before that what he said and did arose

not out of any willing on his part, nor even out of boredom, but out of a sense of situation. And where did that sense come from if, as it seemed, he took no share in willing it.

There is an obvious answer to that last question. It came from Kingsley Amis. After all, Dixon is only one of Amis's characters. Amis is doing all the thinking and talking, really. But that is not the point he wants to make here. Amis is not one of those novelists, referred to in the Introduction to this book, who think it is enormously helpful to let their characters know that they are living in a book, not in a world jointly populated by themselves and their readers. On the other hand I have claimed that they don't seem to live very much in a world at all, if by a 'world' we mean, as we usually do when we are discussing novels, a dense network of experiences, memories, places and relationships. I have also claimed that they are very much the expressions or objects of their author's sense of the absurdity of the world, and of his anger, irritation, and so forth, that that is what the world is like. So Dixon's awareness that his behaviour is automatic, and doesn't seem to issue from anything that could be described as his own motives or intentions or requirements is probably related to the way he is being manipulated by an author who is using him to say things and do things over which he himself has no control whatsoever.

Dixon's 'automatic' behaviour in this scene with Margaret Peel is not an isolated occurrence. Over and over again in the novels, characters feel either that, like Dixon, they are not responsible for themselves, that they are doing things and saying things that have nothing to do with them and don't concern them; or that they have split personalities, in which what they are doing and what they are thinking are so far apart from each other that there is no logically explicable relation between them. Another good example of this is the episode, also in *Lucky Jim* (ch. 7), in which Dixon cannot rid himself of the notion that both he and Margaret are figures on celluloid, acting in a film that Margaret has scripted. She is acting much better than he is because he can't ignore the triteness of the dialogue, and speaks his lines with increasing exaggeration and insincerity. Examples of what I call the schizophrenic syndrome abound, increasing significantly in number and severity the closer the hero gets to sexual intercourse. Sexual contact is an almost sure-fire precipitant of this curious mental disturbance. Take Maurice Allington, for example, in *The Green Man*. Screwing Diana Maybury, his imaginative lucubrations revolve around performing a piano sonata at the same time as he is lunching off a plate of sandwiches (not altogether off the beam if we remember that he fills in much of the rest of the time counting to himself in units of thousands, with the object of calculating the time 'to an accuracy of within two seconds per timed minute'). Or Patrick Standish with 'Joan' in *Take a Girl Like You*. He divides his mind between declining the Latin *Dies* in the singular Common, and working out a chess problem involving the move (1) P–K4. The sexual operation itself is described in terms of mains-frequency fluctuation attendant on playing a gramophone record at 16²/₃ r.p.m. There are plenty of other such hiatuses between mind and body during the sexual act. For example, instead of declining Latin nouns, Micheldene quotes chunks of the *Aeneid* to himself, followed by a clutch of Greek irregulars, thence to Chaucer, and on to plushy Victorian fourteeners, his mind working 'like a motor' until he withdraws into sheer inanition – 'One of the really good ones, he thought'.

Even allowing for a brake on premature ejaculation, this is an odd way of having sex. But, as I have implied, it is only the intensification of a discordance between thought and action that is widespread in Amis's fiction. At other times it almost takes on a metaphysical rather than a psychological colouring. For example, in *Lucky Jim* (ch. 18) Dixon looks out of the window of Professor Welch's car as it slows at a road junction. On one side he catches sight of his barber, eyeing two pretty girls who have stopped at a pillar box a few yards away. On the other side he sees a batsman being hit in the stomach by a cricket ball. Dixon's response is to wonder 'whether this pair of *vignettes* was designed to illustrate the swiftness of divine retribution or its tendency to mistake its target'. It seems as if the world at large manifests a lack of connection between thought and action (theologically speaking) or cause and effect (speaking in merely physical terms).

Description of such elaborate mental operations is almost invariably funny. And it combines with other features of Amis's comic method which depend for their effect on disjunctions of one kind or another: between what a character is thinking and what he is doing; or between what he is thinking and what Amis is doing with his thoughts – especially when he gets involved in the mechanics of transcribing actual events into written ones. In these latter cases there is once again a discrepancy between what the prose is telling us and what it sounds like when it is performing that function. The most obvious way the prose draws attention to itself is through the transcription of sounds which either do mean or seem to mean something as sounds, but which mean something entirely different, or nothing at all, when they are written down. In *Lucky Jim* this is happening all the time with Bertrand's habit of adding the suffix 'am' to words ending with a long vowel: 'Christine is my girl and stays my girl, got mam.' In chapter 11 the words of a popular song are set down exactly as they sound, with ridiculous effect:

> Ah'll be parp tar gat you in a taxi, honny,
> Ya'd batter be raddy 'bout a parp-parp eight;
> Ahr, baby, dawn't be late,
> Ah'm gonna parp parp parp whan the band starts playeeng.

Just what you do when you 'parp' leaves the mind in a state of pleasurable disbelief, in the same way as we shall never hear Nat King Cole quite as we used to after Amis's transcription of two immortal lines as 'Dorling – it's increddabull – that you should be so – unforgeddabull' (*Take a Girl Like You*, ch. 8). Writing it down, in both cases, subtly yet outrageously changes the whole ambience of the song, and with it the human emotions it strives to express through *sound*.

This is not far away from verbal parody of a more conventional kind, and there is a great deal of this too in Amis, often very funny. Examples taken almost at random are the Dylan Thomas-ish lines of Gareth Probert's play *The Martyr* (*That Uncertain Feeling*, ch. 9); the blurb beneath the pin-up girl in John Lewis's magazine (the 'Jolly Skipper') a double parody, this, both of that kind of blurb and of Amis's own poem 'A Note on Wyatt' (though without the mixed metaphors in the latter case: *That Uncertain Feeling*, ch. 8); Mr Bunn's transformation of commonplace Anglo-Saxon surnames into their presumed Yiddish originals (*Take a Girl Like You*, ch. 15); the notes for Fr Ayscue's sermon (*The Anti-Death League*, pt II); the extract from *The Good Food Guide* about Allington's pub at the beginning of *The Green Man*, plus the brilliant parodies of the eighteenth-century diarists in the same novel; and, perhaps most brilliant of all, the expression of George Zeyer's nominal aphasia in *Ending Up*. The effectiveness of some of these parodies also depends on our recognition of the sounds of the words, before they are written down, and then our surprise at the odd things that happen to them when they are written down. Here again we are being amused by the way things we expect to coalesce, to settle comfortably into position in a single word actually do the opposite: i.e. pull apart from each other, exposing the absurdity of a world that has all the appearance of being a vacuum mechanically inserted between linguistic signs that are performing no useful linguistic function.

Words behave strangely when their sound and grammatical function are isolated from their sense. Combinations of words also behave strangely. Sentences are forced to extend themselves, under the pressure of the anxiety, curiosity or ill temper of whoever has stuck them together, into ever more complex (though they are intended to become ever more accurate) descriptions of what that person wanted to say. Hence planning or forethought or considered deliberation of any kind on the part of Amis is likely to produce almost incredible contortions of syntax. Making arrangements to seduce pretty women almost always bring into being such 'multi-sequiturs' as this:

> In the last five seconds it had become almost overwhelmingly unlikely that she would meet me the following afternoon, because she was now in the uncommonly rewarding position of being able to stand me up without having incurred the odium of having actually broken an arrangement. On the other hand, she was very much capable of following this line of argument and so going along to the agreed corner to find me not there, which would shove me back to the wrong side of square one, not to speak of the questions about why I was so changeable and so selfish, and did I think it was because I was so insecure that I would have to sweat through a part of the shoving. And, being Diana, to have got that far would mean she would know, without having to think about it, that I would have got as far as it too. So I would have to turn up anyway. But I had been going to do that all along.

The curious spiralling effect of language is not merely the product of an aberration in Allington's mind. Patrick Standish finds language and logic spinning away from him in ever-increasing circles in just such a way when he is shaving in the bathroom after an early-morning bout with 'Joan':

While he shaved, Patrick thought about that smile. The addition of a lack of sweetness to a look of intellect and to beauty was overwhelming. '*What Lola wants*,' he sang to himself, '*Lola gets*.' It made no difference to point out that the sweetness was as adventitious as the intellect, because the beauty was not. Beauty was not of an order of being in which it made sense to talk of adventitiousness. '*What Lola goes through the motions of wanting and oughtn't to have, Lola all too often gets*.' You could not have beauty that had a look of sourness or stupidity; we didn't call that beauty. Beauty without *real* sweetness or *real* mind was as beautiful as beauty with. It was only when it came to dealing with the two sorts that you saw a difference. Did you? Did he? In two or three years would there be much to choose between his relations with Joan if he were Mr Joan and with Jenny if he were Mr Jenny? '*What Lola imagines she might be thought original and interesting if she pretended to want, Lola will use her sex on some poor bloody fool to see that she gets*.'

Amis is partial to linguistic puzzles of this kind. His poem 'The Voice of Authority' makes its point through a similar kind of linguistic joke to the ones Maurice Allington and Patrick Standish play on themselves, or have played on them (the words and the thoughts both seem to have got completely out of their control) in these two passages.

The comic violence that Amis's novels are full of is another manifestation of the hiatus between thought and action, between the world as a character might actually experience it and the world as Amis makes him reconstruct it in his own imagination. Jim Dixon beats Neddy Welch's head in with a bottle; he shoves beads up Margaret Peel's nose. John Lewis dashes the bodies of the book-borrowers at Aberdarcy library onto the stone floor of his coal cupboard. Patrick Standish and Graham McClintoch hunt Dick Thompson with long-range syringes filled with acid or a solution of itching-powder. The common factor of all these happenings is that they are entirely imaginary. They depend on the existence of a hypothetical twin for each of the characters concerned, a twin who inhabits the purely mental world of the hero, for purposes of humiliation, violence, the infliction of pain. The twins live in completely separate worlds. Often there is no justification, beyond plain dislike, for the extremity of one character's sadistic treatment of the imaginary clone he has created from another.

How are we to explain these peculiarities, shared by so many of Amis's heroes: the mechanistic behaviour, the schizophrenia, the separation of word and thing, the uncontrollable spirals of logic, and the comic violence perpetrated on the unwitting clones? What moral statement is Amis trying to make by recourse to this wild comedy? Or is it just comedy for its own sake, a totally irresponsible playing with words and worlds? We need to trace these peculiar habits of mind to the emotional attitudes they express; and then back to the likeable–detestable heroes in whom they are incorporated. When we have done that we might be able to understand the basic preoccupations Amis has always shared with these characters, and be able to relate them to whatever there is of 'moral seriousness' in the novels he has written.

The most immediately noticeable characteristic of Amis man is his manic irritability. None of the heroes of any of these novels possesses an ounce of composure. The smallest inconvenience is likely to get him to run up a fever of sullenness, petulance or rage. This can happen quite out of the blue, with nothing at all to explain it. It is experienced in a mild, not very advanced form by John Lewis when his wife has left the house for a few hours to meet a friend. He is left with time on his hands:

> How, then, was I going to spend the next hour ... ? In defending myself, presumably, against a certain feeling. Such defence was never easy, because of its habit of confusing itself with the feeling. How to define this feeling? Depression? Not a bad shot. Boredom? Oh yes. A slight tinge, too, eh, of uneasiness and inert, generalized lust. Yes, indeed. The centre of it might be called boredom, but ... restless.

Lewis gets rid of the feeling by poring over a photograph of a pin-up girl in a magazine, and then having a blazing row with his landlady. Otherwise the feeling of restless boredom, depression, uneasiness and what he calls 'inert generalized lust', it is suggested, would have ended either in the release of auto-eroticism, or prolonged irritability leading to petulance and anger. All the feelings, that is to say, that beset so many of Amis's other characters. Their oscillation between egotism and unrest accounts in large part for our inability to like them, but our inclination to admire them all the same, because they are intelligent and witty and sexually voracious.

By the time we have reached Amis's fourth novel, *Take a Girl Like You*, this feeling of dissatisfaction, of vague uneasiness, has changed to something more definite; though it still breaks in on the hero without warning, and for no apparent reason. Patrick Standish, waiting for Jenny Bunn to come and make love with him at his flat, has been passing the time inventing a list of Twelve Bad Men, a trivial doodling exercise not calculated to stimulate the mind to feats of metaphysical speculation. Then, suddenly, he feels 'a sharp uneasiness' start up inside him. As with Lewis, sex has something, but by no means everything, to do with it. 'His breathing quickened and deepened as at the onset of sexual excitement, but this was not his condition.' Descriptions of various discomforts follow, but, we are told, 'Nothing in his thoughts or his situation accounted for these symptoms which, the accompaniments of terror, stirred in him more than one kind of terror, as they had recently been doing every other night or so while he lay awake in bed.' What Patrick is experiencing is a disturbing physical manifestation of the fear of death, the terrified thought that one day, perhaps sooner rather than later, he will be part of what he mockingly calls 'Charon's quota'. It has happened before, in equally inconsequential circumstances. For example, after he had been speaking to one of his pupils about the school play: 'his heart vibrated in the way it had recently started to do and he had the familiar but never at other times imaginable, feeling of being outside himself, as if his brain had suddenly frozen and become a fixed camera, while his body continued to breathe and walk and turn its head about in a simulacrum of attention'.

Standish's experience is repeated by nearly all the heroes of the later books. Micheldene, Churchill, Hunter, Allington, Bastable all experience in a very physical way the panic that follows on an awareness of the imminence of death. It is interesting that, in the account of Standish's experience, the separation of the mind from the body discussed earlier in relation to Amis's farcical man-oeuvres, has become a metaphor suggesting what a person's state of mind might be like at the moment of death. Elsewhere, when Amis's characters brood on death, or are put into a panic by some such physical sensation as Standish feels here, they tend to associate their experience with the workings of a mechanical device. The brain clicks away like a camera at the automaton the body has become. Life itself becomes a mechanism when viewed from the vantage point of death. Looking at things in this way, Maurice Allington comes to realise 'we're all on conveyer-belts' that represent the process of dying; and we stay on them 'from the moment we're born'. All adult human beings, in Allington's view, have experienced life as a mindless machine hurtling towards destruction. Therefore, he claims, it is difficult to understand why they don't spend the whole of their lives thinking about it. These are almost his exact words. And it occurs to me that that is what most of Kingsley Amis's heroes have been trying to avoid doing ever since John Lewis's 'uncertain feeling' defined itself more clearly as a fear of death. By the time Amis wrote *The Anti-Death League*, in 1972, the subject had become obsessional. All his best books since that time – *The Green Man* and *Ending Up* – have taken death as their unmistakable central theme.

One would suppose that only a person for whom life is something enormously to be enjoyed would inflate the fear of death to such grotesquely obsessive proportions. In both *The Anti-Death League* and *The Green Man* Amis tries to convince us that, in spite of all the ills that flesh is heir to, this is so. James Churchill has his idyllic love for Catherine Casement, Maurice Allington his affection for his father and love of his daughter Amy. But at the heart of these desirable relationships there is also horror, the intimations of mortality. Catherine develops cancer of the breast and has to be surgically mutilated. Old Mr Allington dies. And Amy is almost raped and murdered, because her father's selfish lust has drawn the ghost of Thomas Underhill and the green man to his house. In *The Anti-Death League* Churchill and Hunter are employed in a sinister secret army unit which plans to decimate millions of Chinese by infecting them with a terrible plague (or so they suppose). At the end of the last chapter the chaplain's little dog is pointlessly run over by a lorry: in the village church nearby, his master has just presided over the singing of the anthem 'Lord, Protect Thou Thy Servants'. The League itself has been invented to expose the immorality of worshipping a God who lets the innocent die and arbitrarily kills and maims women and children. As a result the chapter entitled 'The Founding of the League' reads at times like a sort of rehash of the scene of Ivan

Karamazov's argument with Alyosha in *The Brothers Karamazov*. It comes to the conclusion that to return the ticket is not enough; you have to kill the conductor too.

However, because life is shot through with reminders of death, whether one is considering the deliberate extermination of millions of Chinese, or the accidental destruction of a pet dog crossing the road, it hardly seems worth living after all. Even if your own girl hasn't got cancer, so many other fellows' have. And then there are all those newspaper reports about people swallowing raw potatoes and dying of asphyxiation; jumping from burning buildings and being smashed on the pavements below; gaining their sight one day, after fifteen years of blindness, and dying of a virus infection the next. There is a strong and passionate feeling in *The Anti-Death League* that death has rendered life unendurable, and that, in spite of alternative persuasions from Willie Ayscue and Catherine Casement, it is Churchill and Hunter who represent Amis's own point of view. That is one of sheer despair. In a covert way it has crept into Amis's novels from the beginning. After all, many of even his early poems are about death (for instance, 'The Real Earth'). And the first of his (later) 'Three Scenarios' is directly comparable with Max Hunter's verses 'For a Baby Born without Limbs'. In both of the last-mentioned poems Amis's sense of outrage against the existence of deformity and disease is very strongly conveyed. No wonder he wants to return the ticket. But in a post-Christian, irreligious world, the question has to be posed: to whom?

Amis's horror of death, accompanied by a keen sense of the absurdity of lives that are little more than frenetic preparations for it, accounts in large part for the farcical treatment of character, event and language in all of his novels – even those early ones where the obsession went undisclosed. Farce is one way of expressing one's sense of the futility of life. To convert men into machines, and events into a sort of electric current that galvanises them into furious but aimless activity; to play with the words they speak, and that they write down, as if they were basically meaningless coincidences of sounds and ciphers; to invent people all over again and subject them to therapeutic, though imaginary, tortures and humiliations – these are the consequences of not being able to see why one shouldn't spend the whole of one's life thinking about death, or trying to stop oneself thinking about death.

There is a haunting line in one of Philip Larkin's poems about 'the costly aversion of the eyes from death'. It explains a lot about Amis. His novels show that there is both a pay-off and a price to pay for this. The price is his inability to construct a world that possesses any meaning at all, a world that might encourage one to attend seriously to questions of human motive and intention, and their relation to effects and consequences. The pay-off is his freedom to play with the world as he finds it in as irresponsible a way as God, if he had existed, must be presumed to have played when he first created it. To do that in literary terms is to create farce. To do it in reality is, of course, to produce quite another thing: tragedy, melodrama, absurdity – or Christianity.

I mention Christianity because that is the soft underbelly of Amis's own culture which seeks to justify a world he thinks is unjustifiable. The God of Christianity actually makes an appearance at Maurice Allington's pub near the end of *The Green Man*. Allington puts the question to him: why did he make that other, more highly publicised visit 1969 years before? 'Mmm. I must have been bored', he says. 'I thought, why not? Then I thought I was heading straight for disaster. I needn't have worried, need I? He [Christ] hasn't made much difference to anything.' Whatever moral seriousness Amis's novels possess has to do with this point of view. For good and ill, it makes it impossible for him ever to be serious about anything else.

7 V. S. Naipaul

One of the finest living novelists writing in English is not by birth an Englishman. The distinction and fastidiousness of V. S. Naipaul's prose are the fruits of an English education begun at Queen's Royal College, in Port of Spain, Trinidad, and completed at Oxford. Later, in London and elsewhere, he made of that prose a flexible and powerful instrument of narrative, description and socio-political analysis. But his first eighteen years were spent in Trinidad and, as the novels show, to have profited by this experience is to have been prepared in a very special way for the occupation of being an English writer.

Yet an English writer is what Naipaul is. All his writing life he has been based in London. His publishers are London publishers selling books directly to English readers. The rhythms of his prose are English rhythms, and the speech his characters speak, where translation from a foreign tongue (Hindi for example) is necessary, is English speech. In the later books there are several English characters. In two of them (*Mr Stone and the Knights Companion* and *In a Free State*) they are at the centre of the narrative. And the metropolitan standards to which the behaviour of his colonials is almost invariably referred, and which are therefore frequently questioned and critically examined, are English standards – partly viewed in their 'provincial' aspect, partly as the expression of a wider European culture.

Naipaul values this culture, and feels himself to be very much a part of it. Nevertheless he is a Trinidadian and he is an Indian, an East Indian – which means that his early life was shaped as much by his family's Hinduism as it was by the Western ideas he absorbed at Queen's. This accounts for many of the complications in his writing. It also accounts for his uniquely authoritative position as an interpreter of colonial societies.

Lacking contact with the negro Trinidadians, Naipaul lived his early life in an extremely protected environment. To be an East Indian was to be a member of a colony within a colony, artificially undisturbed by the pressures of colonial dependence. As he was to write in *The Middle Passage*, 'Living by themselves in villages, the Indians were able to have a complete community life . . . it was a world of its own, a community within the colonial society, without responsibility, with authority doubly or trebly removed.' Contact with the West, through Queen's Royal College, produced complications, and embarrassments. But this unique experience gave Naipaul something very useful to a writer of colonial life: involvement in a settled, highly stratified community; and awareness of a less rigidly organised but more mobile, even restless society surrounding it. Memories of the complete, inturned society of Changuanas complicated Naipaul's involvement in that other, incomplete, outward-turning society he found in the West. Later his residence in London, and his travels in India, Africa and Latin America, exposed more of the complication, and it became an effective channel for communicating what lay beneath the politics of exploitation and distress.

Naipaul claims that the security of his Indian childhood left him prey to many kinds of ignorance and self-deception. But I think he realised from a very early age that it also protected him from more insidious and longer lasting misunderstandings of the colonial experience – misunderstandings that few other colonial writers have escaped. Being part of a minority within a minority is no bad thing to be if you are trying to achieve an unprejudiced insight into the situation in which both minorities define themselves as such. To be a member of the outer circle, as it were, immediately and rawly exposed to pressures exerted from beyond it, is to be placed in a position of great temptation – the temptation to react abrasively, myopically, angrily and falsely. But the protection afforded against those pressures by being in the inner circle might be not merely comfortable, but useful too, in so far as it serves to depress a sense of grievance issuing from private as well as political sources.

Geographically, Naipaul made the leap from the inner circle to what lay beyond the outer: by way of Queen's Royal College he moved from Chaguanas to London. But in doing this he did not become a metropolitan. He did not become a colonial of the outer circle either. His double vision of the colonial predicament from both inside and outside was much more comprehensive than anything West Indian novelists of the outer circle, such as George Lamming or Edgar Mittelholzer, have been able to evolve. For

Naipaul, the abrasive contact with an 'enemy' outside was not there. He saw the enemy *inside* the colony clearly, because at first he looked inwards to the Indian community, and only *then* outwards to the negro community surrounding it. There he saw the tensions the negroes, or West Indians, had created for themselves out of the colonial situation imposed on them by the West. That situation was inevitable. The negroes, as later the East Indians, had been a part of the colonising process. There are no West Indians, in the literal sense of the word, in the West Indies now. They were all exterminated (as Naipaul shows in *The Loss of El Dorado*). Nobody's people have been in Trinidad or Jamaica, or any island in the sun, 'since time begun', because those who had been there had been murdered. Being an East Indian in a rural backwater of Trinidad, rather than a West Indian negro in the city, Naipaul was in a good position to see that. He understands similar things about oppression elsewhere, in countries where minorities within minorities, colonies within colonies, also exist. It is surprising how many of them there are.

In his early novels Naipaul tried to write about the East Indians of Trinidad in a way that ignored, except by the gentlest implications, the wider West Indian society in which they lived. After all, to do just this was very difficult. Nobody had done it before. His father had tried to do it, but with limited and rather special success.* In any case, nobody outside Trinidad, and few inside it, even in the Indian community, had read Seepersad Naipaul's stories. So Naipaul was more or less starting from scratch. He risked charges of triviality or, at best, exoticism – the expectation that his readers, if there were any, would be interested in the subjects of his stories rather than with the way he treated them. As he explained in an early essay ('Jasmine'), 'Fiction or any work of the imagination, whatever its quality, hallows its subject. To attempt, with a full consciousness of established authoritative mythologies, to give a quality of myth to what was agreed to be petty and ridiculous ... required courage.' This was what Naipaul set out to do in *Miguel Street*, the first written, though third published, of his books. In the event what he did was rather different. Here, and in *The Mystic Masseur* and *The Suffrage of*

---

* See Landeg White, *V. S. Naipaul: A Critical Introduction* (London, 1975) ch. 2, for a full account of the influence of Seepersad Naipaul on his son's early fiction.

Elvira, he gave what he calls 'a quality of myth' to his subjects. But he also implies that there are very considerable limitations inherent in the subject, and these limitations render its mythical elevation something of an absurdity. The subject may be colourful, but it is also impoverished. Naipaul's definition of this impoverishment is the main business of his early fiction. Its quality can be assessed by looking at the way Naipaul shows how the impoverishment of his characters' lives is closely related to their colourfulness. What seemed like a compensation turns out to have been at least as much a cause. There is sadness, as well as comedy, in the 'personality cult' of Miguel Street.

Miguel Street is not Chaguanas. It has nothing of the structured, organised quality Naipaul suggests sustained him during his first eight years of village life. Instead it is a cross-section of what Naipaul calls elsewhere the 'picaroon society', a society in which the sense of community is held in precarious balance with each individual's assertion of merely selfish impulses and desires. 'In the colonial society', he writes in *The Middle Passage*, 'every man had to be for himself; every man had to grasp whatever dignity and power he was allowed; he owed no loyalty to the island and scarcely any to his own group.' This is what we find in the inhabitants of Miguel Street.

Living in the street imposes on its residents no other duty than to be themselves. To be themselves in the most amusing, striking, theatrical, colourful way they can discover. How do they fulfil this duty? The observant and involved manner in which the narrator, a fatherless street arab, recreates the characters from memory gives us the impression that they do it in a wide variety of ways. Bogart commits bigamy in order to produce a child and then, having done so, comes back to Miguel Street so that he can be 'a man among men' again; Popo the carpenter used to make 'things without a name', or purpose, but, now he has retrieved his wife from her lover, and come out of gaol after serving a sentence for selling stolen furniture, he is busy making morris chairs; Eddoes gives up trying to pass his Cambridge Certificate and ends up driving a scavenging-cart; B. Wordsworth is writing a long poem. On the surface they are all different, all projecting images of themselves as eccentric individualists enjoying the spectacle of one another's separateness, the styles they have chosen in order to assert their personalities. But, in a world where the most important thing to be is individual, nobody's individuality has any lasting value. In the end you can only measure individuality against a standard of personal conduct, within a consensus of opinion about what constitutes permissible and impermissible behaviour. In Miguel Street this is imposed from outside, in the form of the law, and the gaol sentences that such a large proportion of the characters receive. These sentences seem to bear no relation to judgements made by people in the street. Their judgements are completely aesthetic, completely to do with style.

Morgan the pyrotechnicist fails to impress the street with his firework displays. He tries to assert his personality by devising an elaborate system of punishments for his children, and then carrying them out before as large an audience as he can muster. But there is no response, no laughter. That is what he wants: to be laughed at, to be a clown – which is to be noticed. But he is laughed at only when his wife finds him with another woman and makes a public exhibition of him. This is merely humiliating. He has been allowed to act the clown only by *being* the clown, by having the ability to project himself as a clown taken out of his own hands. As a result he burns the house down. Morgan's failure provides a context for Bogart's success – or Eddoes's, or Bhakcu's, or Edwards's, for objectively each of them is as big a failure as Morgan. Bogart is sent to gaol, Eddoes drives the rubbish cart, Edwards is made a fool of by an American woman. In fact almost all the inhabitants of Miguel Street are hopeless failures. But most of them fail with style – and, in their terms, that is to succeed. There is no higher criterion of what a man is worth. As a result, when the narrator grows up, even three years later, and is able to view the world with eyes that have taken in more than Miguel Street alone, the people in it look very different: 'It was just three years, three years in which I had grown up and looked critically at the people around me. I no longer wanted to be like Eddoes. He was so weak and thin, and I hadn't realised he was so small. Titus Hoyt was stupid and boring, not funny at all. Everything had changed.' But it had not changed. Only the context in which it was seen had done that. It is the enlargement of this context, working outwards from the picaroon vivacity and insubstantiality, to a more and more responsible, complex and subtle awareness of the circumstances in which human beings find themselves, that enriches Naipaul's art.

In Miguel Street there are few social conventions, and Naipaul has written elsewhere (in *The Middle Passage*) that 'A literature can grow only out of a strong framework of social convention.' In a setting where the only social convention is to be unconventional, there is little scope for the representation of any but the most superficial aspects of character. Of course no society can do without conventions at all, not even one that depends on institutions outside itself to prevent it from falling into anarchy. People such as George (in 'George and the Pink House') are generally disliked, and the way George treats his wife and son have a lot to do with the dislike, so the dislike does have some sort of moral foundation. But George has no charisma. He is not able to project an amusing image of himself; and that might have at least as much to do with the way his conduct is evaluated. Clearly a society that responds to Man-man's nonsensical self-crucifixion by hurling stones at him has next to no moral sense. The crude aesthetic spectacle, not the inner psychological anguish, is what appeals to them. Man-man is taken away to an asylum. Outside authority removes what might otherwise have been a problem to be dealt with by the Street itself. The framework of social convention which allows people to amuse themselves by stoning a lunatic is obviously very weak. Working inside it is unlikely to produce a readable literature at all. Even working outside it, as Naipaul, through his manipulation of the street-arab narrator does, can only produce a handful of amusing sketches. Clearly the subject itself needs to change; the society that is written about, even if it includes Miguel Street, needs to be more mature, more generously endowed with moral and psychological possibilities.

The Mystic Masseur and *The Suffrage of Elvira* go some way towards extending Naipaul's range. Pundit Ganesh, although a self-advertiser in the picaroon manner, is a much more interesting character than any of the people we met in Miguel Street, much more interesting than we might have assumed he *could* be from the glimpse we get of him in the last story of that volume. Indeed the narrator of *The Mystic Masseur* claims that 'the history of Ganesh is, in a way, the history of our times'. If this is so, it is because Ganesh's struggle to assert himself takes place in an environment that includes a great deal more than there ever was in Miguel Street. It includes, above all, an interest in the emotional attitudes of the characters as they are experienced from the inside, and an interest in the way such attitudes can affect and be affected by movements in society around them. Ganesh achieves his reputation as a pundit and politician as a result of a startling connection between his private struggle to improve his status and aspects of the development of Trinidadian society that make its members especially vulnerable to the way he has chosen to project himself, to impose himself on them. There is a psychological and social dimension in *The Mystic Masseur* that was absent in the short stories. There, the street arab's account of what happened on Miguel Street was for the most part a collaborative one. Until the last two stories it was visibly influenced by the vivacity of the morally dimensionless lives that provided its subject. Here the street arab has grown up, and records Ganesh's story with a lightly mocking attitude that goes some way to 'placing' it in a wider context of Trinidadian life.

Ganesh *is* a representative figure. His half-baked Hindu upbringing has left him with a fatalistic attitude: ' "I suppose" Ganesh wrote in *The Years of Guilt*, "I had always from the first day I stepped into Shri-Ramlogan's shop, considered it acceptable that I was going to marry his daughter. I never questioned. It all seemed pre-ordained." ' On the other hand his education in Port of Spain has given him a naive respect for Western learning and a willingness to apply Western initiatives to what appear to be intractable Eastern problems. His first success as a pundit comes when he drives away an evil cloud that has been following a small Indian boy. He achieves this feat by dressing in impressive priestly robes and making liberal use of sacred pictures, incense and a mysteriously darkened room. But he also finds out from a friend in the oil business how to produce an authentic-looking black cloud which he will actually be able to make vanish. In other words, Ganesh applies a skilful mixture of Hindu mysticism and Western technology to affect the boy's cure. And he applies it with a picaroon guile but also a genuine concern for the suffering of the little boy and his mother. It is difficult to draw the line between the confidence trickster and the healer. His Western opportunism allows him to be the one, at the same time as his Hindu acceptance of what will be allows him to suppose with all sincerity that he is the other. That is a more complex picture of a human being than had been presented in the *Miguel Street* stories. It has a psychological dimension and an acknowledgement of the pressures of social circumstances which were absent in the earlier volume.

Ganesh's success, his elevation to the dignity of G. Ramsey Muir
MBE, draws him away from his past, his island – and indeed, as
his name suggests, from his identity. In later novels such as *The
Mimic Men* Naipaul was to concern himself with 'success' of this
kind much more soberly than he does here. That meant he had to
adopt a very special kind of detachment from the circumstances
he was describing. He had to compare and contrast the behaviour
of his principal character with that of many other characters who
might have shared his colonial experience and metropolitan exile.
Immediately, though, Naipaul chose to adopt a different attitude
to a different subject. After the detached comedy of *The Mystic
Masseur* and *The Suffrage of Elvira* – especially the first of these,
where our acknowledgement of Ganesh's human feeling and
concern allows a sympathetic response to mingle with the more
customary satirical amusement – Naipaul seems to have felt the
need to draw more heavily on his experience of East Indian village
life in Trinidad. For the first and only time he tries to re-create in
detail something of the rural Hindu society in which he grew up
and, quite uncritically, spent most of the first eight years of his life.
Only later would he reinsert this single filament of life into the
complex web of colonial experience which in the late 1950s he was
just beginning to understand.

To re-create is to interpret too. *A House for Mr Biswas* offers itself
as a subtle evaluation, as well as a recreation, of one particular
and deeply comprehended society. It shows how individuals are
absorbed into the dense network of such a society, and how some
of them are attracted to alternative habits of life, competing social
organisations. Mohun Biswas's uneasy relationship with his
Hindu past, his eagerness to exchange it for a different, less
conventional and more individualistic (not to say eccentric)
future, becomes fatally and comically entangled in his present.
And so his present becomes something always to be escaped from.
The title of his recurring but never completed story is 'Escape'. It
always begins, 'At the age of thirty-three, when he was already the
father of four children . . .', but can never get beyond these words.
But, since Biswas's presence, however many children he has at
any given time, is what the reader is interested in, there is a
difference between the way Biswas views his life and the way the
reader views it. The difference is in a large part responsible for the
way we interpret Biswas's predicament – in a more subtle and

more sympathetic way than was possible with any of the earlier heroes.

Our response to Biswas's history depends to a considerable extent on the point of view from which we look at it, and what Naipaul has selected as the most appropriate style and tone to express this point of view. The exuberant, but eventually disenchanted vision of the street arab of *Miguel Street* has gone. So has the poker-faced, sometimes sympathetic irony of *The Mystic Masseur*. In *The Suffrage of Elvira* the ironic tone was more strident, less willing to co-operate with the comic events that it recorded. These devices have disappeared from the pages of *Biswas*. In their place is a different balance of sympathetically involved description and a shrewd alertness to elements of fantasy and pretence that play so large a part in Biswas's view of himself. How did Naipaul acquire this equanimity, this ability to represent events similar to the events of his own life with such a skilful combination of humour, affection and sharp detachment?

The answer to the question emerges only after one has noticed the important role that Anand, Biswas's eldest son, plays in the narrative. On an earlier, not particularly well informed reading of this novel, I had noticed how Naipaul involved his readers in the events at Hanuman House and elsewhere without making covert, and therefore sentimental, appeals to their emotions. One part of ourselves wants to become closely involved in Biswas's struggles and disappointments. But another encourages us to keep our distance, so that we can register the absurdity, sometimes the embarrassing quality, of his behaviour. The explanation of this at once engaged and disengaged point of view probably lies in the fact that the connection between Naipaul and his characters centres more than anything else on Anand; and that, through re-creating his own past, in Anand, as a relatively minor by-product of the history of his father, he had at once secured a position of affectionate involvement with his subject whilst remaining distanced from the subject in a way he could not have managed if the subject had been himself. By using Anand, or the sort of vision of events Anand would have had if he had been present on the many occasions where he was not, Naipaul achieves a purchase on the fortunes of his principal character which provokes understanding of him at once deeply sympathetic and wide awake to his extraordinary frailties and inadequacies.

Almost at the end of *Mr Biswas*, when Biswas has moved into his house on Sikkim Street and before he has suffered the first of two heart attacks, it seems that despite the odds something permanent has been achieved. The drift into encumbrance and reality has created a solid past for the children. The house in Sikkim Street is their home. Mr Biswas's own sense of home was destroyed by his father's death. He therefore had to create a coherence and order out of a disordered past and a future that he saw as a void at the end of a dark road leading from no obvious source. But the lives of the children 'would be ordered, their memories coherent' as the events and memories of all the other houses they had known or heard of telescoped into memories of the house in Sikkim Street. 'So later, and very slowly, in securer times of different stresses, when the memories had lost the power to hurt, with pain and joy they would fall into place and give back the past.' To whom would they do this, one wonders? To all the children, the prose is saying. But the acuteness with which 'a nerve of memory would be touched', the precise way in which particular objects are remembered, suggests the presence of a single mind, of one person reminiscing over the past. He it is who recalls 'a puddle reflecting the blue sky after rain, a pack of thumbed cards, the fumbling with a shoelace', and so forth. And, most tellingly, 'the taste of milk and prunes'. Surely this is Anand, in the last instance sipping his milk in the bar of the Dairies, at the opposite end of the counter to W. C. Tuttle's son Vidiadhar. What follows makes it doubly clear that it is Anand who is remembering, on behalf of all the children, the feeling of security and belonging which they all enjoyed in Sikkim Street.

> In a northern land, in a time of new separations and yearnings, in a library grown suddenly dark, the hailstones beating against the windows, the marbled endpaper of a dusty leatherbound book would disturb: and it would be the hot noisy week before Christmas at the Tulsi store: the marbled pattern of old-fashioned balloons powdered with a rubbery dust in a shallow white box that was not to be touched.

Possession of the house on Sikkim Street gives an illusion of security that stretches back to the disordered past in the various Tulsi buildings, and replaces that past with a mysteriously ordered version of it. In fact Anand continues to react to the insecurity in the new house. As the painters are at work on it, the radio transmits songs that were 'forever after tinged with uncertainty, threat and emptiness'. So Anand, along with the other children in later times, profits from the sense of order and coherence that Sikkim Street allows them to discover in the past. But he is able to feel also within that powerfully illusory fiction an intractable fact that is the very reverse of it – the very real anxiety and dread that attended the whole of his childhood.

Anand, we are told, possessed a strong satirical sense, which kept him aloof from the rest of the family. 'At first this was only a pose, and imitation of his father.' But in Anand's case it led not to fantasy but to contempt, and the contempt became a part of his nature. 'It led to inadequacies, to self-awareness and lasting loneliness. But it made him unassailable.' Since Anand is to all intents and purposes Naipaul himself, it is interesting to speculate on the relationship between satire and contempt in his work. In a later book, *An Area of Darkness*, Naipaul is to confront the issue directly, and take himself to task for the way he had cultivated a natural tendency to contempt. Be that as it may, on the evidence of *A House for Mr Biswas* it is difficult to make out a case for contempt in Naipaul – Anand's record of his father's career and his own upbringing. The son's critical awareness of his father is rarely satirical, because it is too often embarrassed and withdrawn into itself. So that, when Naipaul takes over Anand's point of view to record his father's life and circumstances, the tone is not contemptuous (as it is in some of the later short stories and parts of *The Suffrage of Elvira*). But it is observant, wary, gently critical, as well as shyly responsive to both the exuberance and the depression of its subject. The writing as a whole affords a deep understanding of Biswas's struggle to assert himself, and the obstacles placed in his path both by external circumstances and by fundamental aspects of his own nature.

The investigation of Biswas's innermost feelings this approach makes possible can be demonstrated by looking at a crucial episode in the novel, one that makes use of incidents already described in *The Mystic Masseur*. There, we saw Ganesh drive away a black cloud that followed a little Indian boy about, and that seemed to be a visual representation of the guilt he thinks he ought to feel for his brother's death. In *Biswas*, Biswas himself feels guilt for a death in the family, for he bears some responsibility for his father's drowning in a pond near the village. For quite other reasons, however, he too is dogged by a black cloud. It appears to him when he is left alone in a house in Green Vale, an outpost of the Tulsi sugar estates to which he was sent when his venture at the Chase ended in failure. Unusually calm and content with his lot, Biswas sits down to read *The Hunchback of Notre Dame*, and it is at this point that he senses a strange disturbance which takes visible shape in the form of a black cloud billowing over him. As I have suggested, the black cloud has been imported into *Biswas* from *The Mystic Masseur*; and it is interesting that commentators on the earlier book have pointed out that the boy's predicament there is communicated with a greater emotional drive than almost anything else in that novel. Ganesh's interest in it is deeply concerned, as well as ambitiously pragmatic. Something represented by the cloud, now transferred from the experience of a minor character to that of the hero, seems to carry a more than usually potent emotional charge for Naipaul. And the same thing is true of the way that, in *Biswas*, his hero tries to escape from it. Associating it with people, and especially with the landless labourers he feels are threatening him at Green Vale, Biswas tries to imagine landscapes without people at all. He creates a mental desert without oases, 'vast white plateaux, with himself safely alone, a speck in the centre'. *Safely* alone, but alone all the same. Biswas is isolated and exposed in his attempt to escape the ever-looming black cloud, the sense of other people as a threat to his security.

Panic at the presence of other people, and then, to fend it off, a strong, almost compulsive inclination to withdraw from them totally – these are feelings persistently experienced by Biswas. They carry him to the verge of hysteria at Green Vale, then gradually subside, but never leave him completely. Beneath all the comedy of his struggle with the Tulsis and his determination to 'paddle his own canoe' these are the obsessive forces that constitute the ground base of his existence.

The first chapter, 'Pastoral', goes some way towards providing a reason why this oscillation between panic and withdrawal underpins his attitude to life. There we hear how young Biswas lost his next door neighbour's calf in a stream he was not supposed to go near, and decided to hide at home until it was found. But his father, noticing Biswas's absence, believed he had been drowned in the village pond, and died diving into it to rescue him. This was the culminating disaster in a series of such disasters for which Biswas is deemed to be responsible. For he was born with six fingers and an unlucky sneeze, and the pundit had warned his family not to allow him to go near water. Fate, then, and his own deliberate disobedience had combined to thrust responsibility for his father's death onto Biswas's shoulders. From that time forward, even more than before, Biswas is made to feel his culpability, which arises not so much out of anything he has done as out of the very fact of his existence. Being what he is, he is fated to bring disaster to his family. Now that his father is dead, the family have to move, sell their hut and the bit of land surrounding it and go their several ways, staying with poor relations dotted about the vicinity. A neighbour who bought the land from them discovers oil on it and makes a fortune. This completely destroys Biswas's past, for 'when Mr Biswas looked for the place where he had spent his early years he saw nothing but oil derricks and grimy pumps, see-sawing, see-sawing, endlessly, surrounded by red No Smoking notices'. When huts of mud and grass are pulled down, 'they leave no trace', and there is no trace either of his navel string and sixth finger, which were both buried in the ground there. The pond is drained, and the stream directed into a reservoir. 'The world carried no witness to Mr Biswas's birth and early years.'

In spite of the presence of his sister, Biswas's only effective link with those early years is through his mother, Bipti. But his marriage to Shama and withdrawal to Hanuman House cut him off from her for almost all of his adult life. The fact that she is alive, though, continues to be immensely important to him. When she dies he is severely shaken. 'He was oppressed by a sense of loss: not of present loss, but of something missed in the past.' Shama and the children are 'alien growths, alien affections' whom Biswas cannot feel are any substitute for what he has lost. His feeling for his mother represents a part of him 'which yet remained purely himself, that part which had for long been submerged and was now to disappear'.

The significant point about Biswas's ever-receding and for the most part buried past is that it is a Hindu past. The pundit's warning, the scare about the six fingers, the sneeze and the water, the burying of the navel string and the circumstances of Rhagu's homecoming (he sees the reflection of his new-born child in a pool of oil that has been poured into a brass plate) – all of these things are aspects of Hindu superstition which ripple the surface of a primitive, caste-structured society, regulated by custom, tradition, and fear of change. It is the kind of society Naipaul characterises in his later essay 'Indian Autobiographies' as incapable of rebellion, 'a society which has not learned to see and is incapable of assessing itself, which asks no questions because ritual and myth have provided all the answers'. The answers provided in Biswas's case are highly unfavourable. They carve out for him a sinister rôle in the fortunes of his family, and it is therefore no wonder that he wants to cut himself loose from them and the myths and rituals that have produced them. At the same time the security these things afforded him before his misadventure with the calf continues to exert a compelling influence. Hence his reaction to his mother's death, the other side of the coin to his virtually ignoring her while she was alive. Biswas is fearful of the past, his identity in it as a curse and a destroyer. But he is regretful at its loss: psychologically in the replacement of it by his life with Shama and the Tulsis; physically in the total destruction of its geographical landscape. By contrast with the past, the present is insecure and frighteningly open-ended. Biswas's individualism, his insistence that he should have the freedom to develop his own personality, makes the inner ambitions he aims to satisfy seem fantastic and unrealisable when they are compared with the old acquiescence in his Hindu fate, which demanded no more of him than that he should accept the burden of being what he was born to be.

Biswas has to settle for a life which is awkwardly shot through with memories of a Hindu past and the complex ambition roused by a modern Westernised present. Neither of these things is a simple 'version' of what it purports to be. Biswas's rôle in the Hindu past is peculiar and, on one level, undesired. His commitment to the secular, deritualised present is incomplete, hedged in as it is with the hybrid Catholic/Hindu rituals of Hanuman House and private involvement with the modernising, 'liberal' Hinduism represented by Mrs Weir and the Aryan Association. He is fearful of both the past and the future, despite the commitment he feels to both of them. Certainly his situation is more complex than he is ever prepared to admit to himself. The assumption after Bipti's death that this one part of his life, now irrevocably past, is more purely himself than the present and future that are represented by his own family is simply one of Mr Biswas's self-deceptions – a failure to locate himself in one network of relationships by overvaluing another, which has conveniently sunk out of existence. He is as much his son's father as he is his mother's son, even though the startling prominence into which his rôle in the latter relationship is thrown as a result of the mother's death leads him to underestimate the former. By opting for the one rôle, Biswas is really giving in to a simplification of his own person. What he is must include both of them and more. Nevertheless, his sense of loss, 'of something missed in the past', is real. He will feel it again when he ponders the growing-up of his children. Having missed his own childhood he now muses on the fact that he has missed theirs. By speculating on the future as a 'void' to be filled with the 'life' he wants to create for himself, he leaves behind a past occupying more and more of the actual span of time at his disposal. It takes him all his life to discover that the life he was indefinitely postponing for the future actually lies in the past which he had thought a preparation for it.

Of all of the past, non-Hindu as well as Hindu. But it has been the Hindu past from which he has sought to escape. Unsuccessfully, for it has persisted in diluted and grotesque forms into his present with Shama's family, and even within his own family in Port of Spain in the second half of the novel. And that past is always shrouded in darkness when Biswas tries to imagine it, or when traces of it persist into the present. Raghu's death occurs in the dark: 'the low trees [round the pond] were black against the fading sky'. After diving once into the pond, Raghu says he 'believes there is something down there . . . but it is very dark'. Meanwhile Biswas 'was alone in the dark hut, and frightened'.

It is remarkable how often the image of the dark hut recurs in *Biswas*. Only a short time after Raghu's death, when the neighbours are threatening the rest of the family, one of the older children defending the hut moves between the window and the door – so frenziedly 'that the flame of the oil lamp blew this way and that, and once, with a plopping sound, disappeared. The room sank into darkness. A moment later the flame returned, rescuing them.' It is an image Biswas associates with his Hindu past; much as he associates the image of a void, like the one he imagined at Green Vale, with his liberated future. The image of the hut occurs again in a powerful passage of reminiscence when Biswas is living at the Chase. He remembers a time, far in the past, when he was a conductor on one of his uncle Ajodha's buses:

It was late afternoon and they were racing back along the

ill-made country road. Their lights were weak and they were
racing the sun. The sun fell; and in the short dusk they passed a
lonely hut set in a clearing far back from the road. Smoke came
from under the ragged thatched eaves: the evening meal was
being prepared. And, in the gloom, a boy was leaning against
the hut, his hands behind him, staring at the road. He wore a
vest and nothing more. The vest glowed white. In an instant the
bus went by, noisy in the dark, through bush and level
sugar-cane fields. Mr Biswas could not remember where the
hut stood, but the picture remained: a boy leaning against an
earth house that had no reason for being there, under the dark
falling sky, a boy who didn't know where the road, and that bus,
went.

In his excellent chapter on *A House for Mr Biswas* Landeg White
singles out this paragraph for detailed commentary. He fails to
relate the description of the hut to Biswas's own family hut, also
frequently viewed in the darkness, also having disappeared and
left no trace after the family's eviction from it at the very start of
the narrative. But he does carry the description forward to
compare it with a moment during Biswas's occupation of the
overseer's house at Green Vale when he visits Hanuman House
and sees Anand standing under the arcade, 'staring like that other
boy Mr Biswas had seen outside a low hut at dusk'. This happens
only a little before he returns to the darkness of his own
living-quarters at Green Vale ('The dead trees ringed the
barracks, a wall of flawless black') and experiences the inner
darkness that originates in the black cloud. Later still, when
Anand is living with his father in the house at Green Vale, the
hallucinatory cloud becomes a real one when a terrible storm
breaks. A high wind strikes the house and 'the window burst open,
the lamp went instantly out, the rain lashed in, the lightning lit up
the room and the world outside, and when the lightning went out,
the room was part of the black void'. This is the most terrible thing
Biswas can imagine: the room invaded by darkness; the blackness
and the void become one. Before he remembered the boy outside
the hut, viewed from Ajodha's bus, Biswas had been thinking of
the future as something to be feared, 'a blackness, a void like those
in dreams, into which, past tomorrow, and next week and next
year, he was falling'. Both past and future, in their different ways,
are looked back on and forward to as areas of darkness, voids from

which any purpose or significance has for long been dispelled. The old world of Hindu ritual and the new world of secular self-determination are equally unsustaining, equally empty of meaning and purpose. Seen as Biswas sees them they are both bound to disappoint. For his position, committed neither to the old nor to the new, sceptical of the Hinduism of his youth but unable to forge for himself a secure place in the new world of mass journalism and social welfare, renders him peculiarly vulnerable, peculiarly isolated from either source of security. Landeg White describes his position well by speaking of a journey 'from a world where he is a creature of fate to a world in which he becomes a victim of circumstances, from an order which seems irrelevant to a disorder in which he is a nonentity'.

In a memorable passage from *An Area of Darkness*, Naipaul has referred to this movement within the darkness as a specifically Hindu experience. Having travelled, as he says, 'lucidly' over the area which was to him the area of darkness, 'something of the darkness remains, in those attitudes, those ways of thinking and seeing, which are no longer mine'. The extent to which Naipaul still has lodged within him a habit of responding to the world which might owe a great deal to his Hindu past and ancestry we shall have to reconsider when we read *The Mimic Men* and other later novels. In *A House for Mr Biswas*, Anand dramatically rejects his Hindu inheritance, merely making use of the brahminical initiation ceremony in order to avoid going to school. Naipaul too, by the time he had reached Anand's age here, set no store at all by the Hindu rituals. At the beginning of *An Area of Darkness* he tells us that all that survived of Hinduism in him was 'that sense of the difference of people . . . , a vaguer sense of caste and a horror of the unclean'. All of these things, particularly the last, make themselves felt in the novels. They probably have a great deal to do with my use of the word 'fastidious' to describe Naipaul's style, for in this case the style is a direct expression of the writer's temperament. Underlying these fairly superficial things, however, there may be something much more basically Hindu in the attitudes Naipaul takes up towards his subject. Towards the end of *An Area of Darkness*, when he reflects on his frightened and embarrassed behaviour in the Village of the Dubes, he seems to be in the process of discovering this fact about himself.

Biswas, however, betrays how strong is the residual Hinduism in himself by never failing to sense that he has a destiny. The difficulty here, however, lies in the uncertainty of the relationship between an impersonal destiny and a willed individual attempt to accomplish a personal goal. Biswas's marriage to Shama comes about almost as automatically, as fatefully, as Ganesh's to Leela in Naipaul's first novel. In both cases half-hearted initiatives on the part of the two young men are manipulated by relatives of the girls they will marry to create what they (the relatives) suppose will be to their own advantage; and from the point of view of the young men this looks very like the intervention of fate. But both Biswas and Ganesh plot their ways out of the circumstances into which it appears they have been inveigled. Ganesh accomplishes this spectacularly, and at one fell swoop; Biswas only half escapes, by negotiating a series of compromises. These rarely place him at a permanent advantage, until the purchase of the house of Sikkim Street seems to have given him something of the independence no other of the Tulsi in-laws ever achieves.

Throughout *Biswas* a house is what stands for the freedom to exist in one's own right, to accomplish one's destiny, to achieve independence. What is felt to be ordained and what is willed to be, come together in the securing of this all-important asset. The house is therefore related both to Hindu ideas of destiny and order, and to secular objectives of status and independence. As White has pointed out, for Biswas both of these things must be flawed because neither can fully contain the energies of his complete personality. It is no wonder, then, that the house he eventually secures is at once such an accomplishment and such a fraud, an emblem of status and a wasting asset. For Biswas it creates a sense of deep, if mistaken, satisfaction. Perhaps, though, Biswas's satisfaction is not so mistaken as it must appear to be to anyone experiencing it without the hindsight our reading of the whole book has given us. The dilapidated structure which has brought it into being is not entirely spurious, in spite of the confidence trick played on Biswas by the solicitor's clerk who sold it to him. It really does represent an achievement, as we discover as early as the Prologue (and this affects our response to Biswas's house-buying and building ventures throughout the narrative):

How terrible it would have been, at this time, to be without it: to have died among the Tulsis, amid the squalor of that large, disintegrating and indifferent family; to have left Shama and the children among them, in one room; worse, to have lived without even attempting to lay claim to one's portion of the earth; to have lived and died as one had been born, unnecessary and unaccommodated.

The simple fact of owning his own house means many complex and even contradictory things to Biswas. But above all it means the satisfaction of the claim to which he refers here. It is a claim to a life in which he will be able to feel that he is *necessary*; and in which he will be accommodated not only in the sense of being 'protected' by having a roof over his head, but also in that of being 'taken into account' through having achieved an independent status, a separate existence of which the physical structure of the house is a merely external sign. That is why, when he has bought the house, and has been alerted by a neighbour to the clerk's plans to build another house on a vacant lot next door, he prevents this outrage by giving careful attention to the boundaries on the deeds. He plants a laburnum tree there instead.

Biswas has to ask himself: what does a life mean to the man who lives it? Each man's life is different from another's, but, if the difference is to be in his own eyes a significant one, does he not have to have planned that it should be so? Or is he merely a creature of fate, helpless to direct the course of his own future by individual effort and intelligence? Can a picaroon sharpness and initiative cut itself free of the Hindu fatalism that has caused him to kill his father and ruin his family's prospects, and then become dignified, in the sense of conferring a sense of self-importance and self-respect, in a way that goes far beyond its picaroon origins. A man is pulled in two directions: eager to conform to the image others have of him and so to simplify himself in his own eyes; at the same time insistent that there is in him 'something personal and ordained', an individual destiny that complicates his existence and makes it different from the lives of everyone else. Each of these directions demands that a balance be struck, or a decision taken, between how much of one's life is fated to be as it is, and how much must be struggled for by force of will, often in the face of what look like insurmountable obstacles. We live for others and we live for ourselves, but these lives are seldom the same. What is the relationship between them? How does a man reconcile the conflicting demands they make of him? For destiny in this impersonal sense often seems to take the shape of living for others, allowing others to create our personalities for us, to provide us with rôles to play which become our characters, our sense of ourselves. At the end of a life it can come as a shock to confront an achieved existence quite different from the one that, in the act of living, it had been taken to be.

This may or it may not be Biswas's experience, but it is certainly our experience of him. For, by the time we have moved from the initial notice of Biswas's death in the Prologue to the description of his death at the end of the Epilogue we have grown to appreciate the importance of Biswas's 'claim', and have been able to relate it, more closely than he ever manages to do, to the claims others have made on him. For, in his case, if destiny has taken shape in the lives of others, those others must be pre-eminently his wife and children. The attitude to fate and destiny that would draw him back to his Hindu roots and secure him in the 'irrelevant order' of the Hindu colony within the colony has been weakened by the break-up of the family after his father's death. But it is ever-present in the high caste status he is unable to get rid of, and which precipitates him into the clutches of the Tulsi family, as a suitable husband for one of their daughters.

Biswas's marriage to Shama was one that he did not plan and for which he does not feel himself to be responsible. It happened by accident, a combination of naive bravado on Biswas's part and a rapacious slyness on the part of the Tulsis. Biswas had passed a note to Shama when he was decorating the Tulsi shop, and Mrs Tulsi, knowing of high caste and appreciating the prospect of another young man to contribute to the Tulsi businesses, had manoeuvred him into a marriage for which he was unprepared. The result is that, more than ever before, Mr Biswas feels that he is trapped, that events are beyond his control and that he is therefore not responsible for his own destiny, not a person in his own right. 'How often did he try to make events appear grander, more planned and less absurd than they were!' Now that he is absorbed into the appalling protectiveness of the Tulsi household, it seems to him even less likely than it did in his wasted youth that he will ever achieve something that is entirely his own. Earlier he had waited for the coming of a Love that would transport him to a world of romance. 'He deferred all his pleasure in life until that day.' His friend Alec told him not to worry: 'these things come when you least expect them'. What came was Shama and the Tulsis. But in view of the sum total of what we learn about Biswas's relationship with Shama at the Chase, and later in the

house at Port of Spain and in Sikkim Street, are we to suppose that
Mr Biswas missed out on romance entirely? He never describes
his marriage in terms approximating to those of romance, and his
first escape, with Shama, from the Tulsis – when he takes over the
proprietorship of the Chase – is qualified by a reviewed incapacity
to understand it as anything but a temporary arrangement, 'a
pause, a preparation', like his youth before it.

To say that he does not understand it to be more than this is not
the same thing as to say that he does not experience it as
something more. Naipaul's description of the increasing familiarity of the shop, the personally important details of 'slight
improvements' rendering it 'their own, and therefore support-
able', lead us to believe otherwise and enable us to distinguish
between what is happening and Biswas's imperfect comprehen-
sion of what is happening – as a preparation for something else.
His sense of the situation is a constituent of the situation, not, as
he supposes, a comprehensive record of it. Only later will it slip
into place as one of the determinants of an achieved order and
satisfaction in a life seen to be made up of just such 'trivial'
satisfactions, hidden behind apparently overwhelming disappointments. Mrs Tulsi spoke more truly than she knew when
she told Mr Biswas that 'everything comes, bit by bit'; just as Alec
did when he said things come to you when you least expect them.
At the Chase, Mr Biswas himself finds it strange that 'these
disregarded years had been years of acquisition': of a kitchen safe,
a hat rack, a dressing-table – but of more than these: 'It was
strange . . . for him to find one day that house and shop bore so
many marks of his habitation. No one might have lived there
before him, and it was hard to imagine anyone after him moving
about these rooms and getting to know them as he had done.'

Shama's ambitions extend no further than to be unexceptional,
to share none of her husband's originality, which strikes her as a
ridiculous and, indeed, dangerous aspect of his character. Instead
she wants only 'to have her share of the established emotions: joy
at a birth or marriage, distress during illness and hardship, grief
at a death. Life to be full had to be this established pattern of
sensation.' There is nothing appalling about this, and indeed in
the highly traditional and formalised existence at Hanuman
House it is precisely what is required. But Biswas doesn't want to
be part of it. He humiliates Shama by adopting a persistently
rebellious attitude, with the result that eventually he is allowed to

move out of the house and take up a position at the Chase. Shama occasionally surrenders to the demands and standards of the family; she always returns to Hanuman House for her confinements. Indeed it is immediately before one such return that the comment on her 'share of the established emotions' was given. In the context of her preparation for removal to Hanuman House this may not appear sympathetic. It reads like an attack on her complacency. But what follows must make us revise our judgement, for Shama's preparations for her return have not ignored her husband, for whom she must feel the proper respect, and perhaps a little more than that. The instructions she has written down about how Biswas is to cope when she is away, what preparations have been made for him to be able to live as it is fitting he should, betray an easy familiarity with him that cannot exist entirely in the absence of love.

The commonplace also commands its share of affection and the author does not withhold it. The fact that the demands a person makes on life are conventional and crude is not allowed altogether to impoverish the substance of such a life. Eventually whatever order Biswas recognises in his own life is made up of just such moments and achievements. Shama does not stop being commonplace. At the very end of the novel Biswas's death is the occasion for a reunion between her and her sisters. 'Afterwards the sisters returned to their respective homes and Shama and the children went back in their Prefect to the empty house.' We are told no more. Whether Shama's grief, sensed in the restraint of Naipaul's prose here, is the conventional grief she wanted to feel, or whether it takes notice, as ours does, of the meanings of that Prefect and that house, we cannot know. The 'Prelude' suggests that it is more than emotional; that she goes back to the house in Sikkim Street rather than the house of one of the Tulsis suggests that her grief does have to do with Biswas and not just an anonymous husband. At any rate, Naipaul's treatment of the relationship between Biswas and his wife within the marriage ensures that in neither case shall we mistake grief for something else, which the words 'conventional', 'normal' and 'established' suggest. Besides, apart from the value Shama has in herself, she inevitably becomes a part of Biswas's own destiny, a part of the past which, entering the future in a new order, conveys to Biswas the 'significance' of his life and gives it its pattern and originality.

Shama's contribution to Biswas's destiny is illustrated graphically during a visit he makes to Hanuman House from Shorthills, when the family have for long moved out of the house and only the skeleton of the life they had lived there remains. He enters the room in which he had lived with Shama when he was not at the Chase or Green Vale:

> Through the Demarara window he had tried to spit on Owad and flung the plateful of food on him. In this room he had been beaten by Govind, had kicked *Bell's Standard Elocutionist* and given it the dent in the cover. Here, claimed by no one, he had reflected on the unreality of his life, and had wished to make a mark on the wall as proof of his existence. Now he needed no such proof. Relationships had been created where none had existed; he stood at their centre. In that very unreality had lain freedom. Now he was encumbered and it was at Hanuman House that he tried to forget the encumbrance: the children, the scattered furniture, the dark tenement room, and Shama, as helpless as he was and now, what he had longed for, dependent on him.

Mr Biswas is experiencing one of the greatest platitudes of life. We seek the freedom we already possess and live to regret that we didn't use it when we could. For, before he met Shama and the Tulsis, Mr Biswas had sought freedom in marriage, a family and above all a house. These would convince him of his reality, and upon that reality he would be able to found an order and a meaning. These would be different from the unsatisfactory versions of those things he had experienced with Raghu and Bipti. They would give him freedom, not constriction; they would be a spur to independent purpose rather than a bridle recalling him to the inflexible terms of his appointed being. But as fast as these things were achieved they brought with them disappointment and encumbrance. A marriage drifted into and perpetually interrupted. Children born in his absence and named without his knowledge or permission. Houses rented, owned by others, blown down, and finally acquired in ignorance of state of repair and by means of an unrepayable debt. It is ironic that the house Mr Biswas wanted to live in, not to visit, has first to be made to look fit to be visited even if it remains unsatisfactory to be lived in. He dies in it before the debt comes up for repayment, and, although he does not know it, he has achieved an ambition, an ambition which has changed beyond all recognition.

The way Biswas has achieved his ambition has ensured that it takes on a colouring quite different from anything he had ever imagined. He has fought against the traditions associated with his Hindu upbringing. But, at the centre of his reinvolvement with Hinduism, in his relationship with Shama, as well as with the children, he finds an opportunity to assert his individuality even more than he is able to do as the 'Scarlet Pimpernel' or Miss Logie's assistant at the Community Welfare Department. Indeed his search for a house would have imposed a perhaps intolerable strain on his nerves if Hanuman House had not been there in the background. Frequently Biswas looks back on it, as he does in the passage quoted above, as a place in which, or at least in common with which, all the important relationships in his life, after his estrangement from Bipti, had been formed. It is a fine example of what, in the title of one of his poems, Philip Larkin calls 'The Importance of Elsewhere': another place, held firmly in the mind, that 'underwrites' both the poet's and the journalist's existence as they move away from it to experiment with new styles of life. But, in Biswas's case at least, the presence of the House is a bulwark against total collapse, a safety net underneath the tightrope he walks as an independent spirit. When he secures a limited independence at the Chase, Biswas feels that 'the House was a world more real than the Chase'. After his breakdown at Green Vale he feels 'secure to be only a part of Hanuman House, an organism that possessed a life, strength and power to comfort which was quite separate from the individuals who composed it'. And, when Anand is ashamed that his father is a journalist, because of the taunts he is receiving on that score at school in Port of Spain, Biswas replies that he is independent: 'I don't depend on them for a job. You know that. We could go back any time to Hanuman House. All of us. You know that.'

As readers, we are in a position to sympathise with Biswas over his feelings for Hanuman House. We recognise its limitations – the lack of seriousness with which religious observances are performed, the scandal of Owad's instruction at a Catholic school, the chaos, the noise, the pettiness and deceitfulness of Mrs Tulsi, the vulgarity and philistinism of such people as Govind and W. C. Tuttle. Above all we recognise its power to restrain initiative and to substitute for it the naive ambitions that send Owad off to Oxbridge and bring him back a Bloomsbury-tinted Marxist who doesn't even know how to govern the household.

Biswas does well to try to achieve his destiny by pulling away from Hanuman House, and keeping alive his belief in a house of his own. But he does well also to acknowledge the substantive quality of what it is he is pulling away from. For, far more than the newspaper office or the Welfare Department headquarters, Hanuman House is a receptacle for the display of a wide variety of life such as Naipaul has nowhere presented to us before. The brilliant 'acts' of the inhabitants of Miguel Street are gone. In their place has come a network of relationships which changes credibly as the individual figures in it change – appear, disappear, or simply find themselves in different positions – and which reaches back into the pasts of those who have not always been parts of it, as well as into the futures of those who dare to try to press beyond it. The density of the lives that are lived in Hanuman House, however static and ritualised they are in their general outline, feeds back into Biswas's past and connects with that different, three-dimensional reality of his rural Hindu boyhood.

The strength of Naipaul's novel lies in its success in persuading us that the connection has been made. What happens in it is convincing both as the record of a man living his life from the cradle to the grave, and as a memory in the mind of others, creating an order out of what was experienced for the most part as a chaos, gently teasing out the pattern that lay deeply embedded within a life characterised by apparent false beginnings, lazy acquiescence in events, and disappointing achievements. As in all lives, the trivial acts as a pointer to the important, and is frequently transformed into it. Shama's sewing-machine, cow and coffee set, unobtrusively recurring as they do, testify to the increasing intimacy of her presence. Casual mention of Dodd's Kidney Pills at the newspaper office transports us twenty years back to Biswas's schooldays and his friendship with Alec, who has inexplicably disappeared from the scene – as people do. Figures such as Bipti, Govind and Jagdat punctuate the story and make vivid to us the passage of time and the way some people stay the same as it laps around them. Others change. Others again, such as Mungroo, Maclean and Miss Logie, pass in and out of life rapidly and without trace. Insignificant people such as W. C. Tuttle assume a sudden importance. Significant ones such as Seth suddenly dwindle into contemptible shadows of themselves. Hari we only learn to value after his death: his absence from the Tulsi household leaves a gap we can find no one to fill. Mrs Tulsi's death disrupts the whole complex system of relationships we had taken to be permanent. But we get used to the new fragmentation as we get used to the fact that even Mrs Tulsi, about whose 'decreptitude' there was 'a quality of everlastingness', will die. And we get used to the fact that for the Biswas children the house at Sikkim Street was just another 'permanent' arrangement, though we had seen it as a precarious gamble likely to fail at the end of any chapter.

In *A House for Mr Biswas* Naipaul has made full use of two of his strengths as a novelist that are not to anything like the same extent found together elsewhere in his fiction. First, he has placed at the centre of his narrative the fantasies of a man who cannot, or who thinks he cannot, find a place in society, or family, which will allow him to realise what he feels there is in him to be realised. His search for a house is a search for confirmation that he has a place in the universe; it is an attempt to lodge a claim on life which he feels life has a duty to try to meet. In this respect he is not essentially different from Naipaul's later heroes, who are also in search of this kind of confirmation, though they lodge their claims in markedly different ways. But, secondly, Naipaul has provided his hero with a social milieu at Hanuman House such as no other of his later heroes is to inhabit. The relationships formed by Ralph Singh, Bobby, Peter Roche and Jimmy Ahmed are provisional, tenuous and flawed by betrayals. The world they inhabit is an infinitely more dangerous one, in which there is no protective cushion of family or racial group or village community to come between the exposed self of the hero and the pressures of political and racial disintegration. These characters are in a free state, in the good and bad senses of that phrase: unencumbered with religious and cultural restraint on the free expression of their personalities, they are exposed to similar lack of restraint on the part of other individuals who share their freedom.

So far, Naipaul had not set the plot of his novels in 'free state' environments. He had either circumscribed the liberty of his characters by preserving the threat of the policeman round the corner; or he had continued to 'settle' them in societies that are still servile, still bound by superstitions that link them to a traditional mode of life in which the group absorbs the individual – even if it has to carve out a special niche for such individuals as

Mr Biswas, or even elevate one of them to the rank of MBE, as happens to Ganesh Rumsamair. Biswas, and we, are lucky to discover the hero half-way between ritual and freedom. It means that his struggles for independence and personal dignity can be undertaken in a context of settled beliefs and forms of social organisation that afford opportunities not available to his successors. They will have to go much further to assert themselves in more competitive, less enclosed societies, and the consequences of their self assertion will be more spectacular than Biswas's were. But they will have accomplished less for themselves, in their free state, than Biswas managed to do in his more ambiguous circumstances. they will also have imposed themselves on an environment which is incapable of producing those minor changes that in turn generate major psychological results – changes that such places as Hanuman House encourage to take place. So the reader too lacks a foothold in a world that is complex not only in the psychology and moral inclination of the individuals it supports, but also in the matrix of customs and institutions by which it is sustained.

In *The Mimic Men* Ralph Singh reminds us that 'We talk of escaping to the simple life. But we do not mean what we say. It is from simplifications such as this that we wish to escape to return to a more elemental complexity.' The states of mind of Naipaul's later protagonists are usually not simple. Where they are, Naipaul goes to some length to show us how complex are the circumstances in which they have to operate. But that other level of complexity, the complexity of ritual and customary behaviour, regulating a traditional society has been cut away from the foreground of these later novels. And here is a loss. For, in spite of the confusion and snobbery and ignorance of the Hindu society in Hanuman House, something answering to the description of a traditional society did flourish there. That was why we were able to witness the ebb and flow of prestige, position, status and fortune among the members of a large and extended family. But in any part of the world such societies are under attack, and many traditional groups, tribes and ethnic minorities have been shaken apart and thrust into the condition of the free state. Coming to grips with these societies, Naipaul, in his later novels, deprives himself of the novelistic benefits that flow from the description of communities such as Hanuman House. In the search for new social organisations, men are pulled loose from their customary ties and beliefs, and exposed to the insidious temptations of separateness and independence. More than any of the novels that preceded them, these are novels of distress – distress in the face of freedom, the rejection of a given authority where there is no other authority willing or able to take its place.

On the island of Isabella just such a rejection of authority has taken place. When the movement headed by Browne and Ralph Singh wins the election and takes control from traditional politicians, their predicament becomes that of countless other fold-leaders who acquire what at first seems to be the reality of power. It is the predicament Naipaul discusses in his essay on Papa Bradshaw in St Kitts, what he calls 'the drama of the folk leader who rules where once he securely agitated and finds that power has brought insecurity'. The insecurity is not that of the leader alone, but permeates downwards through the 'liberated' colonial society. On Anguilla, for example, where the problems of Trinidad and the fictional 'Isabella' are even further concentrated by virtue of the smallness of the island, insecurity lies at the heart of the problem: 'the problem of a tiny colony set adrift, part of the jetsam of an empire, a near primitive people suddenly returned to a free state, their renewed or continuing exploitation'. It is significant that Naipaul subtitles his essay on Anguilla 'The Shipwrecked Six Thousand', for 'shipwreck' is a word Ralph Singh uses frequently to describe his situation on Isabella. To be shipwrecked is to be abandoned on the fringes of the Empire at a time when the imperial authority is withdrawing. Usually it is to conspire in that withdrawal, to provoke it, in order to enter into what Naipaul calls, in the Anguilla essay and elsewhere, a 'free state'. This is a condition of personal responsibility that persists less and less securely in an environment of chaos, disorder, even revolution.

The society Browne and Singh seek to govern is incapable of responding to the government they have agitated to provide for it. Conditions of colonial exploitation have failed to create anything that can be described as a society, distinct from separate groups of people who feel no genuine loyalty to anything beyond themselves. Isabella is an island made up entirely of Miguel Streets. And, as with Miguel Street, there is no place within the social and cultural mores of the island from which order and self-government can grow. Singh confesses, from his new position as a minister in Browne's government, that 'in a society like ours, fragmented, inorganic, no link between man and the landscape, a society not held together by common interests, there was no true internal source of power, and . . . no power was real which did not come from the outside. Such was the controlled chaos we had, with such enthusiasm, brought upon ourselves.' Miguel Street had its courts of law and its gaols somewhere round the corner – effective within, but not a part of, the small community whose lives they regulated. Before the election, Isabella had its governor, and a bevy of political stooges whose function appears to have been little more than to regulate the pace of the island's life in accordance with that of the larger entity, the Empire, of which it was an insignificant part. Now that the island has contracted out of the imperial system and committed itself to the free state, there is little it can do with its freedom.

Historically, Naipaul sees that the same thing happened with the collapse of the Spanish American empire in the nineteenth century. In Venezuela, for example, between 1809 and 1813 the Revolution came and Spain suddenly withered away. In these circumstances the new republic was 'shivered into all its divisions and subdivisions of race and caste'. No central authority possessed the combination of military and moral force to hold the society together. And so 'Spain was now seen to be more than its administrative failures. It was, however remotely, a code and a reference that the colonial society by itself was incapable of generating. Without such a reference obedience, the association of consent, was no longer possible' (*The Loss of El Dorado*, ch. 10).

What was true of the Spanish Empire in the early years of the nineteenth century is equally true of the British and other European empires, one hundred and fifty years later. Just as the revolution of Gual and Espana was powered by 'borrowed words that never matched' the society to which they were applied, just as that earlier revolution flourished as a 'private theatre of disguises and false names', so now, in 'Isabella' and on other islands in the West Indies, there is the same combination of mimicry and drama. Papa Bradshaw agitated 'securely' in St Kitts for the same reason as the Isabella 'Socialists' agitated securely on their island. While they had no responsibility, they could cultivate and make a weapon of their grievances. Indeed, the grievances of the colonial politician become his reality. He is nothing without them. As Ralph Singh says, 'Our grievances were our reality, what we knew, what had permitted us to grow, what had made us.' With the grievance of the most obvious form of colonial dependence removed, the personality of the agitator is in danger of collapse. The authority he has been pushing against to achieve his country's freedom suddenly gives way, and there is nothing at the other side of authority for him to define himself against. With the removal of what was taken to be the cause of the island's indignity and distress, there comes only another form of disorder. Whatever order remains is imposed by the remaining superstructure of Western economic interest, represented on Isabella by the bauxite agreement and the Stockwell sugar estates. There is little the new government can do about these interests without causing the workers dependent on them more real distress than they had experienced under colonial government. So the new government can only offer a sort of drama, a mimicry of independent activity and talk of the redress of racial grievances. It can act out a fantasy of freedom, functioning within the strict limits the island's relationship with the rest of the world continues to impose. As Ralph Singh sees it, 'The pace of events . . . is no more than the pace of chaos on which strict limits have been imposed. I speak of course of territories like Isabella, set adrift yet not altogether abandoned, where this controlled chaos approximates in the end . . . to a continuing disorder. The chaos lies all within.'

'Controlled chaos' is the subject of *The Mimic Men*. The phrase describes what seems to be the inescapable political condition of Isabella, and it also suggests a common denominator of distur-bance which takes different forms and is differently evaluated by the characters we come to know most closely. In particular it describes the state of mind of Ralph Singh, whose rise and fall as a West Indian politician provides the narrative thread along which are strung the autobiographical reflections on colonialism, power, and distress which occupy so many of the pages of the novel. The content of these reflections is basically what has been transcribed and paraphrased above. A combination of colonial exploitation and violation provides the context within which, as schoolboy, expatriate, businessman, politician, and finally *émigré*, Ralph Singh tries to define his situation – which is a highly developed and intensely self-reflective version of the colonial situation in general. Biswas, with no political aspirations, had felt himself to be related by only the most tenuous threads to the world in which he lived. His search for a house was a search for independent existence, a sense of belonging to the world in a way that conferred upon him a significance he did not feel he possessed as a homeless parasite. Singh, though, possesses many homes, including the impressive Roman house in which he tries to build a life with his English-born wife, Sandra. But for Singh a house is not enough (although the rickety, infirm structure of his father's house might have contributed in some small part to his persistent feelings of insecurity). He has a vision of disorder that he believes is beyond the power of any one man to put right, even for himself. His father felt it too, and embarrassed the whole family by becoming the leader of a religious protest group. But his protest was based on nothing real. It simply fed on the distress of his followers and provided a myth of potentially successful revolt that Singh knows to have been deeply fraudulent. His father's movement was saved from collapse and absurdity by the outbreak of war and his internment. Nevertheless it is because of his father's 'revolutionary' past that Singh is invited to join the Socialist movement by his old schoolfriend Browne; and it is this movement that eventually brings him to power on Isabella.

The causes of Singh's political elevation, then, are fraudulent. But he has nothing within himself that might have enabled him to resist Browne's invitation to join the party, and then the government. Browne, too, the erstwhile coon singer and comedian of Singh's class in Isabella Imperial, is incapable of going further than to exploit histrionically his rôle as president of the island. He 'had talked so much of distress and dignity as discoveries in themselves, but had not thought to go further'. Now, having been elected by virtue of his appeal to these qualities among the people, he finds he can do nothing for them. He cannot alleviate their distress. He has no control over the island's economy, which is totally dependent on connections with other countries and companies far removed from Isabella. He is unable to create circumstances in which real dignity might arise out of the people's own effort. All he can do is make a lot of noise and drama over negotiations with the bauxite companies and the projected (but impracticable) nationalisation of the sugar estates. Ultimately Singh's involvement in the nationalisation issue, which he knows to be another fraud, creates his downfall. His effort (not very great) to protect his position in Isabella whilst going through the charade of negotiations with junior Foreign Office ministers in London, are to no avail, and his manoeuvres achieve no more than an outbreak of racial violence on Isabella. This renders his position on the island precarious. He decides to leave it and make a new life for himself as an ex-colonial politician in a modest hotel in the London suburbs.

It is from this position, as a hotel guest of eighteen months' standing, that Ralph Singh writes his memoirs. They are by no means the first fruits of his literary talent. Long before he had written articles for the *Socialist* which had caused him no trouble. Indeed he discovered he had a gift for writing. But now, in London, he realises the gift was facile, and it takes him a great deal of time to write the book (though not so long as it took Naipaul himself, judging by the dates affixed to the end of the last chapter). Back on the island, at the height of his political success, he had intended to write, he says, 'a more than autobiographical work, the exposition of the malaise of our times painted and illuminated by personal experience and that knowledge of the possible which can come only from a closeness to power'. A little later he defines more closely what he means by the phrase 'the malaise of our times'.

> It was my hope [he says] to give expression to the restlessness, the deep disorder, which the great explorations, the overthrow in three continents of established social organisations, the unnatural bringing together of peoples who could achieve fulfilment only within the security of their own societies and the landscapes hymned by their ancestors. It was my hope to give partial expression to the restlessness which this great upheaval has brought about.

However, Singh believes he will never be capable of writing such a book, because he is too much a victim of the restlessness that is its subject. Significantly he adds, 'And it must also be confessed that in that dream of writing I was attracted less by the act and the labour than by the calm and the order which the act would have implied.' He comes to realise that calm and order can never be the starting-points for such an enterprise as the one he has envisaged.

On the other hand it might be possible to achieve these qualities, qualities Singh has felt to be missing throughout his life, as a *result*, rather than as a *precondition*, of writing about his distress. That is what eventually he does discover. And he discovers it by realising that he must thread a loop through time and imagine himself away from the London of the hotel, the London of his

post-politician phase. He has to go to the London he knew as a
student more than twenty years ago, the London of his first snow,
of Mr Shylock's attic, and of Lieni, the Maltese girl, and the
christening-party given for her illegitimate child. By re-creating
the events of that winter day, Singh makes them 'historical and
manageable'; and in becoming so they provide him with a genuine
literary aim: 'from the fact of this setting, my presence in the city
. . . to impose order on my own history, to abolish that disturbance which is what a narrative in sequence might have led me
to'. He is successful in his new attempt at writing because he
discovers that the effort truly to re-create what has been
fraudulent in the past, to acknowledge the fraudulence and to
explain it, becomes an extension of that past – an extension
beyond the chaos and disorder that was all there was at the time.
Only gradually, in the process of writing, of keeping closely to the
details of his experience whilst reordering them so as to force
himself to understand the contradictions and illusions out of
which they were made, does the truth of his life emerge. The
disorder is acknowledged, the uncertainties of his judgement
(about his marriage to Sandra, for example) are step by step
eliminated. 'So writing,' he concludes, 'for all its initial distortion,
clarifies, and even becomes a process of life.'

   This is the effect the writing of *The Mimic Men* has on Ralph
Singh. Does it have the same effect on his readers? We must
accept, I think, that Naipaul has created a brilliant imitation of
the memoirs of a particularly interesting and self-questioning
colonial politician. The method is convincing, the manner of
contemplating events, brooding over them, interpreting them and
then reinterpreting them, is entirely appropriate to the circumstances in which the fictional writer finds himself. But in a novel
we are looking for other things too. We want to respond to the
density of the world the real novelist, making use of the fictional
writer of memoirs, makes available to us. Much of Ralph Singh's
account of his situation is analytical and discursive. At times it
reminds us of some of the things Naipaul has written in the travel
books – especially *The Middle Passage* and *The Overcrowded Barracoon*
– though of course always we sense the presence of a fictional
character who is made responsible for saying the things that are
said. This is true whether what is being said is theoretical and
polemic, or where it is descriptive and autobiographical. For it is
the business of narrative to re-create incidents, actions, events. It

is not there merely to provide transparent equivalents of these things, which the reader is intended to look through to discover what it is they 'stand for' – somewhere beyond the confines of the narrative itself. If we feel at all strongly that Naipaul's pre-existent view of his subject, the distress of post-colonial politics, crystallises out too readily in the form of hard deposits of analytical material, inadequately related to our interest in the characters and the things we see them do, then we shall come away from the book with a less high opinion of it than we are likely to have experienced after reading, say, *A House for Mr Biswas*.

Discussing his writing about Trinidad five years before he published *The Mimic Men*, Naipaul claimed that although he feared Trinidad, he had never examined his fear and had never wished to do so. 'In my novels I had only expressed this fear; and it is only now, at the moment of writing, that I am able to attempt to examine it.' The novels he is referring to are the novels preceding and including *A House for Mr Biswas*. Among the books Naipaul wrote between *The Middle Passage* (from which the extract quoted above is taken) and *The Mimic Men* there is only one set in Trinidad (the others are set in London and England), and that (*A Flag on the Island*) is mainly assembled out of stories Naipaul had written some time before. I think it is fair to say that *The Mimic Men* represents Naipaul's first effort to examine as well as to dramatise his feelings about Trinidad. Only at the end of the novel, when Ralph Singh is back in London, conducting a comic affair with Lord Stockwell's daughter, is he able to write, 'I no longer seek to explain; I merely record'. Much of what has preceded that confession has sought over and over again to explain and to examine. That, after all, is the function of the novel. Its basic purpose is to interest its readers in the changes in Singh the writer's awareness of all that Singh the student, businessman, politician, and so forth, has achieved.

But that evolving awareness is a very tortuous and subtle thing, and its manner of expressing itself is frequently overdeveloped to the pont of obscurity. The recurrence of certain words – 'distress', 'disorder', 'self-violation' – is excessive. Their presence has the effect of obscuring what is going on. Especially what is going on in the scene that is being summoned to mind. For we have to remember that, when we use such an expression as 'what is going on' of any event in *The Mimic Men*, we may be referring to one or both of two things: what is going on in Ralph Singh's mind as he grapples with his past in the process of writing about it; and what actually went on in the past. Interesting and intelligent as they often are, Singh's reflections on the meaning of what he is describing often get in the way of what is being described, or at any rate they assume an importance in their own right which is often mistimed, since their presence cuts short a description of events which might well have been developed at greater length and to more considerable advantage so far as the narrative impact is concerned. One feels this particularly about the scenes involving Ralph and Sandra once they have arrived on Isabella; and about Ralph's relationship with Browne once the movement has been started and the strategy to capture political power has been put into operation. The best writing in *The Mimic Men* is contained in Part II. Here, Ralph's account of life among his schoolfellows at Isabella Imperial, and with his father and his family in and around the Bella Bella bottling-plant, moves forward with far less interruption than occurs in his account of the development of Crippleville, for example, or of what Browne and Singh actually do when they have achieved power.

Naipaul's decision to encumber those parts of his narrative which deal with Ralph Singh's political life with a great load of meditative brooding and reflection that other parts of it seem to require has an especially deleterious effect on the way the political events are described. Ralph says that one of the few achievements of his government was to restore to the island a sense of drama, and drama 'sharpens our perception of the world, gives us some sense of ourselves'. In conditions of chaos, he claims, 'which would appear hostile to any human development, the human personality is in fact more varied and extended'. But in fact the human personality of Browne, for example, is much more 'varied and extended' in the earlier scenes at school; when, to take a single masterly instance, his Latin teacher goes too far in making a racial joke (based on his nickname, Blue) at his expense; or when he is turned away from Ralph's parents' house because they take him for a nigger street arab. It also so happens that in the 'political sections of the novel the 'government' Browne has formed is never given a face, seems to contain nobody but himself and Singh. How different again from the scenes at school, where not only Browne, but Deschampneufs, Cecil, Hok and Eden are vividly character- ised. And they are not just Miguel Street individualists, but people caught in a racial and class dilemma which both Naipaul and they have pronounced views on and feelings about. Far from bringing drama to Isabella, Browne's movement seems to expel it; and the only passages that enliven the 'political' scenes are those that offer brief anecdotes about the effect of government policy on some aspect of the island's life – such as the plan to cut down on imported tinned margarine by importing tins and importing margarine, and then paying five black ladies in white coats to put the margarine in the tins. But that kind of thing is on an altogether different level of novelistic competence from the powerfully moving (and comic) scenes where Singh senior takes his family for an outing in the Education Department car; or where Hok, the mysteriously refined-looking part-Chinese boy, is forced to acknowledge his negro mother when, on a school outing, she is encountered doing the family shopping.

The most emotionally powerful scenes in this novel return us to a by-now familiar motif in Naipaul's writing. Before he married, Ralph's father had been the protégée of an English missionary and his wife, and after their deaths he had assembled a book about their work called *The Missionary Martyr of Isabella*. Pausing over photographs reproduced in this book, Ralph is drawn to one of them showing his father as a very young man, 'almost a boy', 'standing up in a group in front of a thatched wooden hut; the background was simple bush. The reproduction was poor, light and shadow ill-defined; and in the badly-fitting old-fashioned costume, which appeared to force his neck and chin out and up, my father looked faintly aboriginal and lost, at the end of the world, in a clearing in the forest.' This is one of a number of descriptions, most of them applied to Ralph himself, of a lost boy running or riding or just, as here, standing somewhere that looks like the end of the world. The image of the boy outside the hut in the dark, already familiar to Naipaul's readers from *Biswas* and *An Area of Darkness*, has appeared twice before in *The Mimic Men*. This particular version of it is strongly reminiscent of Naipaul's description (in *The Middle Passage*) of an old East Indian emerging from the solitude of his hut in Coronie, 'a derelict man in a derelict land; a man discovering himself, with surprise and resignation, lost in a landscape which had never ceased to be unreal because the scene of an enforced and always temporary residence'.

The oddly disturbing image of the dark hut and the lost boy, or the old man in *The Middle Passage* episode, gets much closer to the heart of Naipaul's experience of loss, placelessness, 'the lack of sympathy between man and the earth he walks on', than much else of Ralph Singh's analysis of his shipwreck does. But the anger, the sense of baffled protest, needs to be expressed too. And to capture that will require a more direct and less confusedly reflective approach to the issue than Naipaul provides in *The Mimic Men*. Two stories in *In a Free State* come very close to expressing this inarticulate rage – 'One out of Many' and 'Tell me who to kill'. But for Naipaul's most extended study of it we need to press on to *Guerrillas*, his next full-length novel, and the one which probes most painfully into the relation between protest leadership and social revolt, between private anguish and public disorder.

Guerrillas has a much more powerful narrative drive than anything Naipaul has written since the very early comic novels. The organisation of the plot owes something to 'In a Free State', where hints of disturbance grow ever more palpable as Bobby and Linda press forward with their journey through an unnamed Central African state. In *Guerrillas*, however, Naipaul dispenses with the journey, and gradually pieces together relationships among people who play complementary rôles in the creation of violent events which finally overwhelm them. Details of the plot, such as Jane's inspection of the rural commune at Thrushcross Grange, and her gift of a dollar to Bryant, unfold with an unimpeded forward movement. There are brief retrospective passages about Peter Roche's and Jane's separate reasons for coming together and trying to make a new life for themselves on the island, but these are rarely hampered by the elaborate explanatory or discursive paragraphs we come across so frequently in *The Mimic Men*. So the episodes that make up the story move forward vigorously. The 'story' itself, however, seems to be marking time. We sense that something is going on between the episodes, which is not merely connecting them in the rather casual, undisturbing way event seems to follow event, a visit here followed by a visit there. Instead there seems to be an invisible twist in the configuration of the episodes which provides a link, not materially visible, between Stephens's disappearance and Bryant's resentment, and between Jane's infidelity with Jimmy Ahmed at the Prince Albert Hotel and Roche's visit to Stephens's mother up in the shanty town above the city. But for the moment these events seem disconnected, leading in no certain direction.

They seem to have as much or as little to do with each other as
Jane's discovery of a mysterious tenant in a hut at the end of her
garden has to do with anything that follows in the plot. She notices
the man's cutlass and his paint tin, and illogically relates them to
Bryant in the hut at Thrushcross Grange. In this disconnected
episode, the properties of violence are all assembled. In the
distribution of the loosely connected episodes already mentioned,
other opportunities for violence are being brought together in
ways the characters involved are incapable of predicting.

At the centre of any potential disturbance is the half-negro,
half-Chinese figure of Jimmy Ahmed, the leader of the agricultural commune at Thrushcross Grange. But Jimmy is being used
by financial and commercial concerns on the island to stand
between their own interests and black revolution. The intention is
that he will act as an instrument to siphon off radical violence.
And Jimmy knows this. He tells Roche, 'They've got to make me
bigger. Because, if I fail – hmm. I'm the only man that stands
between them and revolution, and they know it now massa.
That's why I'm the only man they're afraid of.' So why does
Jimmy accept this rôle? And why does Roche, a white liberal who
has been tortured in South African prisons, support Jimmy's
activities, which he admits, in an interview near the end of the
novel, are anti-historical? Jimmy's 'back-to-the-land' project is
not viewed seriously by anyone in the book. Jane thinks it is a
cover for guerrillas. Roche eventually realises that it is a
breeding-ground of violence, not because of any deliberate
attempt to make it so, by Jimmy or anyone else, but because it
brings together groups of dissatisfied and envious poor young
blacks in circumstances which are bound, sooner or later, to
create an eruption of hatred.

The reason Jimmy and Roche are prepared to act out the rôles
they have allotted to themselves in the political scenario of the
island is that both of them, in their different ways, have lost faith in
the beliefs on which they had based their vision of life. Jimmy's
expulsion from England after being held on a rape charge has
washed him up on the island with an inflated reputation as a black
leader, and a profound distrust of himself – a distrust that is the
keynote of the letters he spends so much of his time writing,
particularly his final letter to 'Marjorie' back in England. Her
betrayal of him, after what he describes as her 'making him a
man', has loosened his hold on his identity and driven him to the

play-acting at Thrushcross Grange. It has also released in him genuine feelings of compassion for Bryant, the ugly, homeless negro who has invested all his capacity for loyalty in Jimmy, and who must therefore experience great difficulty in surviving any self-betrayal on the part of the man whom he worships.

In fact Jimmy is already self-betrayed. When Jane and Roche are talking to him on their first visit together to Thrushcross Grange, he begins 'to feel unsupported by his words, and then separate from his words'. What follows is familiar – the darkness, the feeling that the world is lost forever, 'and his own life ending on that bit of waste land'. All that is left to him is fantasy: the fantasy of his position at the Grange, bolstered up by the white establishment who finance it and the loyal blacks who make up the commune; and the fantasies he commits to paper in which a heroic view of himself as folk leader alternates with the expression of fear at what the consequences of his actions might be. As he writes to one of his associates outside the commune, 'Things are desperate Roy, when the leader himself begins to yield to despair, things are bad. When everybody wants to fight there's nothing to fight for. Everybody wants to fight his own little war, everybody is a guerrilla.' Jimmy is little more than a prisoner at Thrushcross Grange. His position there is entirely dependent on the absence of revolutionary activity elsewhere on the island. If such activity breaks out he will be held accountable and will have to ride it out as a folk leader and demagogue, or fail to muster the energy and ideological fervour – in which case he will be swallowed up by the violence it unleashes. His fundamental self-distrust makes it impossible for him to do other than make a merely personal, and despairing, contribution to the violence that eventually ensues.

Jimmy is adrift, shipwrecked. In this he is like Peter Roche, whose liberal principles, distorted in the eyes of others since the dramatic event of his imprisonment in South Africa, fail to cope with a situation that involves too great a personal investment in the racial disturbances that follow Stephens's killing. His sponsoring of the agricultural commune, from which Stephens has withdrawn, might have been responsible for this gratuitous act of violence. And his visit to Stephens's house at a time when he does not realise the boy is dead makes him feel suspect in the eyes of the police and turns him in on himself to an even greater degree than would otherwise have been the case. His interview with Meredith Herbert exposes the extent to which he has acquiesced in the demise of his own political identity. Talking about Roche's book on South Africa, Meredith tells him that he writes 'as though certain things merely happened to you, were forced on you', and Roche agrees that in the course of writing the book he had realised that this was true. Perhaps, as he has already claimed, this has something to do with a failure in his upbringing: 'You must understand I have always accepted authority. It probably has to do with the kind of school I went to.' Roche's liberal inclinations have led him to seek a constructive alternative to racial repression – in South Africa, and then on the island. But an emotional commitment to an ordered society has weakened the basis of any conceivable protest he can now make: 'he could neither act nor withdraw; he could only wait'. As much as Jimmy Ahmed, his capacity for action has been sapped at its base. Roche has built his whole life on sand. Like Jimmy, but without the violent hatred that will end in bloodshed, he waits for the inevitable collapse – which may or may not have come with Bryant's brutal and hysterical murder of Jane.

Jane's contribution to the story springs from a quite different character from that of Jimmy or Roche. Her liberal sentiments are less than skin deep. Her presence on the island is simply a temporary phase in her sexual oscillations between violation and acceptance of comfort. The tensions on the island are in the process of turning Roche, her erstwhile comforter, into the new instrument of her violation, and she is preparing to leave him for this reason. Roche's own behaviour seems to have little to do with Jane's attitudes. She sees that he has lost the sense of himself as a 'doer', something she had admired him for back in London (though for quite inadequate reasons), but she makes no inquiries into why this should have happened. Meanwhile the sexual game she thinks she can play with Jimmy is founded on a contempt that in turn provokes contempt. But she feels she can escape from all this. The 'plane to London will rescue her from the muddle she has contributed to on the island. Her good fortune is that she can eliminate the past, except as a series of occasions when her personality has been subjected to violations for which she need accept no responsibility. 'She was under no obligation to make a whole of her attitudes and actions. . . . She was only what she did and said at any given moment.' Therefore, in spite of her persistent sense of violation, fundamentally she remains inviolable, since her belief that everything can be undone removes her from the world of real, serious values the breakdown of which destroys Jimmy's and Roche's belief in themselves. Even her brutal rape by Jimmy fills her with nothing more than a temporary alarm. She feels she can still get back to the security of her class and ultimate self-esteem. Her death at Bryant's hands, encouraged by Jimmy, is simply one more, last, violation of the flesh. Its ambiguous consequences for both Roche and Jimmy go far deeper than anything that she herself experienced could have impressed upon her.

When the riots break out, after Stephens's death, the activities of politicians merit scarcely a mention. The police on the Ridge are an uncertain quantity – potentially menacing; for the moment, kept happy with gifts of sandwiches the coloured maid has presciently taken down to the station for them. Nobody seems capable of doing anything about the situation, beyond announcing a merely formal state of emergency – until American planes fly in. Then everything calms down. As Harry da Tunja says before the end is in sight,

> Those groups down there don't know what they're doing. All this talk of independence, but they don't really believe that times have changed. They still feel they're just taking a chance, and that when the show is over somebody is going to go down there and start dishing out licks. . . . They would go crazy if somebody tells them that this time nobody might be going down to dish out licks and pick up the pieces.

So once again a small colonial community has to be rescued from itself by an outside authority. Neither Roche's liberation nor Jimmy's spurious version of Black Power can save the situation. For the situation is the same as created on Isabella in *The Mimic Men*, and that Naipaul defines most concentratedly in his essay on Jamaica in *The Middle Passage*. In Jamaica, he writes, the pressures were not simply those of race or poverty.

> They were accumulated pressures of the slave societies, the colonial society, the underdeveloped, overpopulated, agricultural country; and they were beyond the control of any one 'leader'. The situation required not a leader but a society which understood itself and had purpose and direction. It was only generating selfishness, aggression, and a self-destructive rage.

On the edges of such a society there are ever-deteriorating reminders of an earlier coherence, achieved at the expense of the many and promoting the cultural pre-eminence of the few. In *The Mimic Men* there are hints of this in the Deschampneufs family history. In *Guerrillas* the descriptions of the Grandlieu mansion and its mistress's behaviour plays a similar rôle. But, at this late stage of the Empire, living with the consequences of what Ralph Singh called 'the overthrow in three continents of established social organisations, the unnatural bringing together of peoples who could achieve fulfilment only within the security of their own societies and the landscape hymned by their ancestors', the possibility of order is slight and, where present, imposed from outside for a brief period of artificial calm. Unsatisfactory as we saw it to be, the primitive Hindu society that existed in a bastardised form in the Tulsi household seems to be viewed by Naipaul increasingly as a desirable alternative to the disorders and complications of modern post-colonial society. There, authority grew from within, and manifested itself in powerful and effective ritual. As late as 1964, Naipaul described in acutely embarrassing terms his flight from the village of his ancestors on the plain of the Punjab: 'So it ended, in futility and impatience, a gratuitous act of cruelty, self-reproach, and flight.' Much of this almost hysterical response to the society from which his present had emerged has to do with what he calls the spirit of negation, which lay at the heart of his experience of India. But it was also his reaction to being brought face to face with a traditional society, regulated by caste and ritual, untouched by the complications of the colonial predicament.

Lately, however, Naipaul has looked more calmly and more sympathetically at the tattered remnant of those established organisations which colonisation all but destroyed. In his latest novel, *A Bend in the River*, the central African town where Salim, a simple shopkeeper, ekes out a meagre existence, has a Latin motto carved in granite outside the dark gates. It is a misquotation from Vergil: '*Miscerique probat populos et foedera jungi*' ('He approves of the mingling of the peoples and their bonds of union'). The granite monument had been destroyed almost as soon as it was erected, 'leaving only bits of bronze and the mocking words, gibberish to the people who now used the open space in front as a market and bivouac'. To such a sorry state have come the Roman ideals, as well as the monument on which they were engraved.

Salim squats among the ruins and among the new, contemporary post-colonial monuments, and observes the anguish of those, such as the Western-educated Ferdinand, who suffer the consequences of the dangerous ideals. But he also observes Ferdinand's mother, Zabeth, whose primitive world is symbolised in the Catholic priest's, Father Huissmans's, collection of native masks. These masks give Salim the impression that the bush is full of spirits: 'in the bush hovered all the protecting presences of a man's ancestors; and in the room all the spirits of those dead masks, the power they evoked, all the religious dread of simple men, seemed to have been concentrated'. They are images of power and authority, of an ordered, structured society gone for ever except in the memory of the workers and itinerant native women such as Zabeth.

That society cannot be brought back. After Father Huiss-mans's death, the *lycée* he served won't accept his collection of native carvings because it is felt to be an affront to African religion. The masks deteriorate in an unventilated room, 'and seemed to lose the religious power Father Huissman had taught one to see in them; without him, they simply seemed to become extravagant objects'. Their fortunes are predictable. An American visitor goes native and takes them away to the US. They end up as the nucleus of a gallery of primitive art. As the town's other motto states, *'Semper aliquid novi'* ('Always something new'). But the authority is all gone from them.

Index